Social Ecology

By the Same Author

Principles of Comparative Economics (2 vols.)

Borderlands of Economics

The Foundations of Indian Economics

Civics

Rural Economy of India

Democracies of the East

Food Planning for Four Hundred Million

Regional Sociology

Introduction to Social Psychology (with N.N. Sen Gupta)

The Theory and Art of Mysticism

Groundwork of Economics

Migrant Asia

The Regional Balance of Man

The Land Problems of India

The Changing Face of Bengal

Economic Problems of Modern India (2 vols.) (ed.)

Fields and Farmers in Oudh (ed.)

Man and His Habitation

The Institutional Theory of Economics

The Political Economy of Population

Social Ecology

Radhakamal Mukerjee

With a foreword by
Klaus Seeland

PRINTWORLD
Publishers of Indian Traditions

Cataloging in Publication Data — DK
[Courtesy: D.K. Agencies (P) Ltd. <docinfo@dkagencies.com>]

Mukerjee, Radhakamal, 1889-1968.
Social ecology / Radhakamal Mukerjee; with a foreword by Klaus Seeland.
p. cm.
Reprint.
Includes bibliographical references and index.
ISBN: 9788124607480

1. Human beings — Effect of environment on. 2. Social ecology. 3. Urban ecology (Sociology) 4. India — Social conditions. I. Title.

DDC 304.2 23

ISBN 13: 978-81-246-0748-0
Originally published in 1945 by Longmans Green and Company, London
First published in India, in fresh typeset form, 2014

Printed and published by:
D.K. Printworld (P) Ltd.
Regd. Office : *Vedasri*, F-395, Sudarshan Park
(Metro Station: Ramesh Nagar)
New Delhi – 110 015
Phones : (011) 2545 3975, 2546 6019; *Fax* : 2546 5926
e-mail : indology@dkprintworld.com
Web : www.dkprintworld.com

Foreword

More often than not, at least as far as my experiences teach me, forewords are omitted to be read. The one to follow, however, I claim, is essential to be read as it explains to the reader why a book written by the eminent Indian sociologist, economist and political philosopher Radhakamal Mukerjee (1889–1968), hailing from West Bengal that was published almost seventy years ago, is reprinted.

The first edition of this book was published by Longmans, Green & Co. in 1945. This was a lucky date as the Second World War came to an end in that year, but it was perhaps not the very moment to publish a scholarly work on social ecology. Moreover, and I could not trace the whereabouts of the copies of this first edition, it seems that either only a few of them have survived the aftermath of the war or only quite a small number of copies were released from the press – maybe due to paper shortage – or a substantial part of the first edition had been destroyed at the end of war. Whatever may have happened, to my knowledge there are a few very rare copies left in university or public libraries worldwide. This, however, does not explain why a reprint of this book was thought to be desirable or even necessary such a long time after the first edition.

I came across this title when scrutinizing social science publications published during the first half of the twentieth century. Just to mention a few, predecessors of Mukerjee's book, as far as the subject title is concerned, were the ones by M.A. Alihan, *Social Ecology – A Critical Analysis,* New York: Columbia University Press, 1938; the third edition of C. Daryll

Forde's *Habiat, Economy and Society – A Geographical Introduction to Ethnology*, New York: Harcourt, Brace and Co., 1937; *Human Ecology* by J.W. Bews, Oxford University Press, 1935; *Culture and Ethnology* by R.H. Lowie, New York: D.C. McMurtrie, 1917 (chap. III, Culture and Environment) and the contributions to the theory of Cultural Ecology of J.H. Steward from the late 1920s to the 1960s. These monographs and articles by some of the renowned social-science scholars who had shed light on the nexus between society, environment and culture throughout the last century show that social, cultural and human ecologies have a rather long-standing tradition of being tackled by ethnologists, social anthropologists and sociologists.

In the second half of the last century social science was broadening its scope of interdisciplinary work on the interface between socio-cultural and environmental issues, including the formation of new or updated theories. Apart from some of the classic proponents in this scientific field such as C.S. Coon, A.P. Vayda, R.A. Rappaport and H.L. Shapiro, more and likewise relevant authors, who have become "modern classics" themselves in the meantime, published a substantial amount of scientific books to cover the aforementioned issues. Contemporary social scientists cover a wide range of approaches towards what Mukerjee had defined as *social ecology* in his own approach. From J.A. Hannigan's *Environmental Sociology – A Social Constructionist Perspective*, London: Routledge, 1995, to K. Milton's *Environmentalism and Cultural Theory – Exploring the Role of Anthropology in Environmental Discourse*, London: Routledge, 1996, to R. McC. Netting's *Cultural Ecology*, Menlo Park: Benjamin/Cummings, 1977, and A. Naess' and D. Rothenberg's *Ecology, Community and Lifestyle – Outline of an Ecosophy*, Cambridge: CUP, 1989, different foci were laid on the subject emphasizing a functionalist, anthropological or philosophical perspective. Conceptual analyses and critiques were contributed by R. Ellen, *Environment, Subsistence and System – the Ecology of Small-scale Social*

Formations, Cambridge: CUP, 1982; E. Croll and D. Parkin (eds.), *Bush Base: Forest Farm – Culture, Environment and Development* and last not least by the selection of papers and articles in *Social Ecology*, New Delhi: OUP, 1994, edited by R. Guha.

Compared to all these works on social and cultural ecology, Mukerjee's book reads like a most inspiring and multi-faceted socio-political essay based on a broad knowledge of cultural history and social science theories. His text is – by and large – amazingly up-to-date and full of political insights and societal introspection which are still valid at present or which have come true during the past decades. It was particularly striking for me to learn that, what seemed to be a visionary speculation at the time when the book was written, i.e. in the final phase of the British Raj in India, gives the reader sometimes the impression as if they were formulated only recently. The salient features of the political development of the Western civilization had been analyzed correctly by Mukerjee, although his terminology sounds a bit awkward here and there. But the reader can easily transform this terminology and detect its contemporary equivalent in it. The wide range of his scientific competence as professor of economics and sociology at Lucknow University, India, can be seen from his twenty monographs that had been published before and referred to in his *Social Ecology* covering the fields of economics, agro-economics, political science and political economy and sociology. His immense knowledge and intellectual capacity transgresses the borders of those academic disciplines he represented and shows that Prof. Mukerjee was not only at home in their world. He moved freely but, as far as I can see, as well always correctly in the fields of ecology, psychology and the theories of evolution and behaviorism.

To come across a scientific book, which is quite antique, was not or could neither be received by the scientific community nor the public, but is still up-to-date in its content, is not only remarkable but needs further explanation. Mukerjee starts in the first chapters from a clearly evolutionary perspective of societal development, stressing the interconnectedness and dynamics of the coming into being of mobility, the evolution of social institutions, the progress of technology as a result of an interaction between environment and culture. His core message highlights that economics as well as politics of any society reflect its ecological background and therefore he concludes by emphasizing the importance of regions and regionalism in order to realize the equilibrium between a society and the potential of its environment. If the reader projects this message to the recent political developments in the European Union (EU), for instance, it becomes obvious that the political intention of the EU policy to strengthen the regions and diminish the political weight of the nation state favor regionally-based sustainability. The term sustainability has, of course, nowhere been used in Mukerjee's book because it did not yet exist in its present-day meaning, but he gives more than one definition of it in his own terminology and by reading between the lines the alert reader can discover the very concept without its terminological label.

It is certainly rare that a long since forgotten book is revived by a colleague after so many years and recommended for a reprint instead of writing another one himself. Mukerjee's book, however, I am convinced, deserves it to be re-issued with a few marginal corrections of errors or some deleted short passages of very minor importance from my hand. It has been proved an adequate diagnosis of what social ecology is all about in the second half of the twentieth century and I cannot see new lines of development in the near future at the moment. This, I think, is a valid argument for a reprint.

Although there are, of course, some (rather few) references to facts in the text which are outdated by now and had to be deleted by myself, I abstained from a thorough editing to keep it as authentic as possible.

Zurich, July 2013 **Klaus Seeland**

Preface

HUMAN ecology is an infant science which has obtained rather quick recognition as a basic discipline for all social sciences. It has emerged as a synthetic study that deals with the triadic balance of the environment–function–organism, and seeks to unify and co-ordinate all the sciences of man. Human ecology, like plant and animal ecology, is a sub-division of general ecology. Social ecology is different in scope from human ecology which deals with the forms and processes of human *individual* adjustments to the environment. The field of social ecology is the study of the adjustments of man's *social* structures and functions, of the processes of interaction between region, occupation and society — the sociological equivalents of environment, function and organism — out of which arise all social phenomena. The community aspect of human ecology may also be called synecology, a term used by the plant ecologists who differentiate this from autoecology that deals with the study of the individual in relation to the environment, physical and organic. There has been considerable disagreement in respect of both the conception and scope of human ecology. The reason is not far to seek. Since human ecology rests on a close working relationship between geography, biology, economics and demography, each one of which deals with some part of the environment–function–organism triad, different investigators have stressed fundamental ecological concepts for sociology from different fields and angles. The time has certainly come for a clarification of the essential principles of social ecology and their scientific utility and fruitfulness for sociology.

I have endeavoured in this volume to present the major ecological concepts and processes which may help in refashioning the framework of sociology. The fundamental unit of study for sociology is the region. The region is at once an ecological aggregation of persons, an economic framework and a cultural order. It is at once a faithful expression of the distribution of population, resources and occupations, and the interrelated cultural unity. The spatial pattern of the community, the typical arrangement of population, services and institutions and social stratification determine the type and direction of social values and culture. The region shows a basic organic unity, first, in respect of its natural differentiation from other regions; second, in the spatial relationships of population; and, third, in the pattern of social processes, relations and values, moulded by the interchange between region and people in the context of history and heritage. Thus the region as a physical and cultural *Gestalt* * is a dynamic system in which are balanced and epitomized in their operation all the formative factors of social life. Social ecology is the sociological method which gives us the region or ecological order as the natural frame of reference for the classification of social phenomena and cultural processes. It has implications for all societies and cultures, but at the same time brings into the forefront social types and cultural variations which influence social behaviours and organizations. In a sense, therefore, the volume may be regarded as an attempt to write a comparative social ecology on which rest the foundations of comparative economics and sociology.

---

* The German term "Gestalt" refes to the wide framework of the "Gestalttheorie" in Sociology and Psychology. Gestalt may be translated into English as "embodiment" (KS).

Region, population and society are not three separate factors. They mutually influence one another and form a natural balance, each part of which can be understood in terms of the other. Resource pattern, population type and growth, and pattern of living are reciprocally inter-dependent. Social ecology considers society as man's response to an increase of population, which initiates and improves division of labour, social organization and the transmission of the legacy of tools, occupations, patterns of living and traditions. On the other hand, society regulates its population growth, social stratification and role of individuals so as to fit harmoniously into the region.

Within each region the unit of investigation of sociology is the community rather than man, the relationship rather than the individual. Georg Simmel, indeed, observed long ago: "Society exists wherever a number of individuals enter into reciprocal relations with one another". Similarly, according to A. Vierkandt, sociology is concerned with the analysis of fundamental relationships between persons, such as leadership, deference, submission, struggle and power. The method adopted is described as "phenomenological" according to the usage of the term by the philosopher Husserl. With this emphasis of inter-personal relations, sociology finds its proper subject matter in the processes of man's role, status and mobility, and turns from speculation to concrete investigation. Just as the region is a typical resource pattern for population and a typical system of interrelated roles or occupations of individual inhabitants, so society is a configuration of interrelated statuses. Status is assigned by the community not merely to individuals, groups and occupations but also to objects, institutions, concepts and beliefs in ecological and social space.

Status, to be sure, is the single primary datum of sociology; it is a reality at once universal, concrete and measurable within the social milieu including animal society. From Comte's explanation of social physics to the Marxian theory of class consciousness and conflict, from Herbert Spencer's account of social differentiation as a universal bio-social process to the Eugenist's correlation of socio-economic status and innate ability, from Sorokin's theory of social mobility to Pareto's concept of the *elite* we have the recognition of status as a universal and basic social uniformity. It is the task of sociology to study the nature of the status system and domination–deference relations as well as the behaviour of individuals (mobility) within their ecological and social boundaries, both quantitatively and qualitatively. Status is the index at once of individual achievement and social continuity, social dominance or distance, the index of differential achievement of individuals, selected by the ecological processes of competition, specialization and segregation in the dynamic social world.

Status and distance both imply the acceptance or recognition by the society of the position or role of the individual and group in collective life. Society is something more than an ecological aggregate of individuals or an economic framework of division and specialization of labour. It is characterized by a legacy of culture, a hierarchy of norms and values which introduce status-seeking, status-gaining, status-losing and status-regaining as universal social processes with their ecological, economic and cultural aspects. Status which is begotten by ecology and nurtured by culture converts an individual into a person, his position, role or job into a wished-for pattern of social behaviour, his mobility into a moral striving and achievement. There is a give-and-take between the community and the person's goals and purposes which make status assignment the *sine qua non* of the social process.

Stratificatory status, rooted as it is in the adjustment of population to the region, weaves the characteristic group pattern, interpersonal relations and ways of living of a people. It not only provides each person with incentives and opportunities to rise in the social scale in order that he may not only attain status, privilege and self-competence, but also expresses an integral system of attitudes and goals and the moral evaluation of the regional community. Each man's ecological and social status is different from his fellow man's. It is defined by his membership of group life; while groups and classes form and reform, and the status system undergoes alteration in obedience to basic ecological, occupational and social adjustments. Not only his own position or status and occupation but also those of his segregated group, whether dominant or subordinate, are in perpetual flux. Social ecology studies the place, occupation and time relations of persons and groups in their processes of competition, co-operation, conflict, accommodation and succession. These reveal both symbiosis and equilibrium as well as disorganization and disequilibrium with contrasted human relations, attitudes and values. In social ecology the spatial position or status of individuals and social groups, indeed, provide the key to the delineation of the community and of social relations, behaviours and attitudes.

The older sociology has either hugged the figment of the metaphysical individual as a self-contained entity or stressed society as an entity *sui generis,* constituting a single social stratum and missed the complexity of personal and social relationships and processes in the concrete stratified community. The more sociology focuses its attention on the universal, measurable and even predictable processes of status and mobility, the more surely does it progress towards the status of a positive science; while it will have a special field and subject matter of its own differentiating it from all other social sciences. The comprehension from a naturalistic and quantitative standpoint of man's spatial position, niche or occupation in terms of ecological or social space to the range of his status and uniqueness of his personality and achievement, and the cultural pattern, sociology, however, would see the process as one single, integral reaction. American sociologists often identify spatial distribution and movements of persons, groups and institutions, abandoning the biological origin of this line of approach. They also differentiate between ecological and social relationship missing the unity of the social process within the setting of the inseparable triad, environment–function–organism. All this has introduced confusion in the application of ecological concepts to sociological analysis. Society, on the one hand, is man's ecological adaptation to the increase of numbers in a restricted environment, and all human interaction can be interpreted in terms of ecological processes. On the other hand, it introduces meanings and values into ecological interaction or economic relationship in the medium of culture, and this makes the fundamental ecological processes, viz. mobility, stratification, distance, dominance and equilibrium far different from what these are in plant and animal communities. Care should, accordingly, be taken in the first place, while using ecological concepts in human social life, of the difference of the order or level of such basic and universal processes or phenomena. This is not difficult, and, indeed, one way by which knowledge advances is the cross-fertilization of concepts of different sciences. Secondly, in studying the origins and operations of status and mobility in a community, sociology should be entirely objective, i.e. it will accept the present and wished-for values and norms that underlie stratification, distance and mobility as given sociological data. It will not seek to evaluate such ends or norms nor to pronounce value judgements on status and mobility, which it will leave to ethics, philosophy, religion and law.

A closer analysis reveals that stratification and mobility are governed by the nature of social reaction, ecological or cultural, which dominates each community. Human relations represent adjustments to an ecological as well as to a cultural setting. Man's ecological adjustments, since these take place indirectly and externally through the limited and selective forces of the environment, are segmental and impersonal. Man's cultural reactions are integral and intimate. These contrasted sets of reactions have profound effects on the genesis and processes of status and mobility, on the type of the community, and on the level and quality of social life and experience. The predominance of one or other phase of social relationship and behaviour has been made familiar to us by the dichotomy of status or custom versus contract in law, of *Gemeinschaft* versus *Gesellschaft* * relations in ethics, of primary and secondary groups in sociology and of regionalism and centralization in politics. Every society is faced with the crucial problem of finding out a harmonious working balance between these contrasted attitudes, ways and norms of living. The antithesis between the ecological and the cultural phase of social organization — *Gemeinschaft–Gesellschaft* — is so significant that sociology itself has been sometimes defined in Germany as *Baulehre der Gemeinschaft*,** and has selected the fact of the *Gemeinschaft* as the primary datum of its study. Neither *Gemeinschaft* nor *Gesellschaft* represent the entirety of social interaction. *Gemeinschaft* humanizes and socializes man in the tribe, the family, the kindred and the folk, as also brings into existence organized human culture and underlies its finest spiritual expressions and products. *Gesellschaft* is equally universal, satisfying other elemental needs of human nature

* The German terms "Gemeinschaft" (community) and "Gesellschaft" (society) refer to the sociologic thinking of T. Tönnies who published his classic "Gemeinschaft and Gesellschaft" in 1887 (KS).

** In English it means: "Construction science of the community" (KS) and culture, viz. those that arise out of exchange and circulation of commodities and services in society. In peasant culture, we find some kind of working balance between familial and territorial groups, between the framework of status and of contract, between the claims of both *Gemeinschaft* and *Gesellschaft*.

In modern urban–industrial civilization *Gemeinschaft* has suffered an eclipse; but though it cannot be wholly recovered, it cannot be also wholly superseded here. An exaggerated stress of *Gesellschaft* means the degeneration and disruption of culture, and is the outcome of a profound unbalance between ecology, economy and the community. *Gesellschaft* goes with the ecological or fractional phase of human relationship and group organization; with contract, with individualism, with secondary groupism and with centralization. To what extent these contrasted principles of human relationship and group life can be blended is connected as much with the particular stage of social evolution, and ethos of the people as with the individual's ethical effort to change the moral practice and tradition of his group and the community. In other words, the mingling of the two principles is coincident with the integral process of culture itself.

What is a problem of education, culture and individual psychology is also a problem in the adjustment of social institutions and means of social control. Man today shows a profound lack of adaptation to his deliberate and impersonal secondary group environment and the great city, which the stress of the ecological phase of behaviour and modern technology and politics have brought about. Increase of population, which is correlated with and is made possible by machine technology, accompanies the universal tendency of dissolution of the smaller order of territorial and functional groups, neighbourhoods and communities. With this wane the more direct and intimate human loyalties and the associated values and joys of the previous social age. The remedy lies as much in the ecological planning of villages, towns and cities and re-orientation of population, industry and rural–urban relations as in social planning for the recovery of many human values and virtues that have been lost in the vast, invisible secondary associations of this dynamic technological age. Social ecology or synecology has, therefore, to work hand in hand with social biology and psychology as well as with technics, in order that man may attain social equilibrium, that he may not be a misfit in the ecological setting and the secondary group where he is destined to live.

Social ecology is a vast and virgin field orienting social phenomena on the basis of the give-and-take between life, mind and region. It may be permissible to refer to three previous works of mine in which some aspects of social ecology will be found treated in greater detail than here. In my *Regional Sociology* (1926) I defined human ecology as the study of social behaviour with reference to conditioning environmental circumstances and indicated the social psychology of regionalism. *The Regional Balance of Man: An Ecological Theory of Population* (1938) stressed the ecological notion of a natural balance, albeit a shifting one, of the region which exhibits an increasing process of interlinking of the living and the non-living world. The fundamental concepts of ecological balance and vital interchange and solidarity of the region are here seen to underlie the laws and processes of population and sustained optimum economy. *Man and His Habitation: A Study in Social Ecology* (1940) illustrates the operation of fundamental ecological processes such as mobility, segregation and dominance in the growth and structure of villages, towns and cities and their mutual relations. Social, mental and ecological patterns are here analyzed in their mutual interdependence in a total ecological situation: hamlet, village or city. The present volume will, it is hoped, contribute to a scientific classification of social–ecological concepts and to the development of a methodology according to which social ecology may form the basis of a new functional and quantitative sociology.

Some materials of this book have appeared as papers and articles in the *American Journal of Sociology*, Sociology and Social Research and Social Forces in the USA. I have also incorporated a paper on the "Levels of Social Equilibrium" presented before the International Congress of Sociology in Paris. In the summer of 1937, I was invited to deliver a course of lectures in sociology at the Institute of Sociology, Great Britain, the universities of Oxford, Cologne, and Vienna and at the Société de Sociologie Masaryk in Europe, and in the USA at the Columbia University, New York, and the universities of Chicago, Wisconsin, Michigan and Minnesota and at the Washington Chapter of the American Sociological Society. I am grateful to the late Prof. R.D. McKenzie at Ann Arbor, professors E.W. Burgess, Allee and Ogburn in Chicago, H.W. Odum in New York, G.H. Kolb at Madison, Walther at Hamburg, and Charles Elton at Oxford for the many valuable discussions I was able to have with them on the methods and materials in human ecology during this visit to the West.

For my own students at the University of Lucknow the main ideas underlying the study have been set forth in a series of special lectures recently arranged in the Faculty of Arts. I have to thank Prof. N.K. Sidhanta, Dean, for kindly arranging the publication of this study. To my pupil, Susil Chandra, M.A., I am indebted for the assistance in the preparation of the index.

Radhakamal Mukerjee
University of Lucknow

Contents

1

Society and Symbiosis

The Ecological Processes in Human Society: Distribution

THE science of ecology is not a definite specialized study like botany, zoology or geography but represents a viewpoint and attitude concerning all relations between life and its environment. It recognizes several fundamental processes which are of universal character, which all possess a general human connotation and which may materially help in refashioning the framework of sociology regarded as a subdivision of the comprehensive science of balance of the human species in its complex restricted environment. The major ecological processes are —

- Distribution
- Mobility
- Competitive co-operation
- Stratification
- Succession
- Equilibrium

Geography has for a long time been studying the physical factors which govern the distribution of population and resources on the world's map. Economics has added to these an investigation of the causes of the localization of large scale industries, business enterprises and markets and the effect of modern forms of transportation and communication as well as emigration as governing the concentration of population in special regions and zones.

The distribution of crops and natural resources, govern the main outlines of rural and urban settlements. The dispersal of population and the strategic location of industries, business enterprises, markets, banks, social and commercial institutions are governed in all essentials by ecological diversity and inequality. The distribution of the natural resources of the earth is so divergent that we have independent culture zones and economic systems. Such zones and systems represent an assemblage of cultural and institutional traits and forms which have an interdependence, functionally differentiating one region from other regions. Man's works, cultural devices, arrangements and experiences are thus inscribed into each region and give it a characteristic expression. Regional and comparative sociology bases itself on the variety of regional conditions, possibilities and adaptations in the arts of living. The classification of social types or cultural zones is the first step for laying the foundations of regional sociology as a branch of human geography and ecology.

Human ecology is a more organismic and comprehensive study than geography. Its unit of study is the pattern of life as an integrated whole that includes plant, animal and human associations which cannot be treated in isolation from one another or from the entire ecological complex in the zones of the world's distribution of biotic communities. Climate, topography and the distribution of food plants, animals and other resources govern the distribution of population, habitations, industries and arts of living. Civilization adds to these not only the means of communication and transport, railways and waterways, locomotives, steamships and such as automobiles, newspapers and telephones, but also social attitudes, customs, tariffs and emigration laws that control human circulation, dispersal or concentration of population.

All these, therefore, are ecologic forces which govern the distribution of human groups and their migration and segregation by residence and occupation. Industry, trade and culture under favourable conditions of transportation and communication and social attitudes that engender both physical and social mobility promote concentration of population. Through competition, division of labour and specialization in exploitation of resources, the human community distributes itself in hamlets, villages, towns and cities, all interlinked in a system of circulation of men, goods and services. Every associated unit, the hamlet, village, town and city, is a function of the ecological processes of division of labour and specialization, circulation and concentration. The nature, tempo and patterns of human circulations within an ecological frame of reference govern in many ways man's social relations, attitudes and ways of living of human groups. Rural and urban ecology thus forms a fundamental division of human ecology, dealing with human circulations and habitations, routes and regions forming together an integral unity made up of ecological, economic and sociological elements and factors.[1]

The ecological processes, though these have been definitely classified, do not act singly. Nor in the human community can these be separated from intangible psychological and moral factors. Thus physical geography, economic and social tradition and the subtle influences of sympathy and emulation in human intercourse are manifest in the ecological processes of mobility, co-operation, stratification and succession in the human social level. As a matter of fact ecological relations and processes are transformed in the human community into stereotyped social and legal relations, ideals and policies.

This is chiefly the result of the community life being on a

---

[1] This has been treated in the author's *Man and His Habitation*.

higher level of integration and experience in the human as distinguished from the plant and the animal communities. But basically the ecological processes of aggregation and equilibrium produce similar spatial and food relations in the social life whether of plants, animals or humans.

Symbiosis or Division of Labour

The community life, whether of plants, animals or humans, is a moving whole. All organisms move towards some betterment, towards more food and light, towards multiplication and dominance. Plants vary in gregariousness. Some stand together in mass formation, others stand scattered among each other. It is those types of vegetation which live in formations or constellations that throw a flood of light on human ecological relations. Many plants live side by side in a formation due to the fact that they make different demands of light, heat, moisture and nutriment, and, incidentally, they often aid each other's survival. Plant ecologists describe this phenomenon as "symbiosis" and stress that very often in the complex plant formation, one or more species stand dominant in the association, and if it be destroyed the whole association gradually disappears. In human society the symbiotic conditions under which plants and animals live are designated divisions of labour, based on differences of age, sex, race and class and the differential capacity of individuals. In animal communities divisions of labour are sometimes elaborate and persistent and connected with the food supply, security and survival of the animals. But it is in the human community due to man's variegation of interests and capacities and inventiveness that divisions of labour have become at once most elaborate, most stereotyped and most changing.

Increased sociality is of great service to plants as well as animals and humans in the competition with other species. In animal life, co-operation between different species which inhabit an ecological area has special advantages because of inter-dependence, division of labour and even conscious defence against the inclemencies of climate and common enemies. For a single species of animals gregariousness promotes unity, efficiency and achievement through specialization and is often the outcome of rapid multiplication and the economic possibility of a colony living together and obtaining food by methods which do not imply solitary effort. Social animals — and man is the super-dominant among them — obtain a better foothold in the struggle for existence through co-operation in defence and offence and acquisition of food. The gregarious animals not only multiply faster than the solitary ones, but also develop certain habits which maintain their population at an optimum abundance so that they can adequately utilize the vital possibilities of their restricted environment. Climatic or seasonal factors, available food supply and breeding places which affect mating, breeding and the number of offsprings, the presence of enemies or parasitic organisms and fulminating epidemics represent selective agencies, external to the organisms which are normally operative as population increases to a maximum. All these ecological factors and forces are operative in human spatial relations. More interesting ecological methods of limiting population density are the rigid territory systems of many of the higher forms of animals. Division of labour between the sexes early establishes itself among all higher grades of animals offering advantages to the species as regards successful production or upbringing of the young. Among many higher animals, sexual relationship and division of labour become linked with a rigid or flexible system of territory, which is required for the adequate provision of food supply for the developing offsprings. Among birds the territory is linked with the evolution of a complex set of instincts of the male and the female, and thus the sexual relations (i.e. monogamy versus promiscuity, etc.) depend largely on their territorial relations. A pair of birds or carnivorous mammals maintain a strict vigil over the parcel of forest, lake or meadow which they occupy in the breeding season, become pugnacious and hostile to members of the same species, the size of the territory they occupy being adjusted to the needs of courtship, food supply and schooling for the developing young. The territory system is well-marked not only in birds and mammals but also in some of the social insects which space out their colonies to prevent overcrowding. In the insect societies we find the emergence of other effective methods of regulating density, viz. the control of sex and reproduction through starvation or variation of the quality of food of the larvae, and periodic expulsion of surplus queens and drones and swarming. All such mechanisms of limitation of numbers contribute towards maintaining animal populations in wild nature in the condition of ecological equilibrium at an optimum density. The optimum population represents the maximum number of individuals of a particular species which can adequately utilize the possibilities of growth, restricted as these are by some deciding limiting factor or factors in the complex ecological environment. Where climatic and ecologic factors are incompatible with a certain average density of an animal population, the species moves out to its optimum habitat. Mobility is a major mechanism in bringing about the appropriate distribution and density of the animal population.

Mobility

The laws of mobility or migration hold good throughout both the animal and human kingdoms. The weakest are pushed to the periphery, the strongest hold the centre and "the corridors of migrations". Griffith Taylor, one of the pioneer workers in racial ecology, represents Central Asia near the Caspian Sea as "the region of stimulus" and the Danubian and the Chinese plains as "the corridors of migration" for early men. All races, according to him, originated in a common cradle-land near the Caspian Sea. The major races are arranged in five zones about Central Asia and the more primitive types have been pushed to the inaccessible regions.

The evolution and classification of the races of man could be interpreted by means of the "age and area", or as Taylor puts it, the "zones and strata" concept applied to the distribution and evolution of other mammals. But if the ecology of migrations helps us to understand the wanderings and differentiations of early man in prehistoric times when the vegetation zones and, therefore, man's food supply moved alternately, together with all their inhabitants in accord with the waxing and waning of the ice ages, it will help towards a solution of the future struggles on earth faced with a chronic food shortage over inequalities of distribution of population and resources. Applied ecology has made us familiar with the problems of the success or failure of imported plants, animals and insects in new habitats. Importation of very dissimilar strains, whether of plants or animals and humans, leads to degeneration. Conversely, plants and crops, animals or stocks imported from similar climatic regions contribute towards successful acclimatization, settlement and agricultural reconstruction. The frontiers of cultivation in world agriculture could now extend to tropical Africa, the Americas and Oceania, for instance, by giving free opportunities of migration to peoples in similar habitats who may introduce adaptive crops and agricultural methods and practices. In vast voids and wildernesses where a short-sighted policy of exclusion or restriction is now followed, neither the white man can toil in agriculture nor are there native stocks, adequate in numbers or skilled in agricultural techniques, to cope with great stretches of unoccupied fertile land. The problems of colonization and settlement have to be solved in the future without any racial bias or colour prejudice through the adoption of the same principles of adaptive assimilation and importation of appropriate migrants from similar climatic regions which are now guiding plant and animal breeding and the biological control of pests in new lands.

Competitive Co-operation

It is well known that the emphasis of struggle in Darwinism is responsible for a onesided interpretation of man's behaviour in the past century which has now been considered misleading. J.B.S. Haldane has given many examples to show that so long as a species is mainly struggling against other species or external nature it usually becomes fitter. But when the struggle occurs within a species, this is not so. Increase in mere size or the development of weapons and instincts useful in fighting is an advantage in such struggles, but this generally ends in maladaptation to other situations and consequent extinction. The Soviet biologist Gause has found by his study of small animals and plants in aquarium tanks that if two species are put together of which one eats the other it is not before long that prey diminishes in numbers to an extent leading to the starvation and extinction of the predator. Similarly, many primitive peoples have faced starvation after they exterminated too many beasts, and have either declined by being compelled to live in close contact with civilized cultures or migrated to virgin jungles. Elton takes the view that it does not always pay a species to be too well adapted. "A variation making for too great efficiency may cause a species to destroy its food and starve itself to death." This important principle may explain a good deal of the diversity that is always found in nature and the fact that most species have some characters which cannot be accounted for on orthodox Darwinian lines.

Modern biology has not only shown that competition defeats itself if it be pushed too far but also found the beginnings of co-operation in the lowliest organisms. Competition or the struggle for living space and food is often associated with the function of order. The struggle for life is subdued into organization by the evolution of linkages between plants and animals of the same and even different species. The aggregation of life in a given habitat is discernible as a complex web with threads of reciprocity binding together all inhabitants for collective subsistence. Social ecology posits competitive co-operation as giving the living community its characteristic pattern and organization.

The Evolution of Co-operation

The tendency of animals to co-operate is rooted in various kinds of adaptations towards more secure and richer living, and has worked as surely and successfully as the tendency that makes for struggle. Like the animal's structure and function, the expressions of social life have an evolution of their own reaching their climax in human society. At first, it is merely physical contact which is the basis of aggregation. Instances of aggregation of physically united individuals are plant colonies which sometimes move as a unity, hydroids, sea-pens, reef-corals, polyzoa and compound tunicates. These are described by Thomson as vegetative societies, for many individuals act as one, there is physiological self-subordination, and there is a *modus vivendi* found for individual types, which, in some cases, cannot survive in isolation. Many higher animals are gregarious without being social. Gregarious nesting as in rooks, for instance, is hardly itself social, but the social note is sounded in the composite nest of republican birds. Similarly, such herbivorous mammals as cattle, deer, and antelopes and gnawing mammals like lemmings and rabbits live in herds and colonies without being social. Yet they gain obvious advantages by living in association that they lack as individuals. A herd or flock can frighten or fight with an enemy more successfully than an isolated individual, and can sense danger more quickly since the most alert members of the herd warn everybody with their cry or signal. As it develops domination–subordination relations, defence, foraging, migration and even offence are facilitated. Genuine social behaviour is met with among colonies of beavers and prairie dogs, and among the social anthropoids. Among these latter the tendency towards co-operation establishes a stable group and nesting and foraging territory, and accompanies the development of kin-care and sympathy, feelings of dominance, deference and emulation and even of guilt and general indignation for anti-social behaviour. Briefly summarizing the factors that determine social behaviour among animals, these are, firstly, the effects of climate and the physical environment. Phototropism is an instance of an aggregation of insects which are attracted by a strong light. The diurnal and climatic cycles lead to the periodic swarming and migration of many species of animals. Secondly, physiological specialization of structure and functions govern the pattern of group behaviour and relationships of many social insects. Thirdly, the physiological rhythms of many animals lead to nesting, courting and mating relationships which seem to be governed by variations of temperature and humidity through hormonal regulation. Finally, psychological factors are involved in animal social relationships in the case of many gregarious mammals which exhibit dominance–subordination relations, attack their enemies collectively with courage or stampede together in a panic, like cattle, horses and sheep, or set out in long arduous expeditions like bisons and lemmings; while in the case of the anthropoid apes parental care of infants, grooming and mutual service exhibit definitely altruistic feelings that bind together the group. Kohler aptly observes : "It is hardly an exaggeration to say that a chimpanzee kept in solitude is not a real chimpanzee at all". Similarly, Forel observes in respect of ants that the same ant which exhibits courage and pugnacity among its fellows takes to flight before a much weaker adversary as soon as it finds itself alone. State-building insects are overcome by profound depression if their nest disappears.

Co-ordination of Different Biological Needs of Individuals and the Group

In the higher scale of animal evolution gregarious life does not involve physiological subordination of individuals but division of labour which results in specialization for particular functions, and sometimes in polymorphism. Individuals live separately but habitually or spasmodically combine for economic purposes, or for offence and defence and develop at the same time kin sympathy. Among the three needs of gregarious existence, viz. nutrition, reproduction and protection of the colony, now one and then the other is stressed among the social animals. In insect societies, Wheeler considers that nutrition is subordinated to producing and rearing as many young ones as possible and all that it implies is the principal adaptative peculiarity of such societies, while among the flocks and herds of birds and mammals nutrition and reproduction are less conspicuous than the forms of social behaviour connected with protection. Grasslands provided plenty of food ready at hand if their denizens could move easily and quickly with the alterations of the seasons. These modified the ungulates in the direction of speed, and also developed the herd instinct for combination in defence or in flight to which their specialized hoofs, teeth and bones were better suited than to fight. Unlike the specialization for the collection and manipulation of food among the social insects, we have the specialization for leadership and scouting among the grassfeeders who exhibit highly specialized forms of protective behaviour in their aggregations. With the development of intelligence there can be a better orientation and co-ordination of the divergent basic needs. Social behaviour of the anthropoid apes and men is accordingly characterized by the imperative character of the needs and interests for the time being for the associations.

Let us illustrate from the social and co-operative life of the howling monkeys which has been described accurately by Carpenter, and which is superior in the extent and variety of social behaviour to the organization among the baboons, chimpanzees and orang-outangs. The howlers live in a clan consisting of about a dozen and a half of monkeys. The clan is not primarily familial. It provides for reproduction, as also for all other activities and ecological relations which are essential to the life of the individual and of the species. It exhibits such functionally important sub-groups as female and nursing infant; female, infants and juveniles; play, defence, directing, and retreating groups; and assemblages about oestrous and parturient females. Such transient social groupings are obviously specialized as to social function and in manifestly important ways supplement the activities of the clan. The clan lives in a restricted territory where food exists in abundance and competition is unnecessary. Within its territorial range a clan moves in a definite order and form of progression: one or more adult males tend to travel in the foremost positions and control the movements of the clan, and females carrying infants predominate in the last quarter of the column. When danger threatens, any male may lead the others; there is no permanent leader. Routes to food and shelter, or to retreats in case of clan conflicts appear to be sought out, followed and learned by adult males. It thus appears that the social behaviour of this group of monkeys satisfies a wide variety of needs of the individual and the clan, and shows co-ordination almost on the human level. It is also significant that a male howler monkey is a comparatively meek and mild socialist and does not show sexual jealousy and struggle unlike a baboon and, perhaps, early man who was probably less altruistic, tolerant and docile.

Mind and Sociality

Mental evolution in pre-man and early man went hand in hand with the variegation of social behaviour on the one hand and socialization of the individual on the other. Human societies, though grounded in the fundamental biological interests and behaviour, cannot be characterized as nutritive, protective or reproductive associations since the social feelings and traditions supervene and regulate all behaviour. It is the evolution of mind which, indeed, paves the way for real social integration. Among the birds and mammals gregarious habits and modes of social behaviour, similar to those of man, are acquired by direct education from the parents or other members of the herd or association or by imitation. The social life of the higher animals is conducive not merely to the production but also the transmission of traditional attitudes and patterns of social behaviour, which are handed from one generation to another.

Such transmission of the social legacy is especially promoted by the use of the voice. While in insect societies contact and odour form the basis of integration as well as physiological specialization leading to a hereditary social compulsion, in the higher mammals sound signals act as chief integrating stimuli though direct physical contact may still form the basis of aggregation. The evolution of the social use of the voice from the angry hiss of serpents and parental call of crocodiles to the choruses of some birds and the sympathetic, loud, indignant uproar of a colony of chimpanzees illustrates stages in the development of integration. Many mammals, as for example, pumas and caracals practically never use their voices except in the breeding season and then chiefly as call notes for the young; in many others, however, there are not merely sound signals but also gestures as well as words. Nothing has contributed more to man's sociality than the development of his gestures and voice.

While the evolution of the brain is a factor of great importance for gregarious life, a great deal depends also upon ecologic conditions and the reproductive habits of the animals. Steiner stresses warmth as a factor in the development of social life and claims that animals cannot co-operate effectively unless they are able to maintain a high body temperature over long periods of time.[2] Social life enables animals to maintain a higher temperature, so that activities are less intermittent. On the other hand, the development of the neuro-muscular system is not the *sine qua non* of gregarious life. The carnivorous birds, mammals and insects, which are richly endowed organisms, live in isolation; it is habits of feeding and other ecologic traits associated with the territory system which account for the difference. Even among many gregarious mammals we find sociality as unstable and recurrent as sex and hunger, the animal becoming solitary and pugnacious during the breeding season, and social and co-operative when they are asexual. Man by his mastery over ecological conditions has not only transformed his gregariousness into a steady and continuous instinct and interest, but has also evolved mechanisms for integration, which, as these have increased his capacity, have altered his psychological reactions to fellowmen.

Ecologic, Sexual and Family Integration

It appears that the methods of the evolution of gregariousness have been differentiated among the higher forms of animal life. Among birds, for instance, flocks usually arise more from the aggregation of individuals even of different species than from the fusion of mated pairs or families. On the other hand,

---

[2] Quoted in Pearse, *Animal Ecology*, pp. 330-35.

among the social insects, higher apes and men, societies rest on the aggregation of family units. Insect societies are single families writ large, while Yerkes points out that gregariousness and degree of the individual on the group tend from lemur to man to diminish and at the same time to give place to a more definite and stable social unit, the family. The highest exhibition on social solidarity and sacrifice of the individual for the common good seem to be shown in groups integrated out of stable family associations. This points to a significant biological role of the family which human social evolution cannot outgrow. Even in bird life the territory system as well as display of noble parental devotion and sacrifice, which indicate distinct social advances, are associated with the short-lived familial existence soon to be superseded by open congregations formed by individual birds even from different quarters and flocks. Both among birds and social insects the family is closed. But in the bands or troops of social apes and monkeys and in the human social organization, the family is open and there are retained primitive aggregative or associative tendencies which, in the words of Wheeler, "hark back to the ancestral fish and tadpole stages". The most stable forms of group life appear to emerge when *ecologic, sexual* and *familial* integration has combined together along with the capacity for sympathy and fineness of brain. The economic result is a rapid increase of numbers in the herd, colony or association, which cumulatively increases the efficiency of obtaining food, establishes a high degree of division of labour and permits tentative new departures to meet environing limitations which the solitary animals could never risk.

Its Combination in the Social Life of Early Man

The ecological conditions which governed the differentiation of man's ancestors from the primates fostered a good deal of co-operation. In his arboreal apprenticeship, man lived in small family groups and already learned the social use of his hands and voice. His perennial sex interest and reproductive activity as contrasted with the sharply differentiated sexual and neutral existence of most mammals are at the roots of his firmer social integration. His instinctive life, his use of tools and speech and the ecological conditions governing his food quest, all favoured a gregarious existence. The expansion of conjugal and paternal sentiment into kin sympathy was strengthened by ecological factors, co-operation in food getting, offence and defence in the Asiatic grasslands. When he descended to the *terra firma* the quest for flesh diet, as the food supply in the forests was reduced, and his relative helplessness in comparison with his predatory enemies further strengthened social habits and interests and directed the evolution of his intelligence towards social requirements. The economic advantages of combination and division of labour were already experienced by many gregarious groups of mammals. With the establishment of grasses in the world in probably late Eocene times, groups of animals adopted them and since they used to be able to migrate easily and quickly to follow their food from over-grazed or sun-scorched regions, they were modified in their bodily organization in the direction of speed. The carnivores also became bigger, stronger and speedier to feed on prey, now so much more abundant, but more difficult to seize. "The answer of the grass-feeders, with their specialized hoofs, teeth and bones, better suited to flight than fight", observed Watts, "was to seek safety in numbers, and thus develop the herd instinct, with its necessity for leadership and discipline, but this, in turn, provoked a like rejoinder from some types of their enemies". Herds of cattle, horses, and deer are able to ward off attacks of large carnivores by associating together. Association among gregarious mammals also tends to develop specialists for foraging and feeding, attack and defence. All these have been formative factors in the development of sociality in pre-man, or early humans amongst whom the lengthening of childhood made special demands for co-operation. Pre-man or early man seldom lived in isolation which would expose them to grave danger. Hunting expeditions led them to combine and adopt some crude division of labour. Thus, small groups of families collecting fruits or hunting small animals rather than single families or big communities represented man's first apprenticeship in co-operation. But co-operation and division of labour of families, hordes and tribes were determined by regional conditions. Hunting, pastoralism, agriculture and their varied combinations were determined by the plant and animal resources of the region, and these governed types of social integration and organization. Man's new way of living enforced by change in the conditions of food supply as the forests retreated, his new taste for non-vegetarian diet, coupled with his physical inferiority to many groups of animals that surrounded him, developed gregariousness among the early hunters. As the grasslands developed the gregarious types among the mammals, man selected a few among them for his own uses, and these could easily accept his leadership in place of that of their own species. Finally, the grasses provided nourishment concentrated in their seeds, and as man learnt to collect these seeds and began to grow such grasses, a plentiful and stable food supply strengthened social life and division of labour and checked his wanderings. Climate and diet stabilized the physical and mental type, while in-breeding developed a strong consciousness of kind. Man's mental evolution was largely the outcome of division of labour and organization, while like-mindedness, sympathy, and child care raised social life at once to a higher level. Beavers, prairie-dogs and social insects have their permanent social products which make the securing and conserving of food and the defence of the colony easier. Man, on account of the intelligent use of his twofold implements, his hands and his voice, has built up a richer external social legacy than the gregarious mammals and insects. This consists, not merely of his tools and artefacts, stores and dwellings, domesticated animals and methods of transport, but also of economic traditions which define the range of competition as keen among members of crowded groups of animals which quickly exhaust their food supply in a limited area.

Evolution of Tools and Traditions in Social Animals

The social animals exhibit "species knowledge" of tools, weapons, materials of nesting and division of labour, traditions of collective homing and migration in search of food and breeding sites, of saving and storing for the community and territorial possession, even of leadership and obedience, and learning–teaching relationship. Such acquisitions make the securing and conserving of food and defence of the community easier, and play an important role in the rapid multiplication, differentiation and survival of animal types. These are mainly instinctive in the animal kingdom. But the large-brained creatures like the beavers, elephants and monkeys show much intelligent social behaviour and economic utilization. In the social life of the primates we find the greatest development of intelligent social action. They can make and use tools; they sometimes combine to raid cultivated fields and orchards and they sometimes migrate in parties, formed of individuals of more than one species, from the plains to the hills in the hot season and return in winter, carrying their young with them as the conditions of food supply change. For the ape the presence of other members of his species, according to Kohler, is the most important stimulus for the promotion of a large number of vital activities. Among apes we see a careful discrimination between kin and stranger in the family group; the relationship of dominance and obedience is also well established in their harems or more extended societies. These are significant in introducing some order and organization in the food quest, offence and defence. Sounds, gestures and emotional expressions, indicative of social feeling, are also clearly discernible among them, and these are understood by the community which can thus rise into a crowd excitement, fear, joy or indignation. Such feelings also serve as effective means of integrating the community, and justify themselves in the course of evolution though these may not have direct bearings on the first, i.e. ecological or economic justification of a society.

Finally, games also form a part of animal traditions anticipating or imitating the serious activity of the species. These have exhilarating social effects and are played vigorously, especially by the birds and apes. Among the latter "there is rivalry and also collaboration in games just as there is rivalry and collaboration in defence and mutual aggression". Yet the mass games played by many birds and other animals, and the sham and sometimes very real battles in which they engage during the mating season seem to be, as Park observes, "fundamentally expressive, merely". Groos also considers them "orgiastic" in character. Due to the lack of development of intelligence the play of the animals cannot develop that sociability or consensus met with in human games. It is thus clear that many forms of co-operation and habits, attitudes and emotional expressions in the social milieu are clearly to be found among animals nearest man in the biological scale. As man's intelligence evolved, speech superseded all other kinds of integrative stimuli, expanded sympathy, intensified affection in small groups, sharpened social distance and aided the establishment of rank and power, learning and teaching. Tools, territories and traditions could now be transmitted from generation to generation, and these served as shields protecting individuals against the severity of external selection. Man's external legacy registers racial gains like the cerebral registrations represented by the instinctive capacities of the social insects, and lifts evolution to a higher level.

Several gregarious mammals and the social insects no doubt bequeath nests, pastures and hunting grounds which are invested with meaning or with suggestiveness to successive generations. When birds or beavers or the social insects live in the same colony or nest from generation to generation, traditions accordingly develop in relation to the permanent social products which evolve animal foresight. Such dim apprehension of the future as that of a colony of birds or prairie-dogs building nests, or beavers digging a canal or constructing a dam which can be adequately used only by the next generation, or of ants and bees storing for the next winter is, however, the result of an instinctive equipment, not of intelligence. On the whole, while man's tradition and external heritage enable him to preserve and transmit his capital of culture and approved standards and customs, apart from the organic inheritance, the social animals have to begin each new colony anew only with the structural and instinctive equipment provided by true or organic heredity. In this difference Wheeler sees the explanation why so little change has taken place in social insects, although they were highly evolved before the origin of man. The insects have also evolved means of communication, although not language, by means of the senses of smell and touch and also through vibration and sound production.[3] Speech is the most potent instrument of transmitting both the past and the present experience to the future. "The word," observes Myerson, "builds up the whole of that social heredity which is so momentous a thing in human life and upon which finally depend the institutions which tools have created — first and foremost the tool of language, and

[3] Imms, *Recent Advances in Entomology*.

second, the tools created by the hand." Man's hand not only makes, uses and changes tools but also grasps and caresses what he loves, and throws away and destroys what he dislikes — material objects and fellow-beings. Man's contact with fellowmen is facilitated by the use of his hands. But while social proximity or distance is expressed by the language of the hand, it is human voice which plays a more decisive role in bringing about, intensifying, or breaking off social relations. Finally, it is man's language which establishes contacts ranging over widely distributed space and time. The evolution of speech among the social animals has, indeed, been a significant factor in the development of sociality. Many animals produce feeding, mating, fighting, signalling and fleeing cries which elicit appropriate responses in other animals and bring about co-ordination of their activities. The infra-human primates have, of course, the largest repertory of sounds in their vocabulary, some of which express and elicit collective excitement or emotion, such as anger, defiance, indignation, fear or solicitude which prepare the group for appropriate behaviour. The difference between animal and human language is that human language can express not merely feelings but also objects. Man has words for both emotions and objects which implies conceptual thought, since an object is related to a class or category, and can thus epitomize his individual experience for collective guidance. Such experience may also refer to both the past and the future while animal language deals only with the features of the present. Human language thus has aided the development of traditions which may be transmitted to posterity. In animal life the adults educate the offspring but experience cannot be transmitted to the next generation. Secondly, the development of tradition which may be handed over by one generation to another aids the improvement of human tools. Many animals can use and change tools. But such tools are generally hasty and imperfect improvisations to meet particular situations. The variegation and improvement of tools can rest only upon language and traditions. Early man was using some kind of language and some tools and implements in different parts of the earth without marked improvement of his condition for well-nigh 500,000 years. It was only during the last 15,000–20,000 years that he built his first village or city, formed his first language, and developed his first culture. Society should be differentiated from culture.

Distinction between Society and Culture

Society is a mere organized aggregation of persons in a limited territory. Culture is an organized aggregation of tools and traditions. Society is a response to increase of aggregation as this endangers the food supply of the community. Many gregarious animal communities show both under-population and over-population. As communities increase in numbers from a minimum to the optimum, the consequences are not only mobility and competition, which Malthus and Darwin postulated, but also co-operation, division of labour and stratification. As a matter of fact both mobility and competition become efficacious means of organizing the communities of the major groups of gregarious animals by establishing specialization, stratification and integration. Sociality is by no means limited to animals at a high stage of mental evolution. But with mental development, culture develops as another and more complex episode in the community's adjustment to the limited resources and values of the environment. Culture fosters the continuity of society by providing the individuals adequate and adaptive attitudes, habits, patterns and techniques for collective living. It provides easy guidance to the community for population adjustment and to individuals for the satisfaction of their varied needs and interests. On the one hand, man perpetuates culture by transmitting to each succeeding generation its tools, territories and traditions through education and training. On the other hand, his culture and education develop intelligence, expertness and kindly feelings, and act as sieves of selection, eliminating anti-social traits and behaviour and fostering variations congruent with them. Thus society enriches and strengthens itself in a dual manner; as sociality thrives it succeeds cumulatively. Simultaneously the psychical bonds become subtler and more intricate, and thus human society, mammalian in its origin, is no mere ecological aggregation, nor a demographic order, nor an economic framework, but it becomes essentially a moral and political community. At the human level the symbiosis which involves division of labour and interdependence of goods and services between the different inhabitants of the region develops into a consciousness of kind. Symbiosis in plant and animal society thus deepens and expands into a unity of culture, a communion or a web of minds.

Disharmony between Sex and Gregariousness

There is one special reason on account of which the necessity of regulating struggle and competition is greater in human society than among other social animals, and thus some of man's earliest traditions are incest taboos and property regulations which promote mutual aid in the small family group of kindred. Man's elaboration of dress and shelter and his stable conditions of food supply have superseded the rutting period of most mammals and kept alive sex as a perennial interest. The association between the sexes has also become closer and more intimate while the social heritage of customs and traditions often supports the excesses and aberrations of sex, so rarely ugly in bird life, for instance. Man's sex habits, attitudes and traditions, intimately bound up with his continuous sex functioning which may be dissociated from reproduction, and stressed and variegated by the evolution of reciprocal means of communication, often run counter to social interest and to physical health and vigour of the individual. In his bewilderment, primitive man sought to placate sex through taboos and fertility rites and, indeed, the predominance of female figures in palaeolithic art can be attributed to this. From the time of the Aurignacian hunters and food collectors man has found the problems of sex and population particularly difficult for him to tackle. The higher social insects, so abundant in individuals, have overcome the same tendency to over-population through the development of monogyny, which, however, has not been inconsistent with racial survival due to an elaborate protective system which enables a single female or queen to overcome most dangers and vicissitudes. In the more primitive wasps, however, all the members of the colony are capable of reproduction like humans, but their fecundity is low and the dangers of over-population are counteracted by frequent swarming. The specialized deployment of the reproductive instinct will not be compatible with man's evolutionary advance in which sex is implicated with some of man's highest ambitions and achievements. On the other hand, man's institutions, habits and ideas now fail to give him the proper guidance of his sex appetites and to counteract the dangers of population outrunning the means of subsistence. This indirectly leads to greater competition between the individuals and a more acute struggle between society and its environment. The disharmony between the functioning of man's sex and his gregarious impulses which is responsible for so much pathological behaviour and for the heavy hand of economic pressure and competition that frustrate many social gains and acquisitions is due to the rapidity of man's social evolution, upwards and downwards, to which he has not had time to adjust himself. An important step of man's evolutionary advance would consist of so educating the instincts and satisfactions of sex that society is troubled neither by dangers of sex repression on the one hand and over-population on the other. In his reproductive life man has not been able to overcome his egoistic instincts of sex by the force of his extra-organismal social legacy. Infanticide, abortion and neglect of the old and diseased, class struggle and war are symptoms of over-population, and represent phenomena of inner dissolution of society (competition and struggle for existence) setting at naught the social achievements of generations. Both class conflict and wars also prevent that national and territorial division of labour, which would have been an appropriate adjustment to increase of population pressure. Man's social heritage thus exhibits often a conflict between this strong and imperative sex appetite, which through an unregulated multiplication, reduces the standards of life and liberty and opportunities of populations and the social customs and traditions, which regulate competition and mitigate the struggle and suffering which follow from excessive numbers. In a symbiotic society of plants and animals, where co-operation is instinctive, impersonal and vital, and not conscious and moral, such maladjustment between the divergent species of organisms living close together in a region and its resources is not possible. The cultural, as distinguished from the symbiotic order, pays the penalty of superseding the ecological and instinctive mechanisms of control of numbers by traditions and institutions which often fail in offering the right biological direction, and become misfits and malintegrations.

2

Limits of Competition and Specialization

The Contrasted, Fundamental Habit Patterns of Competition and Symbiosis

ECOLOGICAL competition or struggle between individuals and ecological symbiosis or co-operation comprising collective regulation of the struggle are the warp and woof of all economic relations and activities and the two fundamental ecological functions, guided by instincts, imitation and training have become assets to man's economic behaviour in the face of the constant menace of over-population.

Seeds and germcells compete with one another for the chance of reproduction. Plants compete with one another for food, space and light. Animals from beetles to elephants exhibit competitive behaviour in respect of food and mates. In the organic world there is not only struggle among individuals of the same species, but different species of animals also struggle with one another for food and living space. At the human level, competition is not only for food, mates and standard of living but also for money and status which stabilize individual achievement and acquisition. In the ecological order different individuals or different species of animals who are common inhabitants of the same restricted environment also exhibit symbiosis. Different species of plants and animals live interlocked lives. Evolution fosters as much individual variations as collective patterns of living. At the human level it is customs, institutions, morality and religion which regulate the competition-success complex and thus prevent competition from degenerating into anarchy and brutal struggle of all against all. Thus society evolves a plan or system by which the gifts of nature and man-made goods and services can be made to go round to all as far as possible. Different societies evolve different plans and systems to accomplish this. The wealth, values and amenities of life are limited. Some societies hold out the promise of all values of life to everybody, but virtually reserve the rewards for the few. Here competition naturally becomes a dominating motive in all activities and an effective agency of social development. Other societies believe in the equalization of the values and hazards of life or concentrate the values and rewards in the hands of one class on the basis of heredity or historically acquired privilege. It is thus the *ethos* or cultural compulsion of a people derived from historical and social experience which regulates the attitudes and habit patterns of competition and co-operation within the community. Motives of rivalry and altruism are strong or weak according to the basic pattern of life laid down in the culture of the community permeating all individuals, classes and groups. In no society is competition carried to its logical outcome of lawlessness or the absence of rules of the game. The tenacity with which the family, the occupational group and the class regulate the activity and scale of living of individuals in every society, the manner in which economic and social classes lose their privileged position or throw open doors of opportunity to individuals of other classes without any kind of a social revolution, and the universal appeal to social and moral traditions, when, in a social crisis or a period of rapid technical change, competition becomes intensified, all testify to the fundamental ecologic significance of co-operation as an aid in social selection and survival in the reduced environment. The treatment of custom as the primary cause of friction rather than a mode of collective adjustment in economic theory and of the standard of living more as an index of the individual's scale of satisfaction than a means of maintaining a maximum population in the reduced environment is as unscientific as it is abstract and futile.

Stratification, a Fundamental Law

Through competition and symbiosis there is one established or more dominant species in every life-community. Stratification becomes, therefore, a fundamental law in the organization of life. Climate determines whether tall trees, scrubs and grasses dominate and in this way plant life is zoned over the earth. There are complex strata, grades and differentiations of plant communities on the globe, broadly marked out by latitudes and altitudes. In vegetative life the dominant is the kind of plant which can succeed in obtaining the largest share of light and moisture. In animal life, the smaller an animal the commoner it is on the whole.

> Animals at the base of a food-chain are relatively abundant, while those at the end are relatively few in numbers, and there is a progressive decrease in between the two extremes. The reason for this fact is simple enough. The small herbivorous animals which form the key-industries in the community are able to increase at a very high rate (chiefly by virtue of their small size), and are, therefore, able to provide a large margin of numbers over and above that which would be necessary to maintain their population in the absence of enemies. This margin supports a set of carnivores, which are larger in size and fewer in numbers. It is because of number relations that carnivores tend to be much more wide-ranging and less strictly confined to one habitat than herbivores.[1]

---

1 Elton, *Animal Ecology*, p. 69.

The ecological process of stratification functions in more complicated and subtle forms in all spheres of human social relations. On the whole stratification restricts competition among individuals to each layer, niche or grade in plant, animal and human communities, and assures collective subsistence for all in the ecological order that represents a system reciprocally interdependent and balanced growth of all grades of vegetable and animal life. As in every plant community there are layers of vegetation each adapted to exist in a lesser intensity of light than the one above, so the ecological pattern of human society shows different social grades, classes and castes and different spatial relationships of individuals. It is wealth and power which usually represent the criteria of social gradation, individuals and classes owing their dominance directly to competition and success in obtaining the largest share of wealth and power available in the community. The individual's locale, job or status brings him in contact with other individuals, and relations of competition, segregation, accommodation or conflict develop. Or, again, each individual's position in a social stratum is constantly threatened by the mobility or invasion of another, just as in the plant community migration or invasion takes place, which may entirely replace or subordinate all the individuals of a former dominant vegetation. Ecological mobility or speed of invasion of an area occupied by another social stratum or group throws light on accommodation or assimilation and resistance or conflict with contrasted social behaviours and attitudes. Thus place, occupation and time relations of persons and groups are fruitful concepts in social ecology, revealing the nature of social contacts in the collective adjustment of population to the region.

Economics usually concerns itself with the equilibrium of population in so far as there is an adjustment between gross density and resources of the region, disregarding economic gradation or the hierarchical system of specialization of labour and service by which each class or occupation seeks to appropriate the maximum net outturns in the ecological organization from its labours or sacrifices. While migration, population control, and improvement of the arts of production are the essential factors in establishing an economic balance, the importance of the spatial arrangement of classes, institutions and services for population adjustment cannot be disregarded.

Reduction of Competition

All plants develop their own growth forms and positions in the vegetable community. The forest like the human community, is built up in strata, tree stratum, shrub stratum, ground vegetation, and overstepping these horizontal boundaries the epiphytes and climbers. In each stratum the needs of space, light, heat and nutriment of the different species of plants markedly differ. Thus stratification in the forest community reduces competition, on the one hand, and introduces service of different species in terms of shade, soil protection and other forms of reciprocity, on the other. Similarly, each animal has its own grade, niche, occupation or specific environment in an ecological area. In every animal community there are herbivorous and carnivorous and scavenging animals. Size differentiates the animals among a series of herbivores and carnivores; while within the herbivores and carnivores of any one size there may be further differentiation according to food habits. Special niches are, more easily distinguished among carnivores, which prey upon large mammals, or small mammals or insects.[2] Elton has discerned an extraordinarily close parallelism between niches of animals in widely separated regions and communities. Thus competition for prey among the predatory groups is attenuated and there even develops mutual tolerance. Commensalism is met with

---

[2] Vide *Animal Ecology*, pp. 64-65.

even among carnivorous species of animals, the larger directly or indirectly aiding the smaller predator in the food supply.

Within the same herd or colony all gregarious animals also develop a spatial arrangement of individuals and groups, exhibit patterns of division of labour which enable them to multiply and maintain themselves effectively in the competition for existence. Sexual division of labour has developed early in this stage of animal development and many of the higher forms of animals combine division of labour between the sexes with a more or less flexible territorial system connected with courtship, nesting, schooling, play and other activities of the species which indirectly assures adequate supply of food, freedom and security for the developing young. Division of labour also takes the form of temporary occupation of certain jobs necessary for the security of the entire community by different individuals. Thus, for instance, among antelopes, bisons, elephants and monkeys or among flamingos and penguins we have sentries who keep watch and leaders who lead a fight or migration and among giraffes and penguins there are creche-minders. The less strong and timid animals, including the females and the young, are surrounded by the herd of gregarious mammals as they roam through the forest. Thus reciprocal competition is restricted, mutual helpfulness grows; and society evolves through the growth of traditions and external legacies. Schjelderup-Ebbe, Allee, Murchison and other observers have been accumulating data which show that there also exists in a flock of birds, a definite order of precedence or social hierarchy. Fifty species of birds have shown an apparently hard and fast system of social ranking which may be characterized as being based on an almost absolute peck-right. In certain other birds such as pigeons, ring doves, canaries, and, perhaps, sparrows a rigid social ranking is superseded by an elastic give–and–take relationship, which is a matter of gradual development. With many birds there is a definite social prestige related to sex. The usual report is that the more showy or larger sex is dominant. In some others there is a positive correlation between ability to learn and social position. Masure and Allee have suggested that high rank in the social order can easily have survival value during times of food shortage, a suggestion which needs to be tested by exact observation.[3]

Stratified Specialization among the Social Insects

The acme of stratified specialization is found among the social insects which include several groups of wasps and bees together with ants and termites. These are differentiated into physiological castes. The number of castes that may occur in a polymorphic species varies considerably. Wheeler has described twentyseven castes, largely among females, among ants while four stable castes are of common occurrence among the termites. Increased co-operation and specialization between members of polymorphic species enable the social insects to live and thrive in large colonies in a limited area and it has been observed that a colony should reach an adequate density before kings and queens are reared. Wheeler observes:

> Nourishment, temperature and other environmental factors merely furnish the conditions for the attainment of characters pre-determined by heredity.

Among many social wasps, bees and termites the difference between the fecund queen and a neuter which devotes itself exclusively to the work of the colony is brought about through regulation of nourishment. Nutrical castration (derived from *nutrix,* "nurse") takes the place in the adult worker of the alimentary castration to which it was subjected during its larval period. It also appears that the females of the wasps, bees and ants, which are provided with a smaller muscular sac filled with

---

[3] Allee, "Analytical Studies of Group Behaviour in Birds", *The Wilson Bulletin,* September, 1936.

sperm during a single act of mating, can control the sex of their offspring by permitting or disallowing sperm to leave the sac and fertilize the eggs. When the colony becomes too small, these insects can thus produce the missing sex and increase numbers. Specialization of certain individuals to perform specific functions for the common good and co-operative activity make the securing and conserving of food and defence of the insect community easier and enable a denser population to live and thrive. On the other hand, since the dangers of over-population and consequent disintegration of communal life are very great in insect societies, these have evolved methods of overcoming such dangers by a flexible system of control of sex and fecundity through nutrition and control of environmental factors. Man practises methods for control of reproduction which are crude as compared with those of the true social insects while he neither understands the causes which determine sex nor can he control it. The building of nests, foraging and apportioning of food among the larvae and adults, economy in its use extending even to starvation and competition with other organisms in securing food supply, all appear to have contributed to the development of worker and soldier castes in the insect communities. An unlimited multiplication in densely populated colonies is avoided through the restriction of reproductive powers to few individuals and their suppression in the rest. It is in this manner that the relatively stable specialization of castes in the insect society is adjusted to the conditions of density and adequate provision of food for the entire colony. Thomson rightly observes in this connection,

> As the workers and soldiers do not usually "grow up", so to speak, they are not tormented by sex-impulses as the drones must be, and it seems to us that the maternal care of the non-reproductive worker ants and bees, and the protective vigilance of the non-reproductive soldier-ants and soldier-termites, illustrate what one might call the shunting or sublimation of the sex-urge.

Among the insects we also find as in human society results of perversion of the caste system in the existence of paupers and robbers or predators within the species which devour dead or diseased insects or prey upon the brood. The instincts to feed, foster, and defend other individuals make the invasion of an animal society by parasites and guests easy. In India a moth and a mouse are regularly associated with the nest of social spiders. There is a considerable number of guests in the nests of ants and termites, myrmecophiles and termitophiles, including various mites, spiders and millipedes; there are many parasites in human society.[4] Other instances of perversion of behaviour are afforded by slavery or dulosis among some species of ants whose workers raid the nests of other species carrying off to their own nests pupae from which workers subsequently develop. Some species are entirely dependent upon their slaves in whose nests their young queens establish their own brood. The character of this exploitation thus varies. One species of ants preys on the brood of another or enslaves it; another species uses its host merely for the purpose of bringing up its own brood; still another merely derives a certain protection from living near its neighbours.[5] The swarming activities of bees, wasps and ants resemble the marauding and colonizing expeditions of men while the development of highly specialized social parasites with no workers which live at the expense of other species resemble human societies which subsist by maintaining a slave or proletariat population to a necessary level.

Specialization and Constraint of the Single Organism

Animal ecology abundantly illustrates how niche, occupation,

---

[4] Pearse, *Animal Ecology*, p. 335.

[5] Wheeler, *Ants*.

territory and division of labour have a direct bearing on the population problems of a herd, colony or aggregation of gregarious mammals, and how an appropriate specialization among the more highly organized social insects is perverted towards social parasitism as in human society. Among the termites caste development does not preclude, as in the human species, participation of individuals of different castes in the life of the community. Here the sexes are of equal social importance, each caste comprising individuals of both sexes, whereas in ants the workers and soldiers consist of female individuals only. Workers and soldiers among the termites seem to be suppressed males as well as females. Thus we find a more marked resemblance with the ecological pattern of human society. A high degree of specialization for the economic efficiency of the social insects makes it necessary that certain functions and interests, specially the reproductive, are relegated to the background or are imperfectly developed. In the termitary some individuals with small brain and eyes and with the reproductive organs in a very rudimentary condition, develop into sterile workers and soldiers; others with these several organs normally developed grow into fertile reproductive forms. Wheeler has also noted that termites, as a result of social life, have shown a tendency to deteriorate in their physical prowess, but tend to attain a higher degree of nervous organization. He has observed a similar, though less pronounced, tendency in ants. He also believes that ants and bees have evolved from ancestral wasps and that each of these has developed the caste system independently. The male and female must have potentialities in their germ cells for all the characters that the species shows. It is the quality and quantity of food that produces the various castes in wasps and bees, but in ants the germ plasm has somehow been reached and modified, so that a heredity basis for caste differentiation has been established. Alice, who has recently considered the question whether the caste system among the social insects is a result of heredity or of the social environment, cites evidence from the lifehistory of cockroaches and termites that with the termites, colony life is an absolute essential for the development of intestinal protozoans which are lost with each moult and which the termites obtain by swallowing a drop of liquid emerging from the anus of another termite, and that aggregation allows aspects of mass physiology to develop, which in turn permits a closely knit and varied social evolution.[6]

Similarly, Castle and Pickens support the theory that functional reproductives of each sex produce respectively a substance that when eaten by the nymphs of a group, inhibits the development of the reproductive organs in the nymphs of that sex. This material is thought to be distributed throughout a group by grooming. Castle stresses the fact that conditions within a termite colony such as the number of individuals, castes already present to a considerable degree influence the time of appearance and nature of new castes. By the removal or addition of a single individual the balance of a colony may be altered so that the appearance of certain types may be delayed, prevented altogether or caused to appear very soon. Such is apparently the influence of mass physiology on the structure and functions of organisms in the termite colony. Among the highest social insects specialization and constraint of the single organism are so extreme that its independent viability is sacrificed to a system of communal bonds. As we pass from the socially primitive to the more specialized groups of social insects, or in the ontogeny of the single colony as we pass from earlier to its later stages, we actually witness, remarks Wheeler, "a notable and increasing degeneration of the individual". Holmgren has shown that the supra-oesophageal ganglion or brain in the mature kings and queens

6 *The Social Life of Animals* pp. 241-47.

of termites shrinks to one third, while the sympathetic ganglia increase to three times their original size. And von Rosen finds that the eyes and optic ganglia of the aged royalty among termites also undergo marked degeneration. Furthermore, the eyes, brain, thoracic structure, and often also the pigmentation of the workers in the most highly socialized ants are less developed than they are in the workers of small primitive societies, which are more like the original solitary vespoid ancestors. Evolution by atrophy certainly accompanies an advance in social integration of the insects.[7] At the human level the social integration is worked out by the unison of minds, by social psychology instead of mass physiology.

Specialization versus Plasticity in Human Society

In human societies a high degree of occupational specialization, though it similarly involves usually certain limitation and loss of vital capacity and of creative initiative among individuals, has evolved interdependence of mental patterns. Man's progress would lie in reconciling the demands of increase of numbers, and specialization in the Great Society on the one hand, with those of freedom and complete development of individuality in the reduced environment, on the other. No doubt an ever increasing specialization in human activities has brought about an atrophy or sub-atrophy of man's sense-organs and tissues. An increasing proportion of population in modern urban communities exhibits congenital or acquired defects of vision, hearing and smell; while degeneration in the epidermal structures, viz. teeth, hair and pigmentation is on the increase. No doubt man's success may not wholly depend on the proper functions of his eye, ear or nose but it is considerably promoted by nice discrimination of colours, sounds and smells. There is also greater activity of man's

---

7 Wheeler, *Essays in Philosophical Biology*, chapter on "Emergent Evolution", p.161.

visceral nervous system and endocrine glands which result in the higher emotivity and greater criminality in the large beehive cities of modern times. The totalitarian states of today have brought about such regimentation of the individual in the face of deficiency of food resources and inter-state rivalry and conflict that societies are now being fashioned like those of the social insects in considerable parts of the world — authoritarian societies of very low intelligence of the average individual combined with an intense and pugnacious solidarity of the whole. International conflict has its counterpart in the hostility of every colony of social insects towards every other colony, even of the same species. Yet man's variability of behaviour and his inheritance of generalized response possibilities are in marked contrast with the structural and instinctive, specialization of the social insects which fit them more admirably than him to an elaborate communism and control of numbers. As compared to the social insects' works and devices, which represent final and relatively stable accomplishments, man's social adaptations represent a diversity and novelty which can only equal the divergence and variability of his psychical characteristics. It is these which assure man's fresh advance, and the test of civilization is how far it can elicit a wholesome heterogeneity of capacities among individuals and at the same time assure the largest participation of all in the social acquisition of a large sized community without that measure of polymorphism which discourages plasticity.

3

Functions of Dominance and Distance

Social Stratification of Trees, Animals and Men

THE structure of a forest exhibits different social layers that are the result of a competition by which the trees come to dominate the canopy and the other species assume subordinate positions in accordance with their competitive equipment. Out of the struggle for raw materials in food-making and for radiant energy comes the sorting of the constituent species of a forest into dominants, subdominants, and subordinates, which form strata or layers of diminishing rank and the process is accompanied by the suppression or elimination of the weaker individuals or species.[1] This is best illustrated in the tropical rain-forest, which exhibits great development of stratification, several tiers of trees being present in addition to others formed by more lowly plants.[2] "In its complex, many-layered structure," observes Braun-Blanquet, "the tropical rain-forest presents a marvellous picture of closely knit community life. Its manifold systematic and ecologic types of plants and communities are the most highly evolved, the most minutely adapted".[3] Each of the different strata have their own species, and these, if they may be said to strive to reach their own level before attaining full development, make no attempt to pass beyond it, even if opportunity offers. In other words, the arboreal species seem

[1] Weaver and Clements, *Plant Ecology*.

[2] Newbigin, *Plant and Animal Geography*, pp. 123 and 160.

[3] *Plant Sociology*, p. 367.

to fall into three or more groups, each possessing not only a particular height limit, but also a related degree of tolerance of the shading due to the canopy of the next tier above. The species present in the topmost tier presumably demand, at least in the full grown stage, complete exposure. Thus the struggle towards light mainly affects the sapling stages. It may be added that some of the occasional herbaceous forms of the lowest tier have iridescent or violet leaves, apparently to help them to make the fullest use of the light rays which penetrate the forest gloom. This again suggests that the members of the different tiers are not all striving to overtop their neighbours, but are definitely adapted to a particular stratum.

Social bonds are also established between plants and animals in the different strata of the forest community. Since in an equatorial forest tall phanerophytes predominate over all other life-forms and vegetal food is concentrated in the upper tiers, climbing animals with prehensile tails (monkeys) and parachutes (flying squirrels, lemurs, phalangers and many others) are most numerous. Even birds here, due to the density of the forest, have limited powers of flight compared with those occurring in other types of habitat. At the ground level movement of bulky animals is difficult while pasturage hardly exists. It is in this manner the equatorial forest governs and sorts the types of animals in its different tiers. Social stratification of both trees and animals thus emerges as the result of competition, segregation and division of labour.

In human society, due to the unique development of speech, education and tradition, division of labour, though grounded merely on economic interests, develops into an integration of behaviour and unison of minds and thus each occupation, each natural area or region, where a class of community pursues its routine of life, develops its own traditions and customs, its own culture. The social significance of division of labour was strongly stressed by Durkheim.

Society created by division of labour is not limited, according to him, to merely economic interests, it represents a unique social order. "Instead of developing separately, individuals concert their efforts; they are interdependent parts of a unity which is effective not only in the brief moments during which there is an interchange of services but also afterwards indefinitely". Specialization of individuals for specific occupations or duties in human society which finds its counterpart in the castes and differences of behaviour among individuals of an animal aggregation is not merely an ecological mechanism of interchange of services and exploitation of the specific environment by the population; it rises to a cultural mechanism for the cultivation and education of appropriate habits, attitudes and interests. The patterns of division of labour and specialization of occupations, professions and services in human society are appropriate for each population adjustment. It is these factors which make individuals available at positions, where competition will give them a status. On the other hand, such status or selection often implies training and develops specialized interests, attitudes and personality traits of the individuals. Each occupation, profession or service plans the life, social aims and attitudes of individuals, and thus the development of different types of personality is quite conducive to man's social adaptation and efficiency, which is in the last resort a phase of the society's population adjustment.

Circularity of Dominance Relationships in Bird Society

All gregarious animals exhibit relations of dominance and distance in which lie the germs of stratification in human society. Animal societies develop notions of a common leadership and allegiance due to a discovery that some members have unusual power, cunning or brilliance which may stand the herd, flock or colony in good stead in the acquisition of food, in attack, defence and migration or in some other form of mutual aid.

Schjelderup-Elbe, Allee and others have observed that flocks of birds and possibly many other kinds of animals are organized according to a "pecking order" in which each individual has its own status depending on whether it may peck other individuals or submit to being pecked by them. Among the chickens studied in the laboratory a kind of simple despotism is general, with the larger, stronger and more pugnacious males usually dominating the females. Among the pigeons and parakeets, dominance or submission changes according to the phase of the breeding and nesting cycles which the birds are in at the time. Thus, the social order here is loosely organized on a give-and-take basis. With all these birds, observes Allee, social ranking has a survival value. High rank in the social order of the flock means much greater freedom of action of the birds, more ready access to food and a generally less strained style of living. It is hard to say whether in nature it means more than this, although it seems probable that in times of food shortage or other phases of environmental stress, the ranking birds, who have the first opportunity at food, might readily fare better than those low in the social scale. The pecking order is far from being a constant and fixed hierarchy.

The causes underlying this hierarchy of the birds have not been successfully investigated and no definite results are available. The factors that determine the position of the birds in the social order are rather complicated and include such personal traits as health, age and pugnacity of the individual birds, sex in general and the reproductive cycle in particular, as well as such ecological factors as size of available space, feeding and nesting habits, and the possibilities of establishing special territories. High position in the social order does not necessarily coincide with group leadership, although at times it does.[4]

---

[4] Allee: *Social Life of Animals*, Chapter VI, also *Animal Life and Social Growth*, p. 153.

The Biting or Bullying Order in Mammalian Society

The organization of the herds and packs of the lower mammals is like that of the bird flock except that it should be called a biting, bullying or mounting instead of a pecking order, or, with some zoologists, a "scale or order of dominance". Among domestic cattle, cows exhibit an order of bossing or hooking privilege which is expressive of dominance. Hudson, speaking of the packs of semi-feral dogs kept on the cattle-breeding establishments in Argentina remarked that from the foremost in strength down to the weakest there is a gradation of authority; each one knows just how far he can go, which companion he can bully when in a bad temper and wishes to assert himself and to whom he must humbly yield in turn.

Serial Subordination in Anthropoid Society

Wheeler observes in this connection:

> A dominance scale of fundamentally the same type has been observed in the troops of various monkeys and anthropoid apes but is, of course, more elaborate, as we should expect from the greater physical and physical plasticity of these creatures.[5]

Yerkes has studied dominance–subordination of the group of chimpanzees.

> Physique, intelligence, temperament and experience, as objectively evaluated and describable in behavioural terms, stand forth as the essential determining conditions of those social behaviour patterns which we have come to designate as dominance and subordination. Highly impressive and socially significant in ape as in man are such biological contrasts as robust and puny, bright and dull, well-adapted and inept, courageous and cowardly.[6]

---

5 Wheeler, *Essays in Philosophical Biology*, Chapter on Animal Societies, p. 246.

6 Yerkes, "The Life History and Personality of the Chimpanzee", *The American Naturalist*, March-April 1939.

Yerkes and Yerkes have found that dominance is not merely a matter of leadership by a given individual, or even of primacy of initiative and control in every situation by a despot. Instead, the system of relationship extends or may extend throughout the group, thus constituting an order or hierarchy. Both among chimpanzees and howler monkeys along with dominance there is serial subordination. Yerkes and Yerkes compare chimpanzees, howlers and baboons as follows in respect of social order or hierarchy: in degree of increasing dominance by a single individual usually a male — howler, chimpanzee, baboon; in degree of increasing co-operativeness in the group — baboon, chimpanzee, howler; and in degree of increasing approach to equality of status — baboon, chimpanzee and howler. Howler and baboon, they conclude, seem to represent radically different natural experiments in social organization, the one being a species of communism, the other a form of absolutism. And they ask: Has dominance itself become dominant in the order, primates, by reason of superior value for survival?[7] Maslow found among groups of rhesus monkeys similar serial subordination. With these primates mounting and bullying are the most reliable measures of dominance, cringing and flight of subordination. The hierarchy of dominance found from the results of the separate pairings is practically perfect in that it shows no circularity of dominance relationships such as that found in birds. Starvation seems to heighten the dominance of the overlord animal. When larger groups are formed, behaviour emerges which is unpredictable from the data on pairing; animals dominant in the pairing are, in the group, beset by alliances of their subordinates and beaten severely. Dominance traits markedly differ between the chimpanzees and rhesus monkeys. The dominance of the former is primarily friendly, protective, altruistic and playful. That of the rhesus monkeys

---

[7] Yerkes and Yerkes, "Social Behaviour in Infra-human Primates", *Hand-Book of Social Psychology*, p. 1019.

is rough, brutal and aggressive, expressing themselves in ferocious bullying, mounting and assault. Monkeys seem to pay little attention to each other, form only loosely cohering pairs and are generally low in dominance behaviour. Carpenter's recent field studies of the social relations of free ranging primates in their native habitats corroborate Maslow's conclusions in respect of differences in dominance qualities of the different species of monkeys and apes. Furthermore, it seems indicated that arboreal primates show less tendency to pugnacity than the more terrestrial primates. Howling monkeys in the Panama Canal zone were found to range in size from five to thirtyfive animals in each group, with the modal group containing eighteen animals. Within each group there were approximately seven females to every three males. Gibbon groups in the forests of Siam ranged in size from two to seven with the modal group consisting of four animals. The characteristic Gibbon group comprises an adult male, an adult female and a succession of young ones upto a maximum of five. When a young one has been with the parent group until four or five succeeding young ones have been born, it has then matured sufficiently for it to separate from the parent grouping and become a part of the nucleus of a new group.[8] Thus group integrity or splitting (apoblastosis) is associated with ecological factors, conditions of food supply and striking species differences with respect to degrees of dominance and pugnacity among the primates.

The Biological Significance of Dominance

A pecking or bullying order or a relationship of dominance or distance in a flock of birds and a herd or pack of mammals gives the individual dominant or sub-dominant animal an advantage in mating, food gathering, especially during drought, or in the course of migration, and also invests the

[8] Carpenter, "Free-Ranging Primates", *The Scientific Monthly*, 1939, pp. 318-25.

animal group with a certain stability and a degree of organization. These are especially necessary for defence, foraging and even offence. Thus the gradation or stratification of the animal community, which nourishes and maintains dominance–subordination relationship, contributes towards better organization and success in the struggle for existence.

The Role of the Leader in Animal Society

Dominance implies not merely control or coercion but also good leadership which involves integration and co-operativeness. The leader of the animal herd, flock or colony, indeed, plays a valuable role in the food gathering and defensive activities of the animals. Among some mammals, leadership of the herd or band rests with an old and experienced female, as for example, among giraffes, antelopes, reindeer and cattle. Often she is the sentinel of the herd who never betakes herself into rest without calling upon some other animal to relieve her.[9] Many instances have been adduced where the death of the female leader is followed by disorganization and easy capture or massacre of the herd and where she successfully organizes attacks, flights and defences, lends assistance to the wounded members of the herd and even sacrifices herself for the herd. With many other mammals, e.g., elephants, seals, gnus and baboons the male is the leader and sometimes a jealous one, that drives other males out of the herd, which becomes a large harem; although in some cases a few individual defeated males are tolerated. Leadership here is also strong, vigilant and effective though it weakens in the mating season when there may be continual bickering. Striking examples of successful leadership are also afforded by herds of bison among whom the bulls form a ring with the cows and calves within when they are attacked

---

[9] Alverdes, *Social Life in the Animal World*, p. 122.

by enemies and fight their battles. Among many mammalian species, again, the males unite to form one herd and the females another. Herds or packs, separated according to sex during seasons other than the mating period, are found among wild sheep, bison, boars, stags and bucks with their respective male or female leaders. In such cases the young ones usually belong to the female packs. Speaking about the packs of red deer under the female leader, Darling observes:

> Matriarchy makes for gregariousness and family cohesion. The patriarchal group (among deer) can never be large, for however attentively the male may care for his group he is never selfless. Sexual jealousy is always ready to impinge on social relations leading to gregariousness. I contend that the matriarchal system in animal life, being selfless, is a move toward the development of an ethical system.

Female Societies, Animal and Human

With many of the herds of mammals the duties of protection, care and schooling of the young are in fact borne by the females. Patriarchy among the mammals is, on the whole, less stable and is more pugnacious and combative and the association often disappears during the period of sexual rut, or when danger appears the male head makes off and rejoins the herd when it is past. Similarly the flocks of male birds are more pugnacious than the females. The male among the higher vertebrates is usually larger, stronger and more pugnacious than the female and therefore becomes, as Wheeler remarks, a much more serious social problem than he is among the insects.

> The male acts like a violent ferment in vertebrate group life, increasing both its constructive and destructive mobility and accentuating its dynamically stratified organization.

Female societies, like those of the hymenoptera and lower mammals, and bi-sexual societies, like those of the termites, are, indeed, peaceful and harmonious, but also stationary and incapable of further social evolution. Many mammalian societies thrive by rejecting the aggressive males of the species except in the mating season. Many insect societies, again, maintain their organization by reducing or eliminating the number of males which is subtly and carefully adjusted to the needs of food supply and reproduction. It is only in the termite and human societies that we find males consorting with females in the colony throughout life and that workers and soldiers are of both sexes. The male has been socialized in the termitary but not in the human society. It is probable that man's social evolution in the future will chiefly consist of the chastening and discipline of sex and aggressiveness on the one hand, and the utilization of power and vitality of the human male for constructive purposes. Man today is too much of a destroyer, a law breaker and war maker to assure the safety and continuity of his species. Can he reach the social subordination of the male as in the termitary, the most perfect type of society that has evolved in nature, without sacrificing his plasticity?

There is no doubt that not before long centuries of evolution partially tamed the human male that early human society could be integrated and stabilized. Ecological factors played an important role in such socialization. Man's arboreal ancestors who subsisted upon fruits and nuts in the forests could guard their harem and maintain their male dominance amidst, however, constant bickerings and sexual fights. As man's immediate ancestors came down on *terra firma* and adopted omnivorous food habits, both polygamy and promiscuity were eliminated and a far greater co-operation between the sexes than there is among the higher apes was discernible. As the baboon or gorilla troop foraged together for fruits, nuts and herbs, the harem had a chance to survive as the male leader or overlord could guard the females from the attentions of the younger and less dominant males. But as early man became largely dependent on a more variegated diet including animal foods, food collecting or hunting which demanded long absence from the cave or tree shelter could not succeed until a stable biparental family superseded the harem. For no hunter would pursue his calling if in his absence the females were seduced or abducted. A monogamous family achieved a new division of labour between the sexes in the human family based more on mutual interests and feelings and less on the size, strength and pugnacity of the male as among his primate ancestors. No doubt among several groups of primates such as the chimpanzee and gibbon bi-parental family has stabilized itself and safeguards the care of the young, while the tenderness of the gibbon or chimpanzee mother for their young and solicitude for kin are almost on the human level. In the evolution of the human family, the taboos on incest and adultery have disciplined the rebellious sexual desire of the male and prevented the bi-parental nucleus of society from being integrated by masculine aggressions and fights. Further, the prolonged infancy and childhood of man have contributed also to the pronounced socialization of the male through intensive social conditioning by the mother. Matriarchal or matrilineal social organization, though not universal, has been a significant phase in the evolution of a sane and balanced communal life as displayed in the order and social solidarity of the hymenoptera. In matriarchy masculine competition and strife were largely regulated, the male sexual aggression was subordinated, division of labour was slight and social equality was promoted in many respects. The patriarchal society provided a more elaborate division of labour and was as full of internal conflict as it was progressive. Conquest, domination and slavery, all emerged in the patriarchal communities as factors of social selection and progress. But a rigid social stratification based on conquest and subordination itself became a serious hindrance to progress. In patriarchy there gradually developed much more subtle and specialized relations between the directive and dominant and the subordinate social groups and individuals. Social evolution, however, through equal opportunities and benefits to all minimizes social distance and elicits a collective participation in the hazards and gains of society. Yet the directive classes in all civilized societies possess greater wealth and higher plane of living as well as markedly superior traits which differentiate them from the rest of the community. Social progress which is directed by the *elite* of society depends largely upon the interests and objectives of the latter. Its stability rests upon an equitable sharing of the benefits of progress between the *elite* and the community as a whole. On the other hand, it is through a process of selection that both the dominance of the *elite* and the acceptance of their aims and attitudes by the rest of the community are determined.

Ways of Expression of Dominant Behaviour

In both animal and human community stratification is the outcome of competition, selection and division of labour. It brings into existence dominance–subordination relationship and behaviour and is an effective means of organizing the community. At the human level, however, feelings of dominance or subordination are distinct from factual dominance or subordination. Real dominance may be accompanied by inferiority feelings. Thus in many societies women are expected to conceal dominance feeling in relation to men by compensatory "ladylike" behaviour, and conversely persons with feelings of weakness compensate by dominant behaviour.[10] In the animal society dominance feeling is causally related to dominance status, while the feeling itself due to

---

[10] Maslow "Dominance Feeling, Behaviour and Status", *Psychological Review*, 1937, 44: 404-29.

inadequate mental development is inchoate. Animal psychologists consider that reciprocal evaluation in the animal world is largely dependent upon physiological factors (including learning), and that "interpersonal" contact of animals is probably personal (in so far as it refers to species) but not individual. Secondly, dominance–subordination relationship, once established, is much more stable in human societies, and conditions the behaviour and affects the hereditary dispositions of individuals belonging to a dominant or subordinate class, sex, age, race and nation. For this reason there are found marked resemblances in persons belonging to widely different groups both of which are dominant or suppressed. The *elite* of all races and nations show a similar psychological background and modes of behaviour which persist as long as the dominance factor does not change.

Among the universal ways of expressing dominance–subordination are the infliction of death, physical suffering, humiliation and sexual aggression, on the one hand, and prostration, bowing, supplication and sexual submission on the other. It is noteworthy that such behaviours are discernible also among the infrahuman primates. Thirdly, in human communities dominance–subordination is determined by social heredity and cultural compulsives, and not by individual qualities such as size, strength and agility as among the animals. There are, however, many primitive tribes, as for instance, the Eskimos, among whom status depends upon personal qualities and achievement. Finally, the causes which govern dominance or subordination factors in the human as contrasted with the animal societies are much wider and deeper rooted as these are in the totality of social and cultural aims and not merely advantages in terms of quest for food and sex. Among many savages, however, the advantages in respect of food and sex enjoyed by the dominants in animal society hold good. Many tribes of primitive people have food taboos which forbid certain edibles for the tribe, but which the elders only can enjoy; while the latter also monopolize the young girls leaving for the young men hags and widows. Even in civilized society the consumption of food during war or famine often comes under the control of dominant social groups. Class standards of consumption are saturated with dominance–deference relations. This illustrates one of the ways by which man expresses his dominance or mastery. Biologically speaking, man appears to have a tendency to enjoy physical dominance or mastery whereby others run when he attacks, give up their hold on what he seizes and yield to him in matters of food and sex. Thorndike observes:

> By association this enjoyment may become attached to less obvious forms of mastery, such as giving verbal orders, directing the acts of men remote in space or time, or receiving prayers and tribute. There is also a tendency to enjoy submission to the proper sort of master. This too changes by association. The captain may enjoy doing Napoleon's will as truly as he enjoys having soldiers do his own will.[11]

The framework of culture, rights and duties and moral code and religion enter into man's dominance–deference attitudes and behaviours by instilling habits and ideals of both mastery and submission and thus man's dominance or deference becomes a matter of easy conformity in the smooth-working mechanisms of human roles and statuses. Contrasted are the habits and behaviours adopted in different societies for winning dominance and social position. These are related to the practical and utilitarian purposes of the societies which direct and mould individual achievement and stamp it with the seal of social approval or esteem. In some primitive societies men seek dominance through success in headhunting and war. In others men will distribute food and trophies to their companions or display food, ornaments and weapons

11 Thorndike, *Human Nature and the Social Order*, pp. 733-34.

or collect cattle, slaves and even children to win distinction and status. Some primitive groups such as the Zuñis of New Mexico appear not to welcome evidences of outstanding ability or originality among the individuals and associate prestige with mediocrity. "The best thing to be said about any individual is that no one ever hears anything about him." So far do they carry their negative attitude against individual superiority that if a man wins a race in their annual athletic contest, they do not permit him to run again the next year. A modest amount of prestige may be obtained by buying one's way into secret societies, or by learning a great deal of ritual material, but even this confers no great honour or merit. Similarly, the Arapesh tribe of New Guinea favour the co-operative and submissive behaviour of men. Though there are leaders as soon as the son reaches puberty the big man retires from active competitive life which he has had to lead and which the society assumes, usually correctly, to be eminently uncongenial and difficult to him.

No doubt different peoples with contrasted culture patterns condition self-assertive and dominant or co-operative and submissive attitudes of children and mould them in conformity with their customs and social attitudes. The fear of punishment or disapproval, the force of tradition as well as the advantage which is derived by individuals in social and economic intercourse harmonize their incentives and goals of life, behaviours and ways of living with the pattern of their particular social structure.

The Roles of Social Distance

Domination–subordination relationship and behaviour are always supported by the maintenance of different degrees of social distance between individuals, groups and classes. In the same race, community and group there is found social distance between individuals which is rooted in differential psychology and the play of co-operation or competition in social space. Individuals who may be brought near to each other by temperamental affinities or pursuit of common satisfactions and goals of life may be separated as the result of competition when such satisfactions and goals are limited for appropriation by their very nature and one seeks and obtains them at the expense of another individual. Social distance may be maintained among individuals within the same group without personal rivalry, antagonism or bitterness. Leadership, or a serial domination within a group, is based on differences in traits and capacities, and its aim is to maintain a certain degree of distance. But so long as leadership helps the group in the pursuit of common values the distance is tolerated. A shrewd leader also endeavours to fraternize with the group to maintain his domination. Every individual plays several social distance roles:

1. as individual to individual in a system of competition or co-operation. Attitudes of emulation, rivalry or antagonism, and of friendship or comraderie develop in such a social situation;
2. as individual to the leader. Attitudes of aggression, domination and extroversion, and of inferiority and submission emerge in such a social situation;
3. as individual to an individual belonging to another race, community or group;
4. as race, community or group to another race, community or group. Group relationships are anonymous, indirect and impersonal. Thus it is often found that between person and person, e.g., between a worker and an employer, or between a Britisher and a Nazi German, amicable relationship or social proximity may subsist, but in the same social situation the worker and the employer as belonging to rival industrial camps, and the Britisher and the German as belonging to warring nationalities are sundered by great social distance. Orgies of social bitterness and antagonism

and racial and national passion and hatred are seen to emerge recurrently in the social situation; and

5. an insecure economic status implies an inferior social status with regard to freedom and the values of life. Thus it engenders opposition to and increases social distance between groups; as for example, a trade or industrial union and an employers' organization which stand opposed to each other in social competition.

Measurement of Social Proximity and Distance

As between individuals, so among groups, communities and races, degrees of social proximity can be roughly measured in terms of interdependence, intermarriage and acculturation. Men and women tend to marry their biological equals rather than their opposites. Thus marriage represents the relationships of closest social proximity. Even within the same nation-group intermarriage and social intercourse between the different social and economic classes are largely limited. Social distance is quickly and alarmingly increased in periods of unemployment and depression creating the conditions of an upheaval or revolution. On the other hand, an equalization of incomes and standards of living between the classes and freedom of social mobility and cultural and recreational contacts contribute towards more social proximity, and may ultimately bring about social amalgamation and assimilation.

Social distance is especially marked in all communities characterized by unequal distribution of wealth and diversities of race, culture and functions. Nowhere, perhaps, is social distance more marked than in Hindu society where not merely castes choose occupations for individuals but maintain a rigid social distance from other groups and occupations. The *modus vivendi* is represented by the strict prohibition of marriage and inter-dining outside the caste, coupled with avoidance of physical contact with the "untouchables" who belong to such groups and function as scavengers, agricultural serfs, tanners, criminals, vagrants and primitives. It is estimated that there are a substantial amount of people belonging to depressed castes in India, i.e. 20 to 25 per cent of the total Hindu population; a legacy of Hindu social distance adopted through the centuries. In certain parts of India the distance between high and low castes is safeguarded by the social taboo that prevents the latter from approaching wells, entering temples and even traversing roads meant for the exclusive use of the upper castes.

Untouchability, unapproachability and unseeability where contact, approach from a distance and even mere sight respectively cause pollution to the upper social orders, represent three grades of segregation of the depressed castes in India. A whole host of social conventions in respect of touching food and water for the upper castes, domestic service and entry into the inner apartments of their homes, access to public roads, markets, wells and temples and even being visible at stated periods of the day or only at night time has developed in these submerged castes an inferiority complex from which rescue is certainly difficult. The depressed castes not merely accept these different degrees of segregation insisted upon by the upper orders according to the caste and the social situation but also a rigidly prescribed low standard of living, which is the symbol of degraded status. It is heartening to note that the reform movement led by Mahatma Gandhi supported by the sanction of his eagerness to fast unto death has to some extent destroyed the atmosphere of uncompromising segregation and intolerance of the upper class Hindus.

Social distance in acute form is also met with in the Southern States of North America and in South and East Africa. In these countries the colour bar has presented a serious obstacle to social mixing and prevented Blacks and Oriental immigrants to obtain equal opportunity in agriculture, industry and business. Thus not only differences of culture, race and functions but also differences of colour enter into social ranking and distances in different culture patterns. Social distance is enforced both by legal measures as well as by public opinion. Social ostracism is as much a means of prevention of social mixing as legal prohibitions to enter certain public grounds and paths, to reside and carry on business in certain specified areas or to use public conveyances.

Even where laws are not operative in bringing about social segregation, race and group prejudices have enough strength and persistence to prevent social intercourse with the "undesirables". In the Oriental villages and cities, each caste, community or profession from the highest to the lowest is often found segregated in its particular section or quarter. The absence of competition prevents encroachments of one culture group, race or community upon another. Where, however, low ranking communities or groups move into the more esteemed quarters of the city, the upper cultural groups or classes gradually withdraw as a means of maintaining social distance. Residential property in such areas of transition gradually depreciates due to the advent of low ranking groups and migration of high ranking ones.

This process is seen on a larger scale in the big cities in the West of the USA where Blacks and disesteemed immigrants who are usually at the bottom of the socio-economic scale occupy the low prestige sections and districts of the cities, but who, as their economic condition improves tend to move into the more esteemed pockets. Sometimes Blacks move into an adjacent district leaving it to white residents to recede. In the city of St. Louis, for instance, the older Black settlement gradually moved *en masse* from the east side towards the more esteemed western section of the city, the area vacated by them inviting new Black immigrants to move in. The gradual movement westward of the Blacks had speeded up the migration of the early American settlers along with all their institutions while other foreign immigrants such as the Irish, Germans, Poles, Jews and Italians all responded to the universal desire for the improvement of economic status by migration into higher prestige areas. "A middle-class family living half-way to the earthly paradise of the West End finds its fortunes suddenly improved and moves out a mile farther." A study of sixtynine migrations of churches in that city also showed that all of them, whatever their conscious motive, were carried along on a general tide that bore westward the kind of population to which the older Protestant churches were accustomed. Up to 1870, the churches moved short distances in the river districts. During the period from 1870 to 1890 occurred the virtual abandonment of the "downtown" section by the English-speaking churches. The older populations fought a continually losing battle against the invasion and often moved their institutions barely in time to escape the encircling movement. Between 1910 and 1920, the struggle had shifted west of Grand Avenue, and today the Protestant churches are menaced by population changes as far west as Kingshighway Boulevard.[12]

For the city of Chicago, Burgess has shown how social distance is maintained by different settlers by continuous recession from later comers who occupy a lower position in the socio-economic scale. In many American cities the order of social distance which underlies mass invasions and recessions is somewhat as follows: Irish, Germans, Scandinavians, Czechs, Poles, Jews, Hungarians, Italians and Blacks.

Social proximity and distance of all kinds are measurable. Personal distance is measured by the number of contacts, especially leisure time contacts, the extent of mutual co-operation and interdependence extending from the physical

---

[12] Douglas, *The St. Louis Church Survey*, pp. 69-71.

to the ideal plane and the maintenance of direct and informal relationships between individuals. Bogardus has suggested the following device, for measuring distance between social groups. Subjects are requested to express choice for races of people according to degrees of understanding and intimacy. The instructions read as follows:

> According to my first feeling reactions, I would willingly admit members of each race (as a class, and not the best I have known, nor the worst members) to one or more of the classifications under which I have placed a cross.

Seven classifications are offered, viz.,

1. to close kinship by marriage;
2. to any club as personal chums;
3. to my street as neighbours;
4. to employment in my occupation;
5. to citizenship in my country;
6. as visitors only to my country; and
7. would exclude from my country.

The Social Contact Distance is the average value of the categories in which a race is placed, or the arithmetic mean of the ratings, and the Social Contact Quality Index is an average rating of numerical weights when classification 1 is given a value of 7 and each succeeding classification is reduced by 1.[13]

No doubt the method of measuring social distance will have to be varied according to the differences in social situations of different peoples. Thus for the Orient the categories which may be offered for social scaling should differ from those presented by Bogardus and be somewhat as follows:

1. to endogamous relationship within a caste, clan or brotherhood;

---

[13] Bogardus, "Social Distance and Its Origins", *Journal of Applied Sociology*, 1925, 9: 216-26.

2. to membership of the same caste, clan or brotherhood;
3. to inter-dining;
4. to other forms of social intercourse;
5. exclusion from the neighbourhood, village or city; and
6. exclusion from the country.

Further, the interplay of specific social habits has led to a more stable system of attitudes as regards social gradation in the East than in the West.

Social Distance and Social Progress

Both in the East and in the West the measurement of attitudes in respect of social ranking will throw a flood of light on the interpretation of social behaviour and the means of controlling it for social harmony and justice. In human ecology the crucial problem of social ranking is to maintain the dominance and segregation of that class or the *elite* in society which best represent the cultural objectives of the community as a whole without at the same time thwarting the upward social movement of individuals or groups who actively participate in that culture. Thus a dynamic society must obtain a dual interpretation and satisfy a dual test. First, social stratification is to be defined in terms of distance between individuals and classes which live apart and not merely live together, while the compatibility of the principles that govern social distance with the cultural aims of the community is to be subjected to collective scrutiny and judgement from time to time. Second, the freedom of individuals and classes to move in space and cut across the cross-sections of the society has also to be considered in the context of these very aims. It is an ecological paradox that social distance and individual freedom are both indispensable for social progress and survival.

4

Ecological and Social Pyramids

The Universality of Stratification and Integration

WE have seen that a forest formation is divisible into tiers or strata of trees, shrubs and herbs which constitute an orderly arrangement of dominants, subdominants and subordinates. Similarly the animal community is composed of dominant, and subordinate animals arranged in a system of eating and being eaten, which ensures optimum living conditions for all and the stability of the ecological climax consisting of interlaced plant and animal communities. In an ecological climax there is a limited number of dominant species. As long as the environment remains constant these do not permit subdominant species to attain controlling positions.[1] The climax is a harmonious, integrated whole but not inflexible. Human ecology similarly pictures individuals, social functions and institutions arranged in a system of hierarchy of control which assures the selection of each in the best interests of the community through its appropriate location and power and contributes to social integration and stability. Society, in order to obtain stability, imposes relatively rigid relationships between the different social strata. On the whole the result of social stratification is a hierarchy of domination and submission, with the lower strata carrying the more irksome burdens for the community. The picture is aptly described by Wiese-Becker:

---

[1] Pearse, *Animal Ecology*, p. 167.

> Each layer in the pyramid dominates those below it, even though the upper layers are usually smaller than the lower. Moreover, the lower the level, the more mechanical and menial the work.[2]

No country exhibits such elaborate superimposition of social strata upon strata than India. The lowest social grades in the hierarchy are represented by the medley of castes representing hunters, fishermen, agricultural or servile labourers, tanners, messengers and scavengers who undertake menial, irksome or unclean jobs. Thus society here gives us the picture of a symmetrical pyramid broad at its base with the more considerable proportion of the population held in low social esteem, and engaged in menial or dishonourable occupations and jobs.

Animal biologists study the development of organs of integration and control in the organism. This is the result of an increasing differentiation of the parts of the animal body in the process of relation and response to the environment. As evolution has progressed the parts of the animal body became related in terms of dominance and subordination, that part assuming the role of control and co-ordination which has exhibited a higher rate of physiological activity. Child finds an axiate pattern in the higher organisms, the processes of living, or certain of them, going on most rapidly at one end of the axis, and from this end their rate diminishes along the axis. The relation between a more active and a less active region, according to him, is the foundation of physiological dominance and control. In human ecology we similarly find areas and organs of dominance emerging at focal points in human utilization and circulation. Not merely does a differentiation of regions take place with reference to the areas of dominance, but all services, functions and institutional units are integrated, co-ordinated and centralized in relation to the dominant institutions, and

---

[2] Wiese-Becker, *Systematic Sciology*, p. 310.

organs of social control. Society's rate of activity increases with population and is the highest at the centres of dominance. In the axiate pattern of human society social relations and adjustments orient themselves in terms of dominance and subordination. Social status and social distance express the orderly arrangement of position and power, which define the activities of groups and individuals as the human community multiplies and seeks accommodation through division of labour, specialization and segregation. The greater the differentiation, the more imperative is the need of integration, centralization and control, and the sharper the social distance and segregation of directive institutional units, groups and individuals. The concepts of social status and distance in human ecology accordingly express the differentials in social metabolism, which determine the specialization of services, institutions and individuals, on the one hand and the co-ordination and integration of society on the other. These measure both differences in the rate of activity of individuals and groups and the orientation aims of the human community.

The Pyramids of Industrial and Agricultural Communities

The pyramidal pattern of an industrial community and of its distribution of industries, occupations, habitations and cultural patterns, like the distribution of population over the region itself, is an outcome of all-pervasive ecological forces and conditions. Through sifting and selective processes, manifest in mobility, differentiation and organization, individuals and classes obtain their appropriate, though shifting, role and status in the divisions of labour, which enable them to make the best use of themselves in the social–ecological order. The ecological organization of the community rests upon an adequate and efficient functioning of co-ordination and control of its dominant functions and interests, and social differentiation and selection leave these in the hands of the directive classes. These come to dominate not only production, but also credit and finance, education and leisure. In a modern industrial city the pyramidal concentration of capital and industry has favoured the concentration of financial and industrial power in a small managerial and directive elite, which is concentrated in the central financial district, the focal centre of the system of communications and of credit of the entire region. It is from Lombard, Wall, Broad and Clive streets that the industry, trade and finance of large regions thus are, to a large extent, controlled and directed. Without the pyramids of industrial government and control of credit, the complex structure of modern industry and trade will break down; yet such an economic structure, based as it is on artificial distinctions and inequalities of opportunities and power does violence to man's deeply rooted instincts and traditions, and invites constant change of occupational status and location.

Mobility is less intense, and distance and differentiation are less sharp in agricultural regions. Though the ecological organization of the agricultural community is characterized by an orderly distribution of land values and rents and of social mobility from the periphery or an outer circle of adjoining villages, more or less independent but still dominated by the village market — the focal point of the whole rural complex — yet rents and land values do not show striking differences of levels; nor population density striking gradients, while the forces of occupational and cultural differentiation leading up from the tiller of the soil to the village landlord and moneylender-cum-grain-dealer, who exercise the managerial functions of co-ordination and control of agriculture and rural finance, are sociologically less significant. Both migration and occupational mobility are attenuated in the villages, and thus social changes are much slower and the cultural patterns, adapted to the old economic routine, regulate public opinion and thwart economic adventures and enterprises. In agricultural civilizations social distances are rigidly demarcated, occupations are stereotyped, but guarantee jobs to all while customary patterns of thought and action also prevent mobility. Here society cannot move quickly towards a new arrangement for the exploitation of resources, a new division of labour demanded by the increase of numbers. Individual and group mobility measures social change, which follows from population increase. Mobility is the outcome of the same processes of standardization of trade and industry and of easy and quick communication which facilitate co-ordination and control. It is facilitated by an intenser social and economic pressure in the community and by individual training and personal enterprise. Where these are absent a quick change of economic and social status and occupational and institutional readjustment are not possible.

The hierarchical structure of dominance and distance of classes and occupation groups reflects the basic modes of co-operative exploitation of the region, and this would change under new conditions of density or with improvement of the arts of production. Occupational mobility and change in social gradation are the cultural modes of establishing new relations of population and resources and correspond in this respect to changes in food-chains and ecologic controls brought about by a change in the relative proportions of animal populations.

Not merely is the division of social classes and political groupings governed in the main on the basis of the principles of dominance and distance but the same principles are at work in the determination of hierarchy in the national or world economy. In the modern world economy, peoples and regions which happen to possess available combinations of iron and coal have easily risen to world power, while peoples whom nature has denied these essentials of modern industrial enterprise have to suffer as hewers of wood and drawers of water. The world is divided today politically into strong and weak, and economically into lenders and borrowers on the basis of the division of coal, iron and oil in the modern fuelpower, metal civilization. Within the same community the dominance of supercapital and high finance is reflected, not merely in tariff, currency and banking policies but even in the relations between the money-market and the city, and between the city and the countryside. Even the division of a village or city into occupational or functional areas, the central location of markets, banks and commercial institutions, and the gradation of house rents and land values in the city, all show a spatial distribution governed by the system of dominance of money power which organizes and integrates the various primary produce and industrial regions of the world. The dominance of metropolises in the world organization has its counterparts in, and, indeed, rests on the central control of myriads of cities and little towns scattered about in the countryside, less intensive but indispensable foci of human utilization, circulation and co-ordination.

In a human community, whether we think of the arrangement of professions, occupations or jobs, the distribution of wealth and power, or of qualitative personality–social traits among the individuals, the pyramidal pattern is evident, and, indeed, this is the great problem of politics or sociology, ancient and modern, viz., how to reconcile the interests and welfare of the many with authoritative and efficient social control and government that naturally gravitates to the hands of the *elite*, whether oligarchy, aristocracy, bureaucracy or dictatorship. Survival of the dominant carnivores in the pyramidal structure of animal life depends not only on their physical characteristics and the strength of those instincts and habit patterns which regulate their territorial system according to which their prey are relatively neither too few nor too many but also on their smaller numbers and lower prolificacy. Where the dominant class in the human community multiplies too fast, the ecological "foodchain" is strained, causing social conflicts, which ultimately lead to the disintegration of the class, or the class creates or finds new opportunities in other areas (through earth hunger, war and conquest) like the carnivores, which tend to be much more wide-ranging and less strictly confined to one habitat than other animals. Social distances between individuals and classes are governed by the principle of dominance. These are crystallized into class standards of living, and are strengthened by custom and public opinion against the constant inroads of economic changes. Social distances are more marked in communities which have been welded together by war and conquest than in those which grow out of tribal or ethnic accretion and assimilation. Conquest, through expropriation of land and check to racial admixture, excludes large masses of people from economic opportunities and prevents their upward economic movement. The social position or status of an individual is determined by his social group or class in so far as it is able to maintain its niche in the ecological pattern. Thus social distance indirectly governs and limits occupation, and the standard of consumption as well as mobility and credit. The *elite* shows the highest standard of consumption, mobility, power and credit, appropriating the largest share of the values and rewards that region and culture can offer. Political power, economic monopoly and social obstruction to upward movements of individuals and groups maintain their social distance, and protect the existing social arrangement against the inroads of social change and the adventures of enterprising individuals who want to modify dominant social norms and cultural motifs.

The Social Pyramid as an Expression of the Scheme of Values

On the one hand, the stability of society and culture rests on the maintenance of social distance between groups and individuals. On the other hand, social distance reflects the disparity of achievement in the individual's or the group's struggle for position, status and power which the collective consciousness sanctions and stabilizes as a scheme of culture. It mirrors the traits, values and virtues which society favours and selects for its own survival. Thus an extra-economic valuation is superimposed upon the ecological processes of spatial and functional distribution of groups and individuals. The importation of social norms makes the interrelations of men and their interactions with the habitat far different from the relations on the mere ecological level. Man's traffic with the environment bears an indelible impress of his conscious strivings, aspirations, and schemes of values. In crowded peasant communities status, wealth and power are measured less in money and more in terms of large families, acres of land and herds of cattle. The economic hierarchy in rural and urban areas is built after different patterns. The prestige of age and wisdom in the Orient, the dominance of the Chinese literati and the Indian brahmins alike testify to social attitudes which stabilize a social gradation appropriate for a peaceful rural civilization. In sparsely peopled new lands, whether back-wood clearings or lumber camps, mining areas or plantations, social selection favours young, ambitious and enterprising persons. In these frontiers of human settlement there is a striking preponderance of adult males, and families are mobile, disorganized and unstable. Here the pioneer woodsman and the squatter, without wives and children, "the baggages of fortune", set the norm. In ancient and sedentary village settlements, it is the patriarch who dominates. Social life is stable, economic change is slow, the family is firmly rooted in the inalienable holding, transmitted through the generations. Social distances are here relatively fixed with the aged and wise at the top of the social pyramid. Classes and occupations are few, simple and stereotyped. The patriarch's virtues, which are conservatism, foresight and sacrifice, are not only the support of successful farming but also the binders of the family and village communal organizations. The dominance of the village elders is the mainstay of co-operation of the primary groups in rural society which ensures agricultural and social efficiency. The village elders are the custodians of rural public welfare; it is they who enforce collective management of irrigation, village grazing in meadows and pastures, harvesting and even social recreations. The ecological organization of the human community grows, under the ministrations of man's group consciousness and experience, its own crop of customs and traditions which overrule competition and individualism and favour social cohesiveness. In new settlements man's ecological organization as well as his social interests, attitudes and habits are different. In virgin lands when the pioneer plants first make their appearance, they are found widely and largely distributed under trying conditions. Here and there they work isolatedly preparing the soil for the more complex forms of vegetation to establish themselves. In a stable plant community the pioneer plants which have readily and quickly converted a landscape become scarce and are killed out by the climax vegetation. This also happens in the human community. Human societies, as these age, weed out the idiosyncrasies of pioneer men and novel institutions that prepare the ground for social stability and differentiation. In a new settlement the woodsman, the miner and the squatter show the mobility and shiftlessness of the pioneer plants. Here it is not the patriarch who is at the head of the hierarchy, but competition favours men with intense individualism, extravagance and speculative spirit which infect everybody from the cottier and the coolie to the big landlord, entrepreneur and wholesale merchant.

Transformation of Ecological Base and Values

The density of population, stage of economic development and social selection thus in different ecological bases favour a peculiar age and sex composition and dominance of characteristic types of individuals and groups. These embody different social attitudes, virtues and personality traits of individuals which are most appropriate for the exploitation of ecologic resources in the particular economic and cultural stage of the people. The longer the period of settlement or more elaborate the division and specialization of labour, the more culture and technique are associated with an occupation, dominating the interests and activities of the individuals through a code, training and morale. This is the distinction between an occupation and an art or profession. In the pioneer settlement or the changing industrial world, where new inventions and shifts of occupations do not permit any stabilization of interests and attitudes, the characteristics and status of arts and professions cannot easily develop in an increasing number of occupations. The contrast between old and new settlements has of course been more sharply drawn here than is found usually in actual societies, and there are also communities, which show transitional features and the mingling of the contrasted social attitudes, individual personality features and formative forces that tend to be stabilized through the principles of social dominance and distance. It is these latter principles which determine the general ecological pattern of society and tend to stabilize it, harmonizing the interplay of thousands of qualitatively different occupations in the appropriation of resources, energies and social values that flow ceaselessly from the mutual give-and-take of man and his environment. The division and gradation of classes, occupations and jobs accordingly represent both an ecological framework for the exploitation of the restricted environment by the population, and a cultural framework for the pursuit of appropriate social values.

In an old agricultural civilization coming under the ambit of the modern industrial system and larger spatial division of labour, the social phenomena of the frontiers of civilization, however, reappear. The village moneylender or the itinerant grain dealer in the East who links the ancient selfsufficient rural community with the outside commercial world that knocks at the gates of the peasant, shows the same individualism, extravagance, speculative spirit and even unscrupulousness, characteristic of the frontier personality type in new lands. He frees himself from any traditions of the family, or business and mercantile codes and becomes an important agency in disintegrating the economic system of the self-sufficient village. The timber merchant, the mining contractor and the plantation entrepreneur in the frontiers of civilization, like the moneylender and grain merchant in the old civilization which is disintegrating under the impact of world economic forces, are alike agents or representatives of city merchants, bankers, and financial magnates. These latter dominate from distant metropolises and cities the prices and movement of crops and raw materials modifying or destroying the customary routine of agriculture and division of labour. Thus the pyramidal control of agriculture and industry, trade and finance is gradually but inevitably imposed upon the world economy through myriads of agents, representatives and subordinates scattered throughout the world who upset the prevailing social order and division of labour.

Succession and Invasion, Ecological and Social

Plant ecologists have made us familiar not only with the phenomenon of zonation according to which plants arrange themselves in definite belts about a central point of excess and deficiency of limiting environmental conditions, but also with the process termed succession according to which there is development of vegetation from initial stage to climax, the same ecological area becoming successively occupied by different plant communities until one group of dominant plants reaches its maximum. In human ecology, too, we find stages of succession in the emergence of dominance of certain central and co-ordinating interests, services and institutions in the local centres of country towns and cities. In the vegetative life each plant form modifies the habitat by reaction, making it less favourable to itself and more appropriate for the invasion of the next higher lifeform until the final stage of vegetation becomes the dominant lifeform in the area. Vegetative succession happens from a less stable to a relatively permanent or climax stage in respect of the climax and the soil type of the area.

In the social world economic history represents succession. Here also the trend is towards progressive adjustment to the habitat, the population being regarded as a biotic community and symbiotically linked for its life and utilization with the plant and animal communities, and the entire ecological complex finding an increasing harmony with the *ensemble* of the ecological and social forces.

In the plant world stabilization is increase of dominance. In the continuous development of the plant formation, which is like that of the growth of any organism, one life-form is marked out as a dominant one which maintains itself as a climax and constitutes the final stage of development of the formation except for catastrophes, such as fire, flood, landslide, etc., until there is fundamental change in climate.

In human ecology the progress from forestry and extractive industries to agriculture, and from crude and intermittent agriculture to successive types of intensive farming and to industry and commerce accompanies a redistribution of population units and social structures and institutions, just as trees, shrubs and grasses are redistributed in the course of vegetative succession, and new dominants or co-dominants emerge which control the habitat. Economic development is fostered by dominance of certain groups, functions or centres which serves as the directing focus or the specialized and central cerebral cortex, co-ordinating and controlling the parts of a higher organism. Finally, the increase of centralization and co-ordination and the influence of the dominant focus accompany a greater stability for the whole economic and social base.

Succession takes place in relation to the region, to each subdivision of the zone, to the village and to the city. The process of succession takes on a new meaning and is lifted to a higher level with the complexity of the ecologic organization and extension of its boundaries. Certain specialized central and co-ordinating forms of services and institutions do not appear at the agricultural level. An oak forest community as a dominant must be preceded by other trees which prepare the ground for its development. It is only in the manufacturing and commercial stage that we find the natural area of economic control and business dominance. Here the city or metropolis is most elaborately differentiated into ecological areas and cultural groupings, which have marked specialization of functions. The focus of centrality and dominance is the small, compact business area, where just those institutions and services of human management are concentrated which depend upon quick information, judgement and action and require a minimum space, such as the highly specialized functions in the fields of finance, credit and industrial administration. These are interdependent and their close contiguity in the business area is of decisive advantage to each utility or service. Despite the pressure from increasing land values, offices of banks and big businesses and industrial undertakings occupy the strategic positions, while other institutions and services accept the role of subordination, deriving their sustenance from their close proximity of the dominant institutions. All institutions and services inhere together or segregate themselves in forming a communal pattern which persists so long as the human situation does not materially change. The area of ecological dominance of the big business becomes the central, sensitive focal point in the total life of the region, the area at once of highest mobility, greatest sensitiveness and most powerful controls. Encircling this area is usually found the merchandizing district, full of wholesale and retail shops in intimate touch with the banking and financial institutions in the business centre. Beyond is often found the intermediate zone filled by various kinds of institutions and mixed utilities, while at the periphery are the best residence sections closely followed by the best retail shops with the intermediate zone of institutions acting as a buffer between them. Residence tends to march steadily into the outlying agricultural belts, first utilized for suburban gardens, bungalows and cottages. There is still another area of industry and residence of the workers who wish to live close to their work.

In a forest community there are layers or strata with distinction of herbs, shrubs and trees. Herb competes with herb, shrub with shrub, and in the dominant tree-layer trees of one species with those of another. A dominant in the plant formation does not compete with a secondary herb of the forest floor. Similarly the urban universe shows competition limited to units of structures and services in each segregated area, such as the area of business and office administration, the shopping area, the area of heavy or light industry and area of residence. Competition usually operates as a basic mechanism in the selection of appropriate population elements and services in each of the subsidiary natural areas. As different species of plants live side by side in a given community due to the fact that they make different demands on the habitat, and show the relation of dominance and subordination, so in the social world there are interdependence of functions and interests and relations of control and subordination between population units, services and institutions distributed in the specialized natural areas of a town, city or metropolis. Apart from the hierarchy in the institutional structure, an increase of population in the city or town leads to the multiplication of churches, temples, schools, dispensaries, restaurants and personal service establishments. On the other hand, with the increase of the size of habitation, such institutions as cloth shops, general merchandize stores, and groceries do not increase in number but increase their volume of sales. There are in these cases economies of large scale establishments while these also permit customers wide choice in the selection of goods to individual requirements and tastes. The age and sex composition of the population also affects the number of different types of service institutions. The type, size and hierarchy of institutions are governed by the density and composition of population as well as by agricultural or industrial specialization of the community. Institutions and services are in ceaseless competition with one another not merely in the same town or village, but within a zone of easy travel or communication. It is through the social–ecological processes of competition, migration and invasion that the pattern of dominance of groups, services and institutions is established. The greater the mobility the quicker is the establishment of dominance through invasion within the zones of influence.

In plant ecology throughout the whole process of the development of vegetation, invasion goes on in all directions, and at all times, and initiates succession. Invasion is a movement of plants or groups of plants from one area to another and their establishment in the latter through ecesis and competition. In human ecology, too, the region, its subsidiary ecological areas, the village, the country town and the city, constantly exhibit the invasion and displacement of population units and cultural groups, of services and institutions. Dominant functions and interests, like those of business and finance, education and leisure establish sporadic subordinate centres in the countryside and exact tribute from the surrounding agricultural community. The establishment of shops and stores collecting the primary agricultural produce from the rural community and distributing finished products of consumption in the countryside and the surplus basic materials in the wider market is a familiar step which accompanies the invasion of urbanism. The pioneers in such an invasion are always small itinerant dealers and moneylenders who spread the net of trade and finance, taking advantage of facilities of transportation and communication. It is in this manner that banks and financial agencies, wholesale shops and mercantile firms, spread out the net of financial suzerainty over a large agricultural territory, establishing subordinate centres of dominance which contribute to link every part of the territory with the central city. Not merely does the city send out banks, mercantile firms and shops and a chain of intermediaries and middlemen, but also cultural institutions such as colleges and schools, theatres and cinema houses, newspapers and media which invade and transform the rural ways of living.

Much of social change and succession can be interpreted and measured by:

a. the number and distribution of marketing and retailing centres in the region which also serve as focal points of professional services and the educational and civic life of the people;
b. the quality of specialized services and goods which are catered by country towns and villages of different sizes and the effects purchases of different qualities have on the rural ways and standards of living; and
c. the articulation of a new pattern of service and institutional relations superseding the old as measured by:

(1) the mobility of the rural population as it resorts regularly or intermittently to the more distant specialized centres;

(2) the presence of such larger and more specialized centres as an index of the standards of living in their constituent sections of the rural territory;

(3) the variegation of occupations, professions and services of the rural population and the increase in number of the non-agricultural persons in the villages and the number of their businesses.

The mapping out of distribution trends by indicating periodically the number and quality of new dominant centres and services will measure the speed of invasion and development of a new social order, i.e. social change and succession.

5

The Dynamics of Human Aggregation and Circulation

The Hierarchy of Habitations

STATUS and mobility are the moving threads weaving the texture of social relationships and behaviours and the institutional patterns in the fly-shuttle of ecological space and time. Social relationship and behaviour, when these become durable and enduring through a replacement of human beings which manifest them, constitute social institutions. Status manifests itself through enduring patterns of behaviour of individuals and groups which we call functions or occupations and families, classes, neighbourhoods, habitations and the state. Mobility is the movement of individuals and groups by which status in such functions, groups and institutions is acquired, maintained or lost.

These processes apply to both individuals and communities and are distributed over wider and wider, ecological and social space and time. Thus man's habitations arrange themselves in a stratification of services and institutions which becomes an enduring pattern of the region. Social mobility brings about the rise and fall of individuals in the hierarchy of the community. Ecological mobility, i.e. the physical movement of the competing stream of human populations goods and utilities brings about domination–subordination or the hierarchy of hamlets, villages, towns and cities in a system of interrelated services within the region.

In social ecology we have to study both the neighbourhood and the Great Society and the mutual relationships of their individual units in both static and dynamic aspects. Physiologically speaking, society exhibits a constant circulation of individual units, changing their rank, position and power, and of population in the aggregate, spatially distributing itself at appropriate locations according to a hierarchy of services, products and energies. Social physiology deals therefore with twofold aspects of social life and relationship: the circulation of men, products and energies in the system of interrelated statuses within a community, and the circulation of population, products and energies in the mass among a group of habitations within a constellation, conveniently described as the region.

The ecological processes of mobility, competition and stratification in society by which individuals are sorted out for functions, occupations and classes according to their capacities tend to break up families, clans, castes and social groups, and place the individuals at positions where they would make the best use of restricted economic opportunities. On the other hand, the loosening of family and neighbourhood ties facilitates change of locale or migration by which society acquires a more efficient division of labour and adaptation through territorial redistribution of population.

Mobility is both horizontal and vertical. Vertical mobility is applicable to changes in socio-economic status; horizontal or physical mobility, on the other hand, is applicable to changes of location. Such changes are applicable not merely to individuals but also to classes and groups and are capable of expression in quantitative terms. Mobility or change of the individual's and the group's status and locale is directly proportional to the tempo of social life and functions, and is but the reflection of that intenser psychological stimulation and response of which a quantitative measure is sought by human ecology. Both physical and social mobility are not merely directly correlated with the *physical* freedom of movement or migration of individuals and classes, which leads to the formation of new social habits, interests and relationships but also with an upward social movement which overrides psychological barriers between individuals and groups. Thus the shift through space and through cross-sections of society gives us a quantitative measure of the tempo of social change or succession and of the new social habits and relationships which accompany it.

Agricultural civilizations differ from industrial communities, and villages from cities, in their gradation of functions, occupations and social classes as well as in population movement and general mobility. Occupations are more stereotyped and social ranking is more rigid in the village than in the city, while there is also far less of physical movement of individuals. In an industrial community, no one can be sure of his occupation or role, but quick mobility and adventure, which universal education and development of communication foster, enable individuals to change occupations, jobs and places. The uncertainty of employment, the movement of persons from place to place, and from job to job, and the all-pervasive and incomprehensible nature of the technological process which tears individuals from their families, social groups and traditional places in the soil and village and yet does not assure them any permanent job in the industrial system, nevertheless represent a tremendous strain on the mobile urban mass. With concentration and control of industry in the hands of the entrepreneur classes, it is these which now determine the security or insecurity of employment, and this is true not merely of individuals and classes but of whole districts and regions. A pyramidal structure of the urban–industrial community with its sharp social gradation between the directive and subordinate classes and its territorial division into the agricultural and the manufacturing districts, its city and metropolis, satellite towns and hinterland are typical of every part of the world. It follows the pattern of the distribution of occupations, with an increase and concentration of population and resources demanding for the purpose of economy, central control and co-ordination over an entire region.

Difference between Concentration and Co-ordination

The Great Society exhibits not merely a sharp cleavage of wealth and power between the economic and social classes, but also a striking disparity of resources and opportunities between villages, towns and the metropolis. This is the price that modern society pays for the physical concentration of population and centralization and co-ordination of functions and institutions. These are associated with quick tempo of human utilization and circulation of goods, services and energies, on the one hand, and the variegation and specialization of social structures and functions, on the other, achieving greater and greater mechanical–technic efficiency. The population of a region, Levasseur has shown, is composed of a certain number of scattered nuclei. It gathers about centres or along lines of attraction. Vidal de la Blache aptly observes: "Population did not spread like a drop of oil; in the beginning it grew in clumps like corals. Reefs of population collected at certain points by a crystallization process." Aggregation of population fosters specialization, mobility and increase of the tempo of activity of individuals and co-ordination of functions of the aggregate. These by leading to improved utilization and efficiency attract or pull other men, who come to share in the values and permanent products that the habitation accumulates in successive generations on the advantageous location.

The processes of centralization and co-ordination, which are sociological, have to be distinguished from the primary ecological process of concentration. Concentration refers to the spatial aggregation of the population; centralization and co-ordination are its obverse processes, referring to the spatial clustering of social structures, functions and institutions. Demographic grouping accompanies the tendency towards the specialization, centralization and co-ordination of common interests, whether finance, business or work, leisure, education or recreation. As foci of aggregation, village markets, little towns and cities easily emerge, indispensable links in the distribution and interchange of men, goods and services in a region. Aggregation of population at each stage is governed by the nature and form of collective functions subserved by each communal unit. Even a small purely agricultural community demands centralization and co-ordination of services for the advantage of the peasants living in the land surrounding a village. Wells, temples, *panchayat* houses, threshing floors and social facilities which are subject to community use are, for instance, usually concentrated in the village site. Successful farming demands some co-ordination of movements of agricultural produce and finished products of consumption, and of credit and finance which are served by the wholesale shops and financial houses in the major market centres; while leisure, education and recreation can be successfully organized only in the cities and towns. It may accordingly be assumed that just as resource patterns, natural advantages and features of routes attract population in certain focal or nodal points on natural routes of human circulations, the need of specialization of individuals and classes for catering to specialized common functions and interests and of their co-ordination in few directive hands leads to centralization. Thus are brought about a greater regional specialization, integration and co-ordination of complex services like wholesaling, large-scale banking and specialized retailing centred round the regional city and towns.

The Central-place Scheme of Distribution of Habitations

Walter Christaller in his central-place theory of the distribution of human settlements does not lay adequate stress on the nature of social utilities and functions which are the primary support of hamlets and villages, on the one hand, and the growth and distribution of larger villages and country-towns on the other.[1] The majority of habitations on earth is represented by villages and little towns inhabited solely by an agricultural population. Essential and specialized, central and co-ordinating services and institutions are distributed among various types of habitations, hamlets, villages, little towns and regional cities. The notion that the larger the population of a region the greater will be the size of the central city is as abstract and unreal as the brushing aside of social, religious and recreational rather than economic utilities and services of hamlets and villages, which have kept alive isolation and dispersal along with concentration as irrepressible social trends. Not merely do hamlets and villages have utilities and functions which towns and cities cannot provide, but they also take up certain central services and functions in a system of division of labour between small and large centres with improvement of methods of communication and transportation. There are extensive and densely populated districts in northern and eastern Bengal and Malabar in India, and in Tonkin in Indo-China, which are honey-combed with hamlets and villages and where there are no little towns and cities. In most areas in northern and eastern Bengal the proportion of population living in towns does not exceed 3 per cent. Even little towns derive their collective subsistence from agriculture, while the central functions are distributed among numbers of larger centres or villages. It is striking that

---

1 Ullman, "A Theory of Location for Cities", *American Journal of Sociology*, May 1941.

in the densely crowded and prosperous tracts in eastern Bengal the bigger villages and market centres comprise a much larger proportion of the rural population and are still expanding; while in the decadent areas in western Bengal little towns and larger villages are much less important than small hamlets and villages, while the latter are on the whole declining. This will be evident from the following comparison:

Table 5.1: Number per mille of rural population residing in mauzas with a population of

	5000 and over		2000 to 5000		500 to 2000		Under 500	
	1921	1931	1921	1931	1921	1931	1921	1931
Inactive delta								
Murshidabad	31	32	204	249	528	532	237	187
Nadia	8	14	156	159	579	573	257	254
Hooghly	6	7	130	123	475	482	389	388
Jessore	8	11	71	81	559	527	363	381
Active delta								
Faridpur	81	109	209	257	496	528	214	206
Tippera	43	49	218	254	527	502	212	195
Noakhali	151	157	248	287	458	443	143	130
Bakarganj	121	134	289	306	447	442	143	118

In the larger villages corporate life is more evident, while the central services which are effectively organized are not purely economic. Temples, mosques and fairs attract the population of the neighbourhood, and religious and recreational centres are as important in the East as trade centres. It is also by no means true that trade makes the small habitations fewer and smaller, and the large habitations larger. For no habitation lives by trade alone, and there is also division of labour in buying and marketing functions between different types of centres from the smallest to the largest. Even in the USA it appears that only the very smallest hamlets (under 250 population) and crossroads stores have declined in size and number. The larger small places have held their own. Zimmern observes that crossroads stores are disappearing and are being replaced by small villages.

> It is evident that claims of substantial correlation between the appearance and growth of the larger trading centre and the disappearance of the primary centre are more or less unfounded. Although there are minor relationships the main change has been a division of labour between the two types of centres rather than the complete obliteration of the smaller in favour of the larger.

Thus, the central-place scheme is neither uniform nor fixed; it is different in diverse types of societies and changes with the development of communication and transportation, the type of agriculture and the method and practice of buying and marketing.

On the whole, however, in homogeneous agricultural regions of relatively uniform land surface

a. the larger villages and country-towns are distributed evenly over the land, based on central business functions of storage, financing and co-ordination of supply and distribution of agricultural produce etc.;
b. the adoption of intensive and commercial farming tends to increase the importance of these essential central functions, make the larger centres larger and give a definite orientation to the division of labour between different types of centres in each region;
c. the distances between the larger centres are governed by the cost of transport of agricultural produce and of central storage;
d. the combination of economic with social, religious, educational and recreational services increases the size of the larger centre, whether the large village or little town;
e. the larger the village or town, the larger its service area or hinterland; and

f. the sparser the rural population density, the larger the village service area or hinterland for each size class.

Measurement of Centrality

The "centrality" of cities, towns and larger villages can be measured on the basis of census returns for what may be adjudged central occupations and services in the region. In the agricultural community the central occupations include banking, wholesale trade, specialized retail trade and rent-collection. Centralization of the more specialized interests, functions and structures and concentration of population help each other, each stabilizing the other. As population pressure increases in any human settlement village, city or region, the influx of men to the centres of trade, business, culture, recreation and all purposes of communal life also increases tremendously. The result is that the entire region of settlement shows an orderly distribution of occupations and interests and a characteristic pattern of aggregation of population with centralization of services and institutions at definite locations, definition of natural areas and their boundaries, sifted and sorted by the pressure on space through comparative land values and rents. Thus the population, services and institutions tend to group themselves in a characteristic pattern, depending on resource conditions, routes of circulation of resources and services, advantages of location, and the folkways of the people expressing themselves in collective tastes and preferences.

Agriculture, industry, business, administration, commerce, education, religion and recreation, all struggle for strategic position and distribution, and this accounts for both the ecological trends of migration, dispersal and concentration of population on the one hand, and of specialization, co-ordination and decentralization of services and utilities on the other, tending constantly to segregate into definite zones or natural areas with their spheres of influence extending to the periphery of a region. The location of dominating co-ordinating interests and services, such as centralized administration and religion in the ancient and business and finance in the modern industrial world, determines not only the areas of highest mobility and concentration but also of highest site values and earnings of the buildings which house such services. The distribution of population and the location and boundaries of "natural areas" used for distribution (markets, shops and railroads), for co-ordination and administration (business, banking and office property), for industry and agriculture and for residence determine the value of the space men occupy and the rent and sale value they pay. These afford the human ecologist accurate indices of the spatial adaptation and arrangement of populations and their differential rating of services and institutions. The size and mobility of population, the proportion of population engaged in central occupations and services and the rents and land values in the central areas measure the degrees of "urbanism" and co-ordination which will be found to vary among towns and cities of various types, ranging from country-towns in agricultural regions to industrial and commercial cities, metropolises and "connurbations".

The Flow of Human Circulation

The ecological region, physiologically, is a mobile competing stream of human population and circulation, with centres or nodal points, channels or routes and orbits or boundaries. Structurally it is a constellation of villages, little towns and cities, scattered centres of population, nucleated foci of human utilization, circulation and co-ordination that enmesh it like a web with its variegated strands reaching out to other regions, and linking the lives of men with those of other regions.

The entire region is divisible into small subsidiary ecological areas;-earth with its characteristic economic procedure — forestry, agriculture, industry and trade — with its appropriate configuration of dominant interests and institutions, social relations and division of labour. The ecological segregation in a zonal pattern in large manner determines the cultural grouping.

The variety of human interests and preferences, on the one hand, and the interplay of the ecological processes of mobility, segregation, co-ordination and centralization, on the other, accordingly divide a whole region into distinct ecological and cultural areas and communities, each performing its specific function in the regional economy as a whole and linked with each other in the web of service and institutional relations in which the various circulations orient themselves in a sort of orderliness.

In such an orientation a hamlet, a village, a little town, a city and a metropolis — each plays a distinct and necessary role. Man like other gregarious animals needs settlements of various sizes for ecological and cultural reasons. Bailey describing the prairie dog settlements in New Mexico observes that the prairie dogs are irregularly distributed in colonies over the great plains area. Some of the colonies are extensive, occupying many square miles, while others are limited to a few acres or little groups of one dozen or even half a dozen animals. This observation is applicable to the distribution of human population. Men in a plain region sometimes live in tiny hamlets, comprising a dozen and even half a dozen huts, or in villages and little towns, covering 5 to 10 sq miles in area, or, again, in extensive cities embracing 1,000 sq miles or more.

Primitive man was a hunter like the prairie dog, but unlike the latter his need of defence against wholesale slaughter by maurading human neighbours was far greater. For group struggles to mutual destruction between members of the same species are almost unknown among animals other than men. Thus human safety lay largely in living and dwelling in numbers. Man's protective and gregarious instincts and habits as well as his conquest of the environment and abundance and security of food supply have built up beehive cities thronged with population. On the whole, man is a villager, while his dependence on agriculture has made many towns similar throughout the world. In the web of human services and utilities in which the flow of resources, energies and products orients itself, the smaller habitations play an indispensable role, which modern technology and centralization cannot abolish; and thus hamlets and villages still hold their own in most countries of the world.

The Route of Circulation

Man's habits of settlement have been formed prior to the development of methods of transportation. Thus it is agricultural resources, especially in summer, which have determined the size of human habitations as soon as primitive man weaned himself from the migratory habits of the wolves which hunt in packs, and became stabilized in his habitation. Man's early habitations were built on the margin of woodland or forest near a spring or stream, and drought or rainfall, fertility or exhaustion of soil still determine the scattered or the nucleated type of villages. In the midst of the forest, marsh or desert man's habitations comprise little groups of homesteads from which he moves out to fight with the land and waters for his precarious living. Gradually population increases and improvement of agriculture and methods of transport bring together habitations, large and small, in a system of circulation and interchange of agricultural produce. The large habitations or towns and cities grew up because of the need of protection of life and property, and could be maintained due to agricultural surplus and facility of transport and human circulation in the region. Thus the urban civilization developed earliest in the productive valleys of the Nile, the Euphrates–Tigris and the Indus, where large populations which did not grow their own food could be nourished because of the remarkable development of agriculture and the ease of river transport of agricultural produce. Speaking about ancient Egypt and Mesopotamia, Flinders Petrie observes:

> It has been noticed before how remarkably similar the distances are between the early Rome capital of the Nile Delta (21 miles on an average) and the early cities of Mesopotamia averaging 20 miles apart. Some physical cause seems to limit the primitive rule in this way. Is it not the limit of central storage of grain, which is the essential form of early capital? Supplies could be centralized up to 10 miles away; beyond that the cost of transport made it better worth while to have a nearer centre.[2]

It is the route of circulation which determines the location and expansibility of cities. Water transport is easier and less costly than road transport. Thus in the ancient past great cities were built as a rule on the banks of large rivers or on the seashore for the convenience of transportation. The latter also determined the number of cities and villages within the region. On the whole the waterways in ancient history, the highways in medieval history, and the railways in the modern age have regulated not merely the distribution but also the size of cities.

The Expansibility of Cities

In medieval Europe the city was synonymous with the bishopric and the episcopal city. The population was composed of the clerics of the cathedral church and of the other churches

---

[2] *Social Life in Ancient Egypt*, pp. 3-4.

grouped nearby; of the monks of the monasteries; of the teachers and the students of the ecclesiastical schools; and finally of servitors and artisans, free or serf, who were indispensable to the needs of the religious group and to the daily existence of the clerical agglomerations.[3] Often a warlike king or emperor, sometimes a feudal chieftain or landlord, sometimes the priest becomes the nucleus of the city, each safeguarding the life and property of the city dwellers against banditry and war. With his power and influence the city grows. Gradually man's total needs such as defence, religion, trade, industry and education are satisfied by the city whose growing population has to draw more upon the resources of the region. But most of the cities, along with the manufacture of wares for the countryside and distribution of articles of trade, still carry on farming. As human circulation increases and as resources and opportunities permit, cities specialize in arts and crafts, industry and trade, education and religion. This is a gradual process; thus the formation and development of cities are likewise slow and gradual. On the other hand, war and insecurity, expropriation and confiscation of land lead to wholesale exodus from the villages, while market and "boundary rights" by which urban dwellers monopolize for themselves the purchase of crops and industrial products from the hinterland or establish their own monopoly by the prohibition of all handicraft production in the villages quicken the growth of the city. It is the economic hegemony of the city over its "environs", hinterland or region which originates and spreads the belief in the superiority of the townsman and his culture, that is at the roots of the cityward drift of population. More than economic causes, however, was, invasion and the cyclonic movements of tribes and folks that

---

[3] Pirenne, *Medieval Cities*, pp. 56-67.

have through the ages pulled people together for the purpose of defence and security.

Both in Mesopotamia and the Indus Valley, walls enclosed the world's earliest cities because of the needs of protection of life and property, but in the Nile Valley the natural defence of the desert obviated this necessity. But even in Egypt after the consolidation of the different states Memphis rose in the delta of the Nile as a walled city. The wall not only keeps out the maurading neighbour but also the inundation when the rivers rise in flood. Defence has been the most potent and persistent centripetal force which pulled men together in the ancient, medieval and modern world. Cities enclosed within walls or palisades were numerous in history: Nineveh, Memphis, Mohenjo-Daro, Pataliputra, Sravasti, Kusinagara, Rajagriha, Carthage, Delhi, Rome and Constantinople. Walled cities and towns, cities built on hills like the Acrapolis of Athens and the Capitoline Hill of Rome, the gorods of the Slavs, the kraals of the Africans and the savage or pioneer villages protected by stockade or mud-fort alike testify to the imperative urban needs of defence and safety. "The walled cities of Middle Asia", observes Ratzel:

> enclose in their clay walls much larger spaces than necessary for a city alone. In Buchara, China, among others, fields and gardens, vacant lots, ponds and swamps, groves of elm trees and poplars, extensive cattleyards, cover more than half of the area. In including these areas they reckoned upon the necessity of an independent maintenance in the case of a siege.

But safety does not lie in mere strategic location, wall or fortress, defence and safety. Safety is also sought in the gods of the tribe, the nation, the city and the empire. Religion thus becomes a centripetal urban force and even now draws people together for pilgrimage to the holy shrine, temple or mosque in the city.

People draw more people, and the advantages of the city life cumulatively increase. The city becomes the permament, all-inclusive marketplace, where the most varied commodities and services that the region can provide are available for persons who can pay for them. The priest, the lawyer, the financier, the worker, the artist, the engineer or the cinema-star, all find in the city the best opportunity for regular employment and high earnings, while people who want services and commodities of the best quality also seek them here. Once large-sized urban populations live in peace, prosperity comes from the concentration of crafts and workshops, and, in the industrial age, of mass production and business in their most diverse forms. Factories and warehouses, fairs and markets, banking houses and commercial firms, wholesale and retail shops, predominantly located in the cities, constantly draw people together. Further specialization of economic and social functions is possible due to the aggregation of population and accumulation of resources: specialized industries, trades and manufactures and specialized occupations and professions. Specialization and large-scale production easily assimilate themselves into the machine technology and profit from the adventure and power of finance capital. This in its turn brings to the growing city food and manufactures from other regions enabling it to increase its population further and expand its ecological base. Institutions also segregate and specialize. Such institution as schools, colleges, universities, museums and hospitals attract certain classes of people. Finally, amusements and recreations such as afforded by the theatres of ancient Hellas and India, the gladiatorial games of Rome, the pageants of the medieval European towns and the cinemas, clubs, cabarets and brothels of modern cities appeal to people of every class as the magnet draws the iron filings. Through the ages urban amenities, pleasures and dissipations have been the chief antidote to the drab business routine and strenuous work in the city. Five thousand years ago Mohenjo-Daro had its spacious comfortable private houses with their nicely arranged rooms, guest chambers, courtyards, terraces and bathrooms and its beautifully constructed public drains and cess pits with an elaborate sanitary service for sewage removal. In this flourishing city there was also a huge public bath which in excellence and solidity of construction cannot be improved upon by any modern builder, and which provided a social centre, as in Rome in later times. The urban dwellers lived a most luxurious life as the lavish use of jewellery, necklaces of various cut stones and beads, armlets and bracelets worn by both sexes abundantly testifies, while they also enjoyed the company of the danseuse, graceful figures of whom perfectly cast in bronze or cut in grey stone have been discovered. The myriad-hued glitter and lure of urban luxuries and excitements have in all climes and times supported the economic advantages of urban business, industry and employment.

The Centrifugal Forces

Such strong, centripetal forces which lead to increased concentration of population in a few cities and towns have, however, to meet the constant challenge of the centrifugal forces represented by the dispersal of homes and farms implied in the very occupation of agriculture and man's natural preference for living in primary groups, neighbourhoods and small communities. Before man's habits and interests have become "citified" in the age of metal and steam engine, he has owed the development of his personality and culture to small face-to-face groups in hamlets, villages and little towns where even now the majority of mankind dwells. The village is the matrix of culture, and of the genius of the individual. The village is also the matrix of economy and business. It is a country-made institution, the daily market or periodical fair of the village, which grows into the town or city. And the town or city can thrive only by utilizing and transforming crops and raw materials, populations and cultural resources which the former produces and brings to it in return for its services of control, co-ordination and organization in every sphere of life. It is thus the aggregate and the individual, the many and the one, help one another. Nor does the hamlet or village remain isolated and self-sufficient, as is often supposed; the village itself is considerably transformed by the growing complexity of the structure of civilization. It develops a good deal of division of labour and specialization of occupations. Arts and handicrafts grow into great elaboration not merely through the specialization of particular artisan groups, but also through the division of productive operations among a group of villages. There also develop fishermen villages, dairy villages and industrial villages, although agriculture is not completely overshadowed. The products of village arts and handicrafts sell much beyond the confines of the region or province, and even command international markets. While the surplus production in agriculture guarantees a smooth routine of rural life, leisure and its enjoyment, the surplus from the artisan's home and workshop can purchase all the urban luxuries the village wants from outside. Apart from the periodical markets and big fairs, a system of itinerant traders, carriers and intermediaries serves as the link between village and village, and village and town. In India and further from India among the agriculturists, and in Western Asia and North Africa among the nomadic pastoralists, the periodical fair or market institution is the chief cause of the relatively small number of urban settlements of the market town type. Besides there is the ubiquitous moneylender-cum-grain-dealer, who is often financed by the wholesale merchant of the city and acts as his agent for the distribution of country produce. In the system of interchange of commodities and services, the village store, mart, and granary subserve the purposes of centralization and co-ordination of an agricultural community. With an increase of population and development of trade, industry and commerce, these institutions, which are the prototypes of the urban marketplace, lay the spacious foundations of a big city or metropolis.

The Role of the Village in Human Circulation

But it is not merely an economic interchange. It is also a circulation of man's works, experiences and culture. Man's delimitation of boundaries of his own fields and homesteads, and orderly apportionment of common meadows, woods, tanks and water channels become the foundation of his private rights and of public ownership. His co-operation in defence, in agriculture, irrigation and village management, is the bedrock of government. The storytelling and recital of ballads and hymns round the family hearth become the inspiration of literature, the drawing on the floor and walls and handiwork and craftsmanship of the home that of art and industry. Songs and dances associated with sowing and harvesting ceremonies in the fields become pageant, drama and theatre. Family worship and offerings before the altar are amplified into the worship of tutelary gods and ancestors of the tribe and the nation in city temples and festivals, while the agricultural fasts and festivities, punctuated according to the seasonal distribution of rainfall and sunshine, weave the texture of a country's religion and ritual.

All this influence emanates from the fact that the organized village develops a collective personality in the give-and-take between man and the landscape. In spite of differences in ethnic distribution and historical factors villages grow like plant communities resembling one another in a region, which imposes upon all the same kind of crop rotation, combined with fallowing and pasturage, and the same type of utilization of idle periods in rural crafts, amusements and recreations. Each village resembles its neighbour not merely in its layout and distribution of land but in its agricultural routine and its recurrent social activities and leisure time pursuits. Each village has its common threshing floor, well, orchard, tank, guesthouse and temple, and from the village site radiate narrow bypaths to the farmer's fields, scattered like autumn leaves throughout the settlement, until these meet the fields and ridges of the neighbouring village. Crop and irrigation practices are the same for every village; the preparation of the fields, sowing, watering, weeding and harvesting, are carried on in the same manner simultaneously everywhere. The same rejoicing and the same disappointment visit every village home at each season when the harvest is brought to the common threshing ground. From the common earthboundness with similar experiences of suspense, toil, exaltation and relaxation of congeries of rural communities in similar soils and climates spring an entente, a mutual rapport with the Mother landscape which underlie the unity and stability of culture. It is the village which is the focus of this culture. Such culture is uniform and homogeneous, but it is vital; its vitality is derived from its continuity with life, from man's constant, collective and intimate touch with the soil, the elements and the plantlike things that grow naturally and ceaselessly. Out of this intimacy grows a profound affinity between man's sowing of the seeds and begetting, between harvest and death, between crop and offspring, between the cycle of human labour and fruition and the procession of the seasons, which colours human relations and delineates the external form of culture. All great cultures organically grow out of, and are shaped and dominated by, the elemental values of the landscape which the drab uniformity of the artificial, monetary calculating urban culture cannot erase. Rural life supplies the seeds and even the taproots which sprout forth into differentiated urban trees and flowers of national culture.

The make-up of the urban products remains essentially rural in spite of the fact that myths and legends everywhere cluster round the genesis of the great city, evidence of the wonder and admiration, its mansions and markets, streets and squares excite the rural population.

Man's ecological and social needs demand that he should live in the village. The village has a long memory. Mankind has lived through the epochs in the village, where he has experienced intimate joys and firm loyalties in its primary groups that have largely conditioned his mental and social development. It is the village which firmly establishes and effectively conserves the cultural individuality of a people. In the continuous flow of raw materials, energies and resources, both natural and social, it is the village which produces and conserves, and the city which co-ordinates, synthetises and innovates. Diffusion and concentration of population and the differentiation of functions between the village and the city are equally indispensable for economic and cultural progress. Isolation and dispersal or concentration and co-ordination differ according to resource conditions, social stage, population and culture. This explains the persistence of two antithetic trends in social ecology, viz. ruralization and urbanization, bringing about a disparity of the size of human habitations everywhere. Yet all human habitations, the hamlet, the country town, the city and the metropolis, are links in a continuous ecological process of utilization circulation and interchange, which overreaches them all.

The Tributary Area of Towns

In the agricultural zone the central and co-ordinating institutions are represented by the wholesale shops and financial houses, periodical markets and fairs, temples and schools of the country towns and larger villages. Each institution or service has its tributary area extending to distant parts, which represent the periphery of the rural community. The radius of service area varies for different institutions situated in different centres. Each country town competes with another with its equipment of institutions and specialized forms of service to secure tributary territories.

It is possible to map out the orbits of influence or tributary territories of specific central and co-ordinating institutions and services as well as the boundaries of an agricultural community and region. Ideally each nodal point or central place would have a circular tributary territory as in von Thünen's theory of rent, and the city, the country town or the larger village would be the centre. However, if three or more tangent circles are inscribed in an area unserved spaces will exist; the best theoretical shapes are hexagons, the closest geometrical figures would be circles which will completely fill an area. Christaller has recognized typical size settlements, computed their average population, their distance apart, and the size and population of their tributary areas in accordance with hexagonal theory, as shown in Table 1. He also states that the number of central places follows a norm from the largest to the smallest in the following order: 1:2:6:18:54, etc.[4]

Christaller's figures are computed on the basis of South Germany. But he claims them to be typical for most of Germany and Western Europe. No doubt, the norms for distance apart the size of centres would vary widely according to the cost of transport and central storage and the state of economic development which would determine the value and extent of the various specialized and central services in various regions.

Social ecology studies not only the structure and formation of villages, towns and cities and lays down general biological principles of growth but also works out the norms for distance

---

[4] Edward Ullman, "A Theory of Location", *The American Journal of Sociology*, May 1941.

Table 1: Christaller's table on typical-size settlements

Central Plate	*Towns*		*Tributary Areas*	
	Distance apart (km.)	*Population*	*Size (sq. km.)*	*Population*
Market hamlet	7	800	45	2,700
Township centre	12	1,500	135	8,100
Country seat	21	3,500	400	24,000
District city	36	9,000	1,200	75,000
Small state capital	62	27,000	3,600	2,25,000
Provincial head city	108	90,000	10,800	6,75,000
Regional capital city	186	3,00,000	32,400	2,025,000

between the various kinds of settlements and their sizes as well as the average populations of their tributary areas. Location and resources, the nature of dominating central services and institutions, communications and means of transport, all enter into the size of towns and their service areas as well as the distance between the various centres of settlement.

Both the economic structure of the town or city and its size and service territory are governed by features characteristic of its regional location, such as animal husbandry, agriculture, forestry, mining and industry. Usually a city combines the function of a country town situated in the midst of an agricultural region with large-scale manufacturing activities and commerce, as the region is occupied and intensively cultivated by the rural population. Such a country town or city has a relatively even growth of activities and population, since the purchasing power of the agricultural region increases gradually with improved land utilization, thereby correspondingly accelerating the distributive as well as the central and co-ordinating utilities and functions of the city. On the other hand, a city which rests on a slender or single economic base, such as the extraction of oil, coal or any mineral resource that is fast exhausted, exhibits a boom period followed by rapid decline and even abandonment. Those towns or cities can attain the highest stability and the biggest size as well as tributary area which can combine the most varied functions and interests. As new interests are taken up by the city, these are commonly distributed to suburbs or satellite towns around the centre or core of development of the old city. Many old cities which rose into a good size before the Industrial Revolution have thus developed industrial suburbs which are often transformed into satellite towns extending the orbit of influence of the central cities. On the other hand, many modern cities have grown out of the assimilation or annexation of several villages which have been connected together by new means of transportation that eventually lead to the building up of the intervening lands.

The distinctive features which characterize urban individuality, giving to each city or town its peculiar skyline, its social atmosphere and its pattern of segregation of population groups and dominant services and institutions is the result of centuries of adaptation of the development of habitation to strategic sites and resources and to its hinterland which sustains it by its own raw materials — crops, populations and modes of culture — that are ceaselessly fashioned and transmuted into new products by the urban collectivity. The city, it is true, abstracts the essence of the region, but the sweep and intensity of production from its science and technique and of mental stimulation and invention from interregional intercourse make it possible for the city to transport the products of the region — the symbolic products no less than the concrete products — to distant parts of the earth. Thus the city, though it belongs to and embodies the region, overreaches and completes it. The local and regional peculiarities of language, thought-structure, temperament and manners represent the warp, and the aspiration of the urban mind to create abstract, symbolic forms and appearances comprehensible to all, is the woof out of which the tapestry of civilization is woven. From out the homespun regional threads of consciousness which give the unique colour and texture to the tapestry emerge certain universal patterns of life and achievement wrought by the humanism of the city which make it a precious inheritance of all lands and ages.

Pattern of Urban Growth and Distribution

We would now consider the growth-form of habitation, hamlet, village and city. Like the animal body, man's habitation, the shell of the community within which man lives, moves and works, increases in size and complexity of its organs and structure. The hamlet, the little town, the city or the metropolis grows from its centre or sub-centres, and there are certain ecological laws of its growth which are universal. The universality of these laws derives its origin from the economy of organs and functions, and their harmonious integration. Each growing village or town exhibits different zones or parts with specialized structures and organs, and like the body of a higher organism shows co-ordination and control of the subordinate parts and centres by the central, focal units, which are the most convenient points of contact with the wider world.

Corresponding to the zonation in the plant world we have the spatial distribution of utilities and functions of social structures and institutions and of population units in a few broadly differentiated zones of the village or town, area of business and commerce, of industry and working men's quarters and of retail businesses and residences. On the whole the following features of urban growth and distribution are fairly universal:

1. central services and institutions are quite consistently located near the centre of the city which at the beginning is only a large village or market centre. Banks, business houses and even hotels, cinema houses and stores are drawn towards the centre of the city. In a growing city these occupy more and more space. Thus the central

business site expands on all sides from the inner core of a market or trading port;

2. nearest the central core of the city is the merchandize area which comprises warehouses and wholesale establishments, but the old association between financial and commercial functions does not persist, the merchandize area being gradually pushed into the zone of main railway communications and thoroughfares because of the advantages of transportation;
3. population shows the greatest concentration in the residential areas close to the centre;
4. certain light industries such as millinery, box-making, tobacco, printing, etc. which occupy little ground space but in which time and service are important are localized close to the centre of the city;
5. heavy industries are localized with reference to facilities of transport and communications and usually in the outlying parts of the city. The influence of topography here is important. Transportation lines and heavy industries are attracted by land below the normal level; while moderate elevations attract residences and level land attracts business;
6. as the city grows population declines in the heart of the city, but land values rise which leads to the gradual displacement of occupants in the residential areas close to the centre that move out farther and farther towards the periphery. "There exists," observes Davie, "an unstable equilibrium between the centripetal force of economy in the transaction of business and the centrifugal force of cheap land. The uniform tendency as a city grows is toward greater concentration in the business centre and greater dispersion in the residence sections".[5]

---

[5] Davie, *Problems of City Life*, pp. 61-65.

7. sub-centres of business and finance, stores and shops accordingly develop, taking advantage of the topography, landuse and layout of main thoroughfares, repeating the general pattern of urban growth and distribution;
8. the better class residences tend to migrate farther and farther to the periphery. Concentration of population in the residential districts, contiguous to the central business site, and dispersal in the fringes and suburbs are seen together, evidence of differential capacities and tastes of different social classes of the urban community.

Centralization of certain services, such as finance, business and administration, also is combined with decentralization of certain other functions, such as retail trade and catering of food, evidence of the differential economy of institutions and activities carried on a large or on a small scale.

The Phenomena of Invasion and Succession

The above antithetical processes of urban growth, concentration and dispersal of population and centralization and decentralization of institutions and functions, constantly lead to the movement of a new type of people, institutions and functions which invades a zone or territory previously occupied by another type. Beneath the apparent stability and uniformity of the urban tenure of life the process of group displacement or of change in landuse is in constant operation, silent, relentless and unplanned. The process is an instance of the major socio-ecological phenomenon of struggle — the struggle for advantageous position and status of groups, services and institutions.

There is, accordingly, constantly found in urban ecology the phenomenon of the invasion and encroachment of one zone or area on another, corresponding to the invasion and succession which take place in the development of the plant communities. Whatever the size, shape or nature of a town or city there is a tendency of the central business area to press upon the neighbouring, older merchandize area, to invade the zone of institutions and mixed utilities, and of the residential area to spread out into the surrounding agricultural belts, followed closely by the retail shops and institutions. It is true that in many towns and cities all such areas are not clearly defined and segregated. Some areas, indeed, overlap, but there is always to be found at least the differentiation of the financial and business area, whose growth and outward pressure upon the surrounding retail and wholesale merchandize area which is also found, well defined in most towns, are the most important movements within a town. Residences also constantly tend to segregate into definite districts due to differences of race and cultural make-up, occupations and types of living conditions.

Measurement of Dominance and Invasion

Corresponding to the universal patterning or zoning of functions, institutions and population units are accordingly found universally in the process of radial invasion and succession, reminiscent of the mass mobility of shrubs into grasslands or willows into sand dunes in the course of vegetative succession. Social ecologists can find in the mobility of urban groups, and institutions and the movement of land values and rentals, which are graded in the various natural areas and which in some measure define their boundaries, very accurate indices of dominance, invasion and succession. Round about the temple and the church, the park and the forum in the ancient or medieval city, land values and rents were the highest as competition for space and accommodation was formerly the keenest here. In the modern town or city these are the highest in the business zone. This is the outcome in large measure of collective interests, preferences and conveniences which create differential demands for space and accommodation in different areas of the town and contribute to give a characteristic pattern to the spatial distribution of population units and cultural, vocational and economic interests. Land values thus are a numerical expression and measure of the shifting, selection and distribution of urban communities and their dominant interests and tastes. In so far as land values and rentals indicate man's economic power, standard of living and social status in the modern industrial community, these represent an accurate index of the quantitative measurement of the cultural contours of urban dwellers. Human circulation or mobility of men, goods and services as well as land value are fairly precise indices to phases of the more elusive social life, and their use in the background of the concepts of human ecology will help to make sociology more quantitative and exact.

A fairly precise measurement of the degree of dominance which a centre exercises in successive zones, out towards its periphery, is afforded by the ecological concept of the gradient. By gradient is meant the rate of change of variable conditions such as home ownership, sex and age groups, poverty, divorce or delinquency from the standpoint of its distribution over a given area.[6] In the vegetable communities we find that plants arrange themselves in zones around a point where one or more of the physical factors are concentrated, their location being determined by their relation to the factor or *ensemble* of factors. Similarly, in a growing town or city, we find rates of various social phenomena varying directly or inversely with the distance from the centre of dominance. In the first place, this conception of the gradient has been applied for the measurement of the extent of urban dominance in the surrounding region by studying the circulation of daily newspapers. It is found that like land values newspaper circulation declines gradually and continuously from the

---

6 Dawson, *Human Ecology in the Fields and Methods of Sociology*, p. 295.

dominant centres and sub-centres of the metropolis or city. As all routes or channels of trade and human circulation come to focus in the central business zone of the city, this becomes the most active centre for both ready and quick information and the mobilization of men, services and commodities. As a matter of fact metropolitan dominance is largely based on the sensitivity of its centre of dominance to trade and economic and political conditions in all parts of the world. The circulation of the metropolitan newspapers which is phenomenal is an evidence of this, and it is characteristic that it gradually declines with increased distance from the city, facing competition after a considerable distance is traversed with small town newspapers which assume circulation dominance over their smaller tributary areas.

In plant ecology, zonation is governed, as we have seen, by the quantitative distribution of the environmental factors. Similarly in the distribution of urban social phenomena we find that a certain combination of physical and social factors leads to the concentration of, say, crime and juvenile delinquency rates and maternal and infantile mortality in certain urban areas, and there is a gradual decline of these rates from these centres to the periphery of the city.

Both the dominance of a region from its central city and the pattern of integration of the entire constellation of habitations which make-up the regional complex can be appreciated by combining:

a. a geographical–ecological study of centres, routes and orbits;
b. a social–ecological and quantitative study of mobility and human circulation and of social distance and segregation; and
c. an economic and sociological study of service and institutional relations of the habitations of various sizes in the region.

Gradients or rates of change of social conditions from the standpoint of their distribution over the region can be usefully employed in all such research.

Relation between the Growth–Structure of a City and its Physical Features

The city is in large measure not amenable to human planning and control. Climate, topography, resources, accessibility, transportation and advantages and disadvantages of sites determine the manner and direction of growth of the city and the arrangement of the urban community. As the city grows a multitude of differentiated and specialized utilities such as public buildings, hotels, shops, factories, railways, roads and terminal centres are superimposed on the physical features of the city, representing a fixed man-made environment on which the population is dependent for its work, recreation and movement. Human spatial relations and adjustments are canalized through narrower channels than the adjustments in the plant and animal communities. The city, therefore, limited in its structure and movement within the framework of topographical features and major transportation lines, and moulded by the vast, mobile and competing current of its population, behaves like an inorganic natural product. The continuous processes of mobility and competition, invasion and accommodation lead to the division of the city into certain organic or natural areas corresponding to the formation of the forest community. As a result of this physical segregation by barriers which become more or less permanent features of the urban landscape, individuals develop different sets of interests and traditions. It is in this manner that the natural area of the city with its many sub-formations or associations selects and sorts out individuals, institutions and social functions. The larger the urban population and the vaster the processes of human mobility, competition and accommodation, the less is the "natural area" of the urban community defined by human design and purpose which are superseded by ecological factors inherent in the physical situation, and the more does it resemble the ecological formation of plant and animal communities.

The ecological patterning of population and institutions of the city is sometimes emphasized, sometimes obliterated when the city expands in numbers and structure. Such urban expansion conforms always to biological laws, all growth being either radial, or axial. Animals that live attached or lead a sedentary life show a tendency towards radial or central expansion. Sessile animals, on the other hand, show a tendency towards more or less bilaterality. "There are many instances," observes Pearse, "where a change from an active, free-living life to a sedentary one has been associated with a tendency towards radial symmetry, and many where a change from sessile to active life has been associated with the taking on of more or less bilaterality."[7] In a similar manner bilaterality is superimposed upon the primitive radial plan of a town or city by the opening out of arterial streets and means of inter-communications which leads to a sudden increase in mobility. The expansion then takes place not from the heart of the city, but along the major axes or routes of circulation. Thus as in the case of most animals there is an apparent relation between the growth-structure of an habitation and environment.

Central and Axial Growth

Hurd has studied the growth of cities, its relation to topographical and other physical factors, and finds that the two types of growth, central and axial, are interrelated and vary in importance in different cities. "Central growth," he observes, "consists of the clustering of utilities around any point of attraction and is based upon proximity. It has two aspects, first, the main general growth in all directions from the point of origin; second, the growth from various sub-centres within

[7] Pearse, *Animal Ecology*, p. 97.

the city, such as transportation termini, public buildings, exchanges, factories, hotels etc." Axial growth is the result of transportation facilities and is based on accessibility. A continual contest exists between axial growth, pushing out from the centre along transportation lines, and central growth, constantly following and obliterating it, while new projections are being made further out of the various axes. The normal result of axial and central growth is a starshaped city growth extending first along the main thorough-fares radiating from the centre, and later filling in the parts lying in between. All cities are built up from these two influences which vary in quantity, intensity and quality. Residences are early driven to the circumference, while business remains at the centre, and as residences divide into various social grades, retail shops of corresponding grades follow them, and wholesale shops in turn follow the retailers, while institutions and various mixed utilities irregularly fill in the intermediate zone, and the banking and office sections remain at the main business centre. Complicating this broad outward movement of zones, axes of traffic project shops through residence areas, create business sub-centres, where they intersect, and change circular cities into starshaped cities. Central growth, due to proximity, and axial growth, due to accessibility, are summed up in the static power of established sections and the dynamic power of their chief lines of intercommunication.[8]

Topographical factors and such features of communication and transportation as roads, railways, tramways and termini as well as location of specialized utilities govern the shape and direction of city development, facilitate or hinder mobility and human circulation, and regulate the use and occupancy of land. Central growth taking place both from the heart of the city and each sub-centre of dominance and attraction stabilizes the dominance of the business and office zone at the centre, and

8 Hurd, *Principles of City Land Values*, pp. 14-15, 58-59.

sharpens the segregation between the different natural areas of the city. On the other hand, as the city pushes into the various outlying natural areas by means of railroads, turn pikes and tramways, shops are projected into residence areas and business sub-centres are created. This leads to the overlapping and interpenetration of characteristics of different natural areas or zones. Thus in an ideal scheme, the segregation of the urban community may be represented by a series of concentric circles with one centre. This may be regarded as an ideal presentation of the ecological zones of the urban community. But the zonal pattern is limited and modified by the axial growth, following the structure of the local transportation system. Accordingly new institutions, functions and cultural groupings intrude upon established natural areas as defined by the central growth of the city due to proximity. Thus railroads with their belts of industries, arterial streets with their lines of shops, overlap and cut across the generalized zonal scheme and the total effects are the distortion, obliteration and neutralization of the zonal arrangement and the intermingling of utilities, functions and cultural traits. Certain natural sections of the city develop traditional prestige, which reduces mobility and increases "historical inertia". "Available evidence indicates," observes Quinn, "the probable existence of a significant tendency toward the formation of concentric ecological time-cost zones. These ecological zones ideally take circular form only in unicentred cities; they assume, logically at least non-circular shapes in dual-centred or multi-centred urban communities."[9] It is only inductive and statistical studies of various social phenomena which show how far in a given city the qualitative distinction and delimitation of the natural areas is distorted and modified by the intermingling of utilities, institutions, and communities which axial growth due to accessibility introduces.

---

[9] J.A. Quinn, "The Burgess Zonal Hypothesis and its Duties", *American Sociological Review*, April 1940.

The zonal arrangement is an established physical fact that is the outcome of nearness and distance in relation to the heart of the living organism, whether a forest, an animal community or a city. On the other hand, man always seeks to conquer distance and resist the radial pressure from the centre, while aggregation at the periphery encourages these tendencies. Axial expansion, indeed, reflects man's imperative social needs as it is facilitated today by the use of the automobile, media and telephone and the distribution of electricity. As both these tendencies become manifest, the regularity of the zonal pattern is undermined and the city breaks up into several cities. And, again, in each city or section the process is repeated. Ecology reveals the relations between the growth–structure of man's habitation and the region, and if there be profound modification of man's spatial relations and adjustments in the dynamic give-and-take between the ecological skeleton of society and man's needs, it is but an extension of the all-pervasive life process to human culture which ecology affirms. The ecological process is constantly thwarted and modified by the cultural process, but again and again re-asserts itself.

6

The Ecological Balance of Population

Synecology: The Science of Interdependent Populations

PLANTS and animals are reciprocally dependent upon one another for their function and multiplication in wild nature. Man is able to set up his dominance in the environment by special protection of and dependence upon certain plants and animals which he selects from his environment for his manifold uses. On the other hand, plants which are acclimatized and animals which are domesticated through the efforts of man can occupy larger space than they would have been able to do in the competition with their rival species in wild nature. Human, plant and animal communities make up by their reciprocal relationships a single unit of the living world, which develops and evolves as a whole. It is for this reason that, as Shelford observes, ecology cannot properly be divided into plant, animal and human ecology but is in fact "bio-ecology". We will call this "synecology". In natural communities composed of both plants and animals there is a rhythm and balance of multiplication for all so that the plant community as a whole can make the best out of the environment. Physiological and morphological adaptations and habits and behaviours of animals subserve the purpose of maintaining an average abundance of individuals so that they may maintain their appropriate niche in the ecological pattern.

Plants form the foundation of the food supply of animals in water as well as on land. In any ecological area the available food determines the numbers and species of plants and animals. The plant matrix is divisible into societies, clans, families and colonies and grades of dominants, sub-dominants and subordinates whose social bonds and balance of growth ensure the unity of the climax formation, animals also contributing to the social integration. In wild nature the vegetative succession or change of dominant and subordinate plants implies transformation in the animal populations as well. The food relation binds the herbivorous animals to the plant matrix of the community, while carnivorous animals are similarly linked directly to herbivores and indirectly to plants. The transformation of the tropical forests into shrub and bush land eliminates most of the arboreal mammals as well as many such herbivores as elephants, wild pigs and rhinoceroses together with, through the modification of light conditions, the formidable insects which drive away other species of animals. Plants, Clements observes, may become also active agents or co-actors in the interaction as in insectivorous species. Similarly, heterotrophic plants such as bacteria and fungi universally assume the role of co-actors, and then resemble animals in being influents of greater or less importance. On the whole, animals due to their mobility and manner of nutrition are active influents and dominants in the biotic community but exploit the vast mass of vegetation to a small extent. A given mass of natural vegetation usually supports only a fractional mass of the animals that could apparently live there without seriously destroying plant life. Weight for weight, vegetation dominates the picture. Elton explains that this limitation of the growth of animal life is due to the interrelations within animal communities and in the ecological mechanisms which control animal numbers. Clements, Shelford, Elton and others have developed certain important notions in their analysis of plant and animal relationships: the idea of optimal and limiting factors and the law of diminishing returns; the idea of optimum population of an animal within a limited set of environmental factors which form the optimum conditions for that species; the inverse relation of size and numbers; the balance between the growth of animal population and its appropriate or available food supply from the vegetable world; the rhythm of growth and succession of different species of plants and animals in the ecological system; and the demonstration that plant and animal communities make up a single, integral living universe, that no animal community is isolated from any other one, but is a section of one vast interrelated biotic community covering a region, a whole country or a continent.

The Circulation of Population Elements in an Ecological System

The vegetation constantly changes and shifts; animal communities are still more restless and in constant movement. A marked factor in ecological succession is the changing rate or flow of the population elements in the successive plant and animal communities. Adams observes:

> As a rule in a new unoccupied habitat the pioneers are few in number, but in time other organisms arrive, and as the population grows, the relative proportions of the organisms are under constant changes in both numbers and kinds, as the competitive process advances toward the relative dynamic equilibrium of the climax association. This is the result of the balancing of all the biotic influences in relation to the environment. It appears to be a self-limiting series or system, and the relative stability of the climax is probably only apparent. In some conditions the climax association tends to include or retain numerous individuals of a few kinds; but in others a relatively large number of kinds of individuals persist.[1]

According to Hesse, whether the fauna will be uniform or varied depends on the kind of vegetation. Variety in the plant world favours variety of animal life. Optimum conditions favour

[1] "General Ecology and Human Ecology", *Ecology*, vol. 16 no. 13.

speciation as abundant food favours variation among domestic animals. With an abundance of species, the struggle for existence between animals becomes extraordinarily intense. Certain animals feed upon others and become parasites; others become poisonous in the process of adaptation for this struggle. The number of prey would determine the number of the predators both increasing under favourable conditions of the habitat. A richer development of zooplankton increases the supply of mackerel. In regions infested with mice there is an abundance of buzzards and owls. Savage predatory mammals occur in forest and grassland areas richly stocked with various species of herbivorous mammals; they are not to be found in small islands where they cannot find prey in adequate quantity. Insect parasites multiply in areas given over to particular types of forest plantations and commercial crops like cotton and tobacco or vegetables. Where insects are abundant birds and spiders also crowd together. In every ecological area a stable equilibrium is maintained between producers and consumers, both populations remaining fairly constant, and gregariousness or solitariness of each species of animals in the ecological community is determined by the entire set of ecological conditions. In the biotic community the producers are represented by the green vegetation and the consumers by the herbivorous animals that eat the vegetation, the carnivorous animals that eat the herbivorous animals and the parasites which feed on both the plant and the animal part of the organisation. That organization depends for its abundance and variety largely on the system of eating and being eaten which drives the chemical wheel of life, the vegetation presenting the carbon and nitrogen in assimilable forms for the animal world.

The Organization of Animal Populations in Grasslands

Animals, it is found, congregate in considerable numbers in grasslands, much more so than in the forests. This is obviously because of easier living on grasses, shrubs and bushes for the fleet-footed rodents and ungulates which also actually benefit the vegetation by moderate cropping. This removes the dead litter and stimulates the growth of leaves and buds. Animals from the elephant to the antelope also help towards the dispersal of many species of fruit and seed as their droppings indicate. This is of great importance in the life of the plant community. The abundance of low vegetation in grass and herb associations nourishes a large variety and huge numbers of insects, reptiles and mammals. Of the mammals the herbivores naturally predominate in the grass area. The rodents surpass all others in number of species and individuals. In Tripoli two-thirds, in the Russian steppes three-fourths, in California three-fifths of the mammals are rodents. Because of their small size, fertility and resistance to drought they have the advantage over other mammals. They constitute the principal food for many predatory animals: eagles, hawks, owls, wolves, foxes, certain cats and others. But their high fertility balances all losses. Many of them live in large colonies and commonly give alarm notes that warn the approach of danger. Many also lay up stores which are often elaborately protected, and which have sometimes been taken advantage of even by man in times of famine as in northern India. Ungulates join the rodents as grasseaters according to the location; wild horses, asses, zebras, especially antelopes, giraffes, bison, pampas deer, camels and guancos, and there are in addition the elephant and rhinoceros in the African savannah. Next to the rodents the ruminants such as antelopes, cattle, deer and camelids are the most abundant. In the grasslands of eastern Africa the zebra and the antelope live in huge herds, while bigger herds of several thousand antelopes of a single species may be seen in some districts. Buffaloes and elephants are also exceedingly abundant and usually found in large companies. The large predatory animals — lions, leopards, hunting dogs and wolves — are attracted in turn by these large herbivores; they follow the herds and flocks, congregate like them at the waterholes during the dry season, migrate with them, and disperse again with them over the grassy plains during the moist season.[2] Many carnivores which are ordinarily solitary occur in packs in the open country, such as jackals and hyenas. Such is the abundance of prey in East Africa that lions move about and hunt here in packs that are thought to be family groups. Movement from one place to another by which they find the necessary food is characteristic of most mammals in the grasslands; many of them are swift as also the carnivores that pursue them. Many of the herbivores have played an important role in preventing the invasion of trees into parts of the plains whose soil and rainfall would have supported a forest growth. They also largely check the advance of human settlement in certain zones.

In the grassy areas in Equatorial Africa wild mammals serve as an ample reservoir for supplies of trypanosomes for domesticated animals and for humans who die by thousands. Outside the fly region, however, the wild animals do not show trypanosomes in their blood and in fact the distribution of the disease coincides with the distribution of the tsetse fly. The primary centres for the fly are associated with waterholes and streams during the dry season, luxuriant thicket growth and abundance of animals. A congregation of fly, animal and man is the best incitement of a virulent epidemic. The fly becomes invigorated as it passes quickly from one animal to another in a large congregation and extends the area of its distribution. Thus the tsetse fly has now spread from its place of origin in West Africa over much of the humid tropical parts of Africa. This has driven man and his livestock from his villages resulting in the invasion of wild game, fly and woodland of gardens and grazing areas. On the other hand,

[2] Hesse, *Ecological Animal Geography*, pp. 462-64.

within vegetation-cleared areas or in belts not infested with the fly there are serious overstocking and overgrazing of domesticated animals causing erosion and overdrainage with the inevitable conversion of wide areas from pasture to desert.

Men in the grasslands cannot be as numerous as the animals he rears. For the herds and flocks, and not the fruits of the fields, are the basis of his subsistence, and these depend upon the pasturage which compels him to move more or less continuously with the animals according to the seasonal outcrop of grasses. Pastoralism requires wide spaces for man who cannot increase in numbers steadily and rapidly without encroaching upon the pastures of other pastoral folks, all mobile fighters and raiders like the carnivorous enemies of their domestic stock. The ecological conditions of sheep- and goatrearing, cattlerearing, horserearing and camelrearing are different, and these also have their effects upon man's economy, density of population and social pattern. But man's domestic animals are by no means restricted to their natural climatic and botanical regions; while the uses to which the same animals are put vary among different peoples and cultures due to diffusion of techniques. Yet on the whole the grassland by limiting the distribution and uses of domestic stock, and determining the specialization of pastoralism governs the needs, size and social organization of the pastoral communities. Finally, the uses of animals among the pastoralists determine largely their economic relations with neighbouring cultivating peoples on the grassland margins. In Asia the pastoralists mounted on their horses went out from the steppes and grasslands of Central Asia, ravaged the territories of agriculturists and founded great empires supported by the tribute from agricultural peoples. On the other hand, the Chinese pioneer farmers have tamed the Mongols and other nomads who either withdrew with their herds or accepted the cultivation of oats, millet, wheat and beans in their semi-arid lands. In Africa both cattle herding and millet growing are adapted to the savannah lands. Sometimes the former has superseded or crippled the latter; sometimes both have lived in symbiosis. The cultivators depend upon the pastoralists for the occupancy of their lands, and supply them millet for brewing beer in return. Cattle which are hardly ever used as beasts of burden in Africa are yet bought by the cultivators for the sake of prestige and distinction.

Animal Communities in the Tropical Forest

The composition of the animal community in the tropical rain forest is far different. Mammals are much less abundant, and the majority of them are arboreal that seldom set foot on the ground and are hence relatively small. Monkeys and squirrels are predominant. The ground dwelling mammals tend in the hothouse atmosphere to be small stealthy forms that wind their way through the forest such as the musk deer, the forest antelope, and the dwarfed hippopotamus. The elephant stands out in contrast as a forestwrecker moving through the forest by sheer strength. Many animals are found to help one another, not designedly of course, in the quest of food. Elephant-made trails are followed by hippopotami, rhinoceroses, buffaloes, wild bears, lions, leopards and even hyenas, and are left yet more passable for other animals. The tapir represents this type of trailmaker in the American jungles. The wild boar, following trails made by elephants, get food from the faeces of the latter and from roots and trees which the elephants have dislodged. Baboons follow the wild pigs and obtain scorpions, earthworms and insects which the pigs have turned up as well as eating roots and the like.[3] It is obvious that this kind of eating at the common table is possible because these animals are neither flesh-eaters nor specialists. Further, the disturbance of the soil caused by the elephant, the wild boar and the baboon

---

[3] Hesse, *Ecological Animal Geography*, pp. 434 and 450.

improves the texture of the soil and stimulates the growth of vegetation. Fruits eaten and passed through the animals are cleaned of their outer coverings and fall into improved germinating beds. Studies of stomach contents of mammals, birds and insects, especially those of the predatory and phytophagous species, indicate that each species selects the food available in the greatest quantity, making selections which in a particular locality tend to give an erroneous impression as to the specific nature of food relations. Thus, there is a balance established between the multiplication of each species of animal and its appropriate or available food supply from the plant world. Then there is the prey-predator relationship. Grass and grain-feeders constitute "the key industry" animals of the fauna of both grasslands and forests. The more numerous and the larger the herbivores, the greater will be the number and size of the carnivores that will be attracted in the ecological area. The strong, cunning and long-limbed predatory animals dominate over the animal life of the region although these are numerically small and breed at a much smaller rate than most other mammals. It is noteworthy that their smaller breeding rate is connected with a complement of instincts and habits in respect of nesting, courtship, food quest and play. Territorialism of both herbivores and carnivores orients them in respect to their burrows, dens and foraging grounds, limits their freedom of movement and indirectly stresses the significance of the role played by the plant community in their lives.

In the thick and moist equatorial forest such territorialism also ties man to his narrow clearing in the jungle which, however, constantly menaces his habitation. Man is powerless here against the rank vegetative growth. In the equatorial forests have survived some of the most primitive races of the world, and nomadism is the result of man's utter helplessness. The quick and luxuriant growth of weeds permits only hunting, food collection, or a crude, intermittent system of cultivation in which the primitive peoples move their settlement at short intervals in order to continue to find fertile fields. Man here grows puny and feeble, a constant prey to wild animals, insects and bacteria of the steaming jungle, and his numbers cannot increase steadily, except in margins of forests and in the meadows growing up in the open glades. In the tropical forests the pig which lives on roots and shoots and the fowl which lives on garbage are reared by the forest cultivators who, however, obtain from them but meagre additions to their dominantly vegetarian dietaries. Similarly, though most of the African cultivators maintain in small number of goats and sheep, which are not native to the equatorial forest area, their animal foods are derived mostly from wild game. Contrasted with the more or less nomadic cultivators of the tropical forests, such as the Kenyas and Ibans of Borneo, the Menang Kabu Malayas of Sumatra and the Boros of Amazonia and the settled agricultural tribes such as the Yoruba and Bantu peoples of the Congo basin and the Guinea coast are the primitive food gathering groups in the same climatic zone. In the equatorial jungles of South-East Asia and Africa live several food-collecting peoples who subsist on fruits and roots and also on relatively small game of the forest such as birds, rats, squirrels, lizards, monkeys, and wild pigs, carefully avoiding the large carnivores such as the tiger, panther and leopard, and the elephant. The Semang, Sakai and Jakun tribes of Malaya, the Andamanese, the Punan of Borneo and the pygmy tribes in the Congo basin, among others, derive their food supply principally from wild vegetables, roots and fruits and relatively small mammals of the forest. Their numbers are restricted by their primitive technique, while their internal social structure remains primitive. Yet even in the African jungles side by side with the nomadic food collectors and hunters, occupying considerable tracts and living in small family groups there are the more advanced and numerous cultivating tribes such as the Yoruba and Boloki whose cultivation of yams and other appropriate and prolific root crops represents an excellent adaptation to forest conditions.[4] Much light may be thrown on the population growth and cultural history of the primitives of South-East Asia and Africa by studying the adaptations of their economy to the flora and fauna of the grasslands and tropical forests.

"Checks" of Animal Populations

Grasslands are, as we have seen, most richly stocked with animals, both herbivores and carnivores. It is the smaller gnawing and grass feeding mammals which here are most prolific, and exhibit marked fluctuations of populations. If these animals have their periodic storms of breeding and over step an average abundance, the dominant carnivores are found to increase in numbers and reduce them, or their bacterial enemies multiply even faster than them and bring about a fulminating, destructive epidemic. Thus a variety of ecological controls safeguards the balance, albeit shifting, of animal populations. The snow shoe rabbit of Canada, the lemmings of Norway and the field mice in different parts of the world, all have their cyclical fluctuations of numbers. Predatory animals keep them in check in years of average abundance. But when mass outbreaks occur epidemics stalk the fields and meadows and drastically reduce them. After an epidemic the animals left to breed are not nearly so prolific as before. Their number again slowly rises until they once more become extraordinarily abundant to be again decimated by another epidemic. Thus the cycle continues.

Climatic selection, the territory habit, the predator-prey system, the pressure of population, the recurrence of plagues and swarming or migration are among the ecological

---

4 Forde, *Habitat, Economy and Society*, Chapter X.

mechanisms of natural population control, which maintain an optimum density for each species of animal which can collectively and individually, utilize the economic possibilities of the restricted environment. Recent studies of the fluctuations of animal populations by Elton, Phillips, Forbes and others clearly show a wonderful web, linking and interlinking the physical factors, the plant, the animal, the parasite and even man himself; a web of the most intricate spinning of woof and warp and a rhythm and balance of growth of different forms of life in the biotic community. If we envisage the aggregate of the organisms in both numbers and kinds, we obtain the picture of a pyramid resting on a vast mass of vegetation, which is the foundation of all life. The vegetation provides the basis and energy of all animal life. It alone, by using the energy of sunlight, is capable of building up carbon and nitrogen compounds from simple inorganic materials to serve as food substances for animal and man. It consumes water and checks the run-off of both water and soil down the river and sea. Thus it conserves the moisture and saves the land for building upon it layers and layers of progressively richer population which grows in wealth in proportion as they make greater demands on the land. A fairly numerous, smallsized and rapidly multiplying community of grass and grain-feeding animals forms the broad base of the pyramid supporting grades of carnivores in the middle and at the top, dominant animals which are relatively few, large and slow breeding. The pyramidal organization of numbers and relationships of the natural communities of plants and animals covers the face of the earth before man, the superdominant at the apex, interferes with them by his tools and implements of stick and stone, iron and steel. Man, the most predatory and numerous among the terminal animals, also releases himself from the ecological controls which maintain a balanced growth of animal populations, and introduces for the first time into animate nature the issue of overpopulation.

The Pyramidal Structure of Animal Communities

The original arrangement of numbers and grades in an animal community when it has reached a steady state, nominally gives us the picture of a symmetrical but flexible pyramid. Such an arrangement results from the three general facts:

a. Vegetarian animals are more prolific and abundant than carnivorous ones. Sheep and cattle, deer and antelopes, rabbits and kangaroos are found in huge numbers and multiply at incredible rates while their enemies such as lion, tiger and wolf which bring their numbers to an average abundance represent smaller populations and multiply at a low rate. Similarly, seed and fruit eating birds are more numerous than carnivorous birds: grasshoppers, locusts and vegetarian beetles than their carnivorous allies.[5]

b. Small animals increase faster than the large ones and are the most numerous in the ecological system.

c. Small animals are preyed upon usually by large animals.

The size limits to the food of animals produce foodchains, and these chains are able to exist because the smaller animals, which have the greater burden to bear, are by their size enabled to support it more effectively. Elton observes that each stage in the chain has the effect of turning small food animals into larger ones, and since there are wider limits to the sizes of animals than to the size of the food of any one animal, we usually find some three or four stages forming the foodchain. Sometimes there are more, but there seem to be hardly ever more than six or seven stages in a chain leading from a vegetarian animal to the terminal carnivorous species.[6] Ecologists, classifying the food habits of animals, further divide the herbivores into those of different sizes, or belonging to different plants, and the carnivores also according to the size and nature of their prey.

---

[5] Mitchell, *The Childhood of Animals,* p. 116.

[6] Article on Ecology by Elton in the *Encyclopaedia Britannica,* I4th edn.

It becomes clear that there are in each animal community a great many different occupations or niches (just as in human society), and that each niche is filled by a particular species. In different ecological areas the same niche occurs, and although the actual species occupying them are different, their habits, numbers and size are largely similar.

The study of the congregation and organization of animal life under the most favourable conditions throws a floodlight on the multiplication of man in his generations. Many grasslands represent areas where the maximum amount of life is found crowded together. Mammals are certainly much more abundant in the grasslands than in the forests. It has been pointed out that in the grass areas the rodents which form the base of the animal population pyramid and surpass all others in the number of species and individuals represent from two-thirds to three-fourths of the mammals. Because of their small size, fertility and resistance to drought they have an advantage over other mammals. While the non-rodents bulk larger as individual units, yet the amount of food consumed by rodents may run as high as 75 per cent of what is available. Next to the rodents, the ruminants such as antelopes, cattle, deer and camelids are the most abundant. Attracted by the latter are the large predatory animals which are the least numerous, represented by wolves, hunting dogs, leopards, tigers and lions. The terminal animals such as tigers and lions are the fewest, representing the apex of the pyramid of animal life. As the prey species increase in numbers, these predatory animals bring them back to lower population levels, while they themselves diminish in numbers because of reduced food supply. In no case does one species completely eliminate another in wild nature. In the heels of the larger predatory animals follow the scavengers such as the jackal, the fox and the hyena which live largely on the remains of kills of the former. The richness and variety of mammals in grasslands contributed to the development of early man's tentatives in animal raising and agriculture in these areas, while in the forests where mammals are much less abundant many primitive peoples are still forced to practise a primitive, intermittent agriculture. Man's domestication of animals from the grasslands was chiefly aided by the adaptability and social behaviour which the animals acquired in the sociological structures of mateship, family and herd. He then chose the traits that were especially useful for him for selection and breeding and gradually eliminated the qualities which were dangerous or disagreeable by consistent selection through several generations.

Man's Disturbance of the Balance of Nature

Man himself who has sprung from the primates is an animal who naturally belongs to the margins of woodland or forest glade. As he descended from the trees of the deciduous forest, he took to co-operative hunting as that of packs of wolves and preferred those collective ways of living which ultimately differentiated him from the anthropoid apes. On the edges of the forests the grasslands supplied him with his domesticated animals, especially the cattle and horses. Man's dominance and increase in numbers in the new environment were accompanied by the abundance of cattle and other livestock as his helpmates and co-dominants. The criteria of dominance in the case of plants and animals are represented by increase of numbers and intensity of "biotic" interference. The actual food relations of animals in wild nature have scarcely been investigated. But the processes of interaction which are comparable to metabolism can be judged from the disturbance caused by man in the balance of nature through the complete destruction of the cover of vegetation and elimination of carnivores, which are enemies of all kinds of his domestic animals, and the rapid multiplication of the latter due to his care and protection in the history of settlement.

The balance of nature always shifts since plant and animal populations constantly fluctuate. But the balance is ever imminent, man continuously upsetting and tipping it on the wrong side. The vegetation shows about the same abundance and range of species through the years. The insects which feed on it show an average abundance except sporadically. When there is an outbreak of insect population, birds prey on and reduce it to an average density, preferring those species which have gone out of bounds. The system of eating and being eaten contributes to maintain the average numbers of both prey and predator also among the mammals. But in their case other mechanisms establishing the balance of population are also operative. Most of them have their territories from a fraction of an acre for a squirrel and a mouse to a few square miles for a tiger, elephant or rhinoceros. Territories are maintained pugnaciously as a result of a complex set of instincts connected with nesting, courtship, watering and play of the higher animals. Thus the animals limited within a narrow foraging range do not over-eat their food supply so that a natural balance is maintained between the multiplication of the species and food supply. Migratory instincts arising out of a sense of disharmony with the region, due to economic pressure, oppose the instincts of the animals to remain localized and hold their territory against their own kind and the result is certainly the establishment of a working balance of numbers of the species. Finally, a sudden epidemic outburst caused by a quicker multiplication of predatory parasites diminishes numbers recurrently with some small prolific mammals which exhibit cycles of growth; while reduced and adaptive fecundity does so normally with many other higher mammals. Man alone among the animals exhibits asymbiotic multiplication. His consumption normally outstrips his means of subsistence. For improving his subsistence he raises crops in succession from the same soil, and exhausts its fertility. He ascends the hill slopes with his axe and fire, and destroys the mantle of vegetation in meadows and plains driving out the animals and letting loose the forces of erosion. A new balance is now established but at a lower level. On account of the exhaustion of soil and moisture, and increase of run off the arable land will yield less and grow fewer crops and support less population; the meadow will similarly support fewer and less nutritive grasses for the livestock. These destructive influences aid one another and gain greater and greater momentum in nature.

Soil erosion reduces fertility and crop yield, and increases the run off which further reduces fertility and denudes whole soils. Simultaneously, the watertable is lowered and the land progressively becomes more infertile and arid. Drought and aridity, extending over larger and larger areas in the barren plain, and floods tearing away soil caps over the bare hill slopes and choking streams and water courses by the deposition of silt and debris are alike the consequence of the impairment of the balanced, fruitful relationships among waters, soils and vegetation. The web of life is now overstretched thinner to cover a depleted region and some threads snap. The balance of life is maintained, but at a level much lower for life, whether plant, animal or man. Synecology demands that man should work in harmony with the balanced relationships in nature so as to accelerate and not put brakes on nature's continuous operations of recuperation and regeneration. Renewal and enrichment rather than exhaustion and depletion of the region should be man's conscious synecological goal if he wants to nourish his land–water culture in which civilization is rooted on a continuing basis for his species.

Man's Failure in the Dry Grasslands

Once upon a time the deciduous forest extended over the

entire Ganges Plain in northern India. Now this area exhibits some of the world's highest records of human and cattle population density, the most complete destruction of forests, woods and groves and most severe grazing and browsing of vegetation by millions of cattle, sheep and goats. Generally speaking, the vegetation at present prevailing is savannah-like throughout this densely populated region. But patches of deciduous forests, probably remnants of older, more extensive woodlands, are found in the submontane districts and in those parts of the valley where the rainfall is over 80 inches. Dry grassland and thorn-scrub formations now make up the man-dominated vegetation. In heavily grazed areas the vegetation is found frequently reduced to one or a few species that are avoided by cattle, among which may be mentioned *Butea frondosa*, *Casearia tomentosa* and many *Euphorbiacea*. Here and there heavy grazing as well as dry conditions have so favoured the prickly scrambling *Zizyphus oenoplia* that it forms dense masses impenetrable for animals. *Acacia arabica* also can withstand the rigorous biotic pressure, and is fairly common in the dry tracts or on river banks. With regard to agriculture diversified farming with the aid of irrigation is the general rule. Crop production includes both indigenous as well as acclimatized types of grains and vegetables. The extension of cultivation and the necessity of protection of domesticated livestock have led to the extermination and gradual dispersal of animals on a scale probably unparalleled in the world. There is hardly any region in the world so devoid of animals and birds. At the same time with the destruction of the smaller carnivores, the rabbits, rats and mice have multiplied, destroying foodgrains and fodder and becoming pests as the consequence of surviving the relationship with man. In the new environment created by man and his co-dominants, the livestock, there has been, indeed, a unique deterioration of faunal standard, and man has in effect lost more than he has gained. Throughout the Ganges Plain it is really a case of the giants being superseded by the pygmies — the wild elephant, the rhinoceros and the buffalo, the lion, the tiger and the wild bear, the black buck, the *nilgai* and the wild ass, the mongoose, the fox and the wild cat, the peacock, the weaver-bird and the great bustard, the florican, the quail, and the partridge either have become extinct or are fast disappearing; and what have multiplied are the mosquitoes and sandflies, ticks and mites, which make life a burden, the caterpillars, moths, locusts, ants, beetles and insects of all sorts which attack the crops; the sparrows and the *saragas*, the squirrels and the rabbits, the mice and the rats, which do great damage to the crops and seem to be yearly increasing in numbers and in their ravages, not to mention the wasps, scorpions, spiders, fleas and bugs. In the deciduous monsoon forest zone in northern India, especially where rainfall is less than 20 inches, the phenomenal increase of human population as well as the disharmonious multiplication of cattle, sheep and goats have now brought about both an acute imbalance of human food supply and resources as well as retrogression of vegetation from the original climatic climax to the dry grassland or thorn-scrub stage, involving the supersession of valuable forage plants by relatively worthless annuals and weeds which die and leave the ground almost bare in summer when forage is most needed for the bovine population. These are the cumulative effects of crime against vegetation through several generations — brand tillage in the hills and hill slopes, encroachment of arable land on forest and grove everywhere in the valley and close and persistent browsing and grazing by herds of co-dominant animals. Fodder famine has been chronic while the forces of erosion have been let loose on an alarming and ever widening scale. Erosion and over drainage have resulted in the destruction of valuable watersheds, loss of stock waters and lowering of water tables, driving out certain wet zone crops such as sugar cane and indigo and leading to the steady expansion of sanddunes. All this has brought about a serious crisis in agriculture in a large compact zone of "badlands". A man made desert is now establishing itself in the heart of one of the most fertile regions of the earth. "Animals are better shortperiod indicators than plants,"observes Shelford. In the Ganges Valley one sees the pushing of the desert species of plants into what was once a prairie and plain, and of the wet community animals, which have over-eaten their subsistence due to increase of population in the plain, into the prairie and the desert with attendant effects upon the habitat. Where human and bovine population through increase has spilled over into or invaded grasslands and desert areas, recurrent human and cattle famine, desiccation and expansion of the desert show the complete failure of man's deciduous forest culture. The far reaching consequences of the interlocked relations between plant, animal and human populations and of human biotic interferences are perhaps nowhere better discernible than in northern India.[7] Detailed surveys of these in both deciduous forest and grassland environments in India may reveal whether man and his co-dominants, the domesticated animals, and his subdominant plants, crops and vegetables can succeed in the grasslands at all. The indication now is that man's standard of living, health and social organization show deterioration as his population increase also receives a setback in the dry grassland environment.

Unlike other mammals who thrive best in the grasslands, man is a failure here, and this failure he brings about more quickly where his religion and social custom eschew a common sense view of animal keeping and lead to an indiscriminate

---

[7] Mukerjee, *The Regional Balance of Man*, Chapters VI and VII.

increase of uneconomical and superfluous cattle as grazing co-dominants.

Biological Status of Population

Animals show physiological failure or unfitness in a physical environment by an increase of mortality and reduction of average longevity. This reflects itself in the age composition of the animal population. A population, whether animal or human, which is demologically progressive exhibits an age structure strikingly different from that of a stationary or decaying population. Whether a population replaces itself quickly and shows a large excess is indicated not by the excess of births over deaths but by the relative excess of the proportion of females surviving through the reproductive ages and relative deficiency within the youngest and oldest age groups which are most exposed to mortality. If we represent the figures relating to the age distribution of a growing population in the form of a diagram, put males on one side and females on another and make each step in the pyramid proportional in area to the number of each sex within each age group, we will find that in the pyramid the lower steps all project markedly beyond those which come next above, giving an appearance of solidity. In a stationary and decaying community the pyramid is attenuated at the base, the lower steps being smaller than the higher. Increase of mortality, especially infantile and maternal mortality, and reduction of birthrate are the *sine qua non* of a decrease of population. The following figures would show that in a large compact region in the Ganges Valley (south-western United Provinces) which now exhibits increase of aridity there has been a decrease of density of population at the beginning of the 20th century.

In the whole province there is a much higher mortality of the females at the reproductive ages and the conditions have become worse since 1921 leading to a rise of the sex ratio in

	Index of Aridity	*Percentage of Gross Cultivated Area which is irrigated*	*Density of Population Per Sq. Mile*			
			1901	1911	1921	1931
Muttra	15.5	31.8	526	452	427	461
Aligarh	17.0	45.9	617	599	546	602
Agra	17.0	25.3	572	551	498	567
Etah	18.2	38.1	500	504	483	501
Mainpuri	21.2	42.2	495	476	447	448
Etawah	21.5	28.3	477	449	434	442

deaths. Data in respect of the gross and net reproduction rates are not available. If Kuczynski's method of determining whether a population is replacing itself or decaying by means of a calculation of the net reproduction rate be diagrammatically represented, we shall find that in a demologically progressive society the population pyramid is wider and stronger at the foundation and the steps representing the number of female children born and surviving by whom the present women replace themselves are larger at the base or the earlier reproductive years. The pyramidal pattern of age and sex distribution of population, which reveals a trend of increase, rests on a successful occupational and ecologic balance by which the force of natality can be made to overcome the force of mortality, in the case of the most vulnerable section of the population, viz. women during their crucial period of child bearing. Decrease of maternal mortality, increase of marriages and rise of fertility are *sine qua non* of an increase of population. In the study of all kinds of plant and animal populations, it has been found, that at different stages of growth or with different modifications of the environment there are different proportions of newly formed, young, reproductive and older individuals, whose life process is restricted, specialized and often reduced both as regards their own *intensity of life* and their *function within the population.*[8] In the case of human population the life process of the reproductive females is restricted by environmental limitations in a peculiar manner and this is crucial in the biological status and movement of the population.

The Depletion and Disintegration of the Region

Man, no doubt, can transform the ecological base to an extent which cannot be imagined in the case of vegetable and animal communities. That plants and animals also reshape their environments has not received adequate recognition. The higher plants and microorganisms living in the soil cause changes in the soil, often of a very radical nature, e.g. with respect to reaction (hydrogen ion-concentration), nitrification, etc. Everywhere plant communities prepare the soil for some active phases for the development of a new vegetative succession which again initiates another cycle, causing changes in the landscape culminating in a particular type of climax vegetation in the area. Even if the climate remains for ever unchanged, there is no reason to assume that the new existing climax formation will be the same a few centuries hence. The present formation is thus a stage or step of a series of events going back to the dim past. Invasions have taken place, competition has ensued, certain species have become established as permanent constituents of the various associations, while others have died out or taken subordinate places. Great migrations of plants have taken place from distant parts of the world and at intervals of thousands of years apart. Plant dispersal and invasion radically change the composition of vegetation, aided of course by change effected by weathering and erosion, by animals and by the hand of man. Everywhere cattle, sheep and goats, on the other hand, keep the climax from developing. Goats are especially destructive,

---

[8] H. Johan Hjort, *Restrictive Law of Population*, p. 16.

eating grasses and shrubs down to the soil surface. The beaver's tree-cutting and dam-building activities are well and widely known, but some of the far-reaching effects of its engineering operations are not so clearly recognized. The beaver builds a dam and slows the water of a stream. Silt may be deposited, and swamp, marsh or peat soils develop. So long as the beaver is on the job, however, the waterlevel is maintained. It is only after the animal has moved that the streamway can be altered to something else. Marsh attributed considerable importance to the beaver as a factor in the development of marsh and forest land, and the destruction of streams important to their existence, which lead them to seek new catchment basins of streams to work their havoc. Contrasted with the havoc caused by the beavers are the beneficient activities of such burrowers as rabbits and field rats which help in building up soils and making drainage and irrigation channels, thus checking erosion and runoff. Burrowing animals not only add to the soil plant nutrients but also bring about aeration, drainage and increased water percolation in the soil. The actual waterholding capacity of the soil is considerably increased largely by the mixing action of their digging. Similarly birds keep insects, rodents and other pests of man, cattle and crops under control. Many of the mammals which unlike the birds are resident and usually active throughout the year aid in controlling insects and rodents. Rodents become a menace to crops and fodder and promote soil erosion when all their predators have been exterminated by man and excessive numbers of his livestock have eaten up the vegetation and laid bare the soil. Similarly, birds also become destructive when the balance between the bird crop and the fruit crop or harvest has been destroyed by the complete destruction of thickets and hedges. Successful agriculture consists in utilizing not only the flora and fauna of the soil, but also birds, rodents and other wild creatures whose aid should be enlisted in man's favour. Like man wild creatures seek to hold their own territory against the competition from their own kind. Inside of its own territory each animal so comports itself as not to spoil its own living. Animal territory safeguards the balance between animal numbers and food supply, and its guarantee in so far as it is compatible with agriculture enables the farmer to benefit from the presence and activities of animals. Most primitive peoples, as Elton remarks, have settled down into a more or less harmonious relationship with the animals and plants of their region. The Red Indians of North America or the natives of Siberia usually took care not to kill too many of the animals upon which they depended for food so that the stock would not become exhausted. In Australia totemic beliefs prevented the exhaustion of certain wild cereals, which might have spelled starvation. In New Zealand the Maoris conserve their forests because these provide the numerous birds that form important sources of their food supply. But it is otherwise with civilized man. Civilized man, the toolmaker and builder, changes and remakes his environment. His weapons and artefacts are as varied as his needs are infinite. While his technology and artefacts tremendously increase his capacity and speed of exploitation of resources, the expansive demands of his industrial standard of living show profound disharmony with the maintenance of integrity and balance of the region. On the other hand, his reckless multiplication leads him to seek quick results, become improvident of nature's resources. With regard to the resources of the grassland many groups of herdsmen adopt practices of rotational grazing and fallowing for enabling the grasses to recuperate. According to the Mongols in Central Asia no pasture ought to be grazed year after year by the same kind of stock — sheep for instance. A pasture ought either to be rested altogether from time to time or grazed by some other kind of stock like cows or horses. If it gets no rest or change, the steady accumulation of the urine and dung of the same animal ceases to be fertilizing and becomes "poisonous".[9] In the grass areas of Marwar in India there is the practice of *oran* according to which some pasture land is held in reserve, dedicated to a demi-god whence pasturage is excluded in normal seasons. The cattle may graze here only during a serious fodder famine. It seems that civilized man is less heedful in husbanding nature's resources. He wastes nature's assets of soil, water, vegetation and wildlife for achieving immediate efficiency, and thus upsets the balance between agriculture and Nature's cycle of recuperation and regeneration. He too often disturbs Nature's adjusted and balanced growth by elimination or addition to the existing state of things, thus setting in motion wheels of change which make the life of his later generations harder.

Limitations of Man's Dominance: Climate and Disease

Man through the evolution of his tools has largely controlled the ecologic conditions of his multiplication and dominance. Man, in the first place, through the exercise of his toolbearing habits can migrate to other regions where the physical conditions favour his survival. But he does not always exercise his choice wisely. Or economic pressure compels him to migrate to and settle in environments where temperature and humidity in combination increase disease and mortality and contribute to his physiological degeneration. In most parts of the tropics the white man's colonization has been a striking failure. His settlement in the great North American and African grasslands has also met with reverses, and probably has no ecological surety behind it. Secondly, man has protected himself against

[9] Owen Lattimore, *Mongol Journeys*.

the inclemencies of climate through the elaboration of clothing and shelter and prevented or mitigated disease and suffering which cause mortality and inefficiency and stand in the way of his multiplication. It must, however, be conceded that cultural control of diseases and insect pests cannot altogether supersede climatic control, and that under certain conditions the vigour of insects and man's bacterial parasites increases in inverse proportion to man's vigour. The capacity for acclimatization of different races is limited and also variable. The Chinese succeed where other people have failed. The South European is more successful than the North European; the Latin than the Anglo-Saxon. "Those whose diet is light and simple fare better than those who are hearty eaters and much of whose food is meat."[10] Similarly another recent writer observes:

> For unknown reasons certain coloured peoples seem superior in the tropics to certain white peoples and similar variations appear to exist among the white groups.[11]

It is probable that the varying experiences of races in the tropics are due to the cumulative interdependent influences of climate, physiological adaptations, diets and living standards. Migration and colonization as well as agricultural reconstruction have on the whole succeeded best when crops, animals, agricultural practices and races have moved out into regions similar to their homelands. Under similar environmental conditions races show greater physiological vigour and immunity from the attacks of endemic diseases as his breeds of domesticated animals can withstand epidemics and pick a living better even where fodder is scarce.

Both the optimum and the limits imposed by temperature,

---

10 Ward, "White Race in the Tropics", *Annual Report of the Smithsonian Institution*, 1930.

11 Price, *White Settlers in the Tropics*, pp. 198, 235.

humidity, sunshine, wind and other factors for successful colonization by different peoples vary appreciably. According to Huntington the physical optimum for Europeans involves a mean temperature of about 65° F for day and night together; a relative humidity averaging about 80 per cent ; and an inter-diurnal variability averaging not far from 3° F. The best physical and mental work is done at temperatures between 30° and 70° F and there is a startling deterioration in all work done as the temperature rises above 70° F. The investigation of the relations between mortality and climate in United States shows that the hot wet coasts of the Gulf of Mexico are very much less healthy than the cooler states of the North. Florida has the worst deathrates and the Nebraska-Iowa the best. Griffith Taylor considers 50° wet-bulb and 75 per cent relative humidity are near the optimum for white folk. Unfortunately few countries publish wet-bulb data, but the usual dry-bulb reading under these conditions is close to 53° F. In presenting a tentative scale of discomfort for the white folk, he notes that wet-bulb temperatures of 65° to 70° F are often and temperatures above 70° F are usually "uncomfortable". According to his estimate, equatorial low lands are always "uncomfortable" while the monsoon regions, the tradewind areas and the margins are uncomfortable for much of the year. As regards the optimum rainfall for European settlement, there is not much to choose anywhere from 40 to 50 inches. In his history of exploitation of the earth, man has subtly and effectively utilized the region and its dominant species of plants and animals for the increase of his food supply. His ecologic control became manifest when he understood successively agricultural water supply and the mineral salts, and recently hydrogen ion-concentration as the limiting factors in agricultural production. From irrigation and agricultural chemistry which have enabled him to reap abundant harvest in old and exhausted lands, in arid areas, in salt encrusted lands or in marsh bottoms, he has now turned to plant and animal breeding and the control and elimination of weeds, pests and parasites.

The climatic optimum is a genuine biological trait of each kind of crops and animals. But as man proceeded steadily, on his "cold-ward march", gradually moving into cooler climates, he produced varieties of plants and animals which are adapted to the new habitats. Thus on the whole there is found today a close agreement between the climatic optima for crops and domestic animals on the one hand and for the most active and advanced types of men on the other. The optima for winter wheat, oats, potatoes, corn, cattle, horses, hogs and hens conform fairly closely to those of the most active men of the world.[12] Man's dominance is largely the outcome of his use of tools, clothing, fire, and shelter, and of his power to select and breed crops and animals adapted to climates close to his own optimum, and this has resulted in a gradual transformation of the ecological organization of plant and animal aggregations entirely in his favour. He has also eliminated his dependence upon living plants and animals by using Nature's store directly. He has exterminated species of plants and animals which compete with him for the means of subsistence, shifting his dependence from animals to green plants, and from secondary, mainly animal foods to primary, chiefly vegetable foods as his population pressure has become heavier. Man in the monsoon region, where half the world's population lives, consumes little beef or meat because of the excessive land requirements of secondary food. In China due to overpopulation he has appreciably reduced the numbers, of cattle, buffalo and horses and rears in preference pigs and fowls which supply animal foods and at the same time do not encroach upon human subsistence. Everywhere he has selected for domestication and

[12] Huntington, Williams and Valkenburg, *Economic and Social Geography*, pp. 142-44.

improvement by breeding species of cultivated plants and livestock which are better adapted to the temperature–humidity combination of his own habitat, and for resistance to its insect pests and diseases.

Climatic Controls for Cereals

But in the fields of plant and animal breeding and importation of exotic strains and breeds man's efforts are still largely limited by climatic controls though the processses of selection and improvement of all sorts of plants and animals are proceeding with marvellous speed. The temperature controls for the major foodcrops are roughly indicated as follows: Barley grows in regions with an average annual temperature as low as 30° F. Oats, wheat (in Canada), and potatoes are also possible in such regions if they have a relatively hot (continental) summer. The optima for barley and Canadian wheat are near 40°; for oats and potatoes near 45°; for United States maize near 49°; and for European wheat 51° F.[13] Rice thrives best in tropical or sub-tropical regions and needs a large amount of water in the soil at certain stages of its development. Its temperature limits are much wider than those of the crops of the white folk. Rice in Asia is grown anywhere from Arabia to Japan, and the summer temperature is everywhere 84° F. Some varieties of rice mature in 60 days, i.e. about half the time needed by most varieties of rice and thus it is possible to grow two crops in a year or to use the land for other purposes when the crop has been harvested. Due to its very short growing season rice can ripen perfectly even where the mean winter temperature is below 32° F. Though 95 per cent of the crop is now raised in the Indo-Japanese lands, all over the world the finest qualities are both grown and consumed in high latitudes, "super-Carolina" being

---

[13] Griffith Taylor, *Environment, Race and Migration*, p. 425.

grown in Lombardy (45° N).[14] Food crops reach in general from the equator to 70° northern latitude, but each crop has its more specific limits with its own conditioning effect upon population and culture: rice extends from the equator to the line of 54° of mean annual temperature, maize to 50°, wheat to 43° and barley to 36° F.[15]

Ecological Principles of Colonization

Trees and grasses serve as the most reliable natural "indicators", revealing conditions favourable for the production of cultivated plants of similar habits in regions where agriculture is not established. On the other hand, cultivated plants grown in similar habitats easily invade neighbouring regions and this has considerably helped towards successful migration and colonization of peoples in the past. Thus the agriculture of rice and tea spread out from China into Siam, Burma and eastern India while the agriculture of beans, corn and millets is even now spreading from the loess to the oases of Central Asia and Mongolia. The migration of the Europeans in North America was aided by the "hill" planting of native American crops. Among the crops which the white settlers adopted were maize, cotton and tobacco. In each case the plant was well perfected aboriginally. Sauer observes in this connection:

> The white man took the ritually used tobacco of the Indian and made it one of the first great crops of oversea commerce. He has kept it in large production by the aid of the fertilizer chemist. He discovered that maize was a far better feed grain than he had possessed before, and he built on it a world trade in lard and pork. He took the upland cotton of Mexican origin and by the invention of the gin gave the world its first cheap vegetable fibre. Each of these cultural adaptations

---

14 Lyde, *Continent of Asia*, p. 478.

15 Gregory, et al., *Physical and Commercial Geography*, p. 183.

> resulted in a great forward surge of population. Together they account in the main for the expansion of American settlement to and beyond the western limit of the eastern woodlands of the United States.

If we accept the synecological view of migration and colonization we have to explore the possibilities of utilization of the open spaces of the world by the introduction and successful cultivation of crops from similar climatic zones. Large manless regions in the monsoon areas or fringes in South America, Africa and the Netherland's East Indies may successfully grow rice, maize or sorghum, and the agriculture of the rice complex may add considerably to the world's food supply, provided the Chinese, the Indians and the Japanese are encouraged to settle in these voids. Similarly, rice may also contribute to population increase in the equatorial rainforest though here land reclamation and drainage scheme should precede the entry of oriental farmers. In the empty grasslands in portions of Brazil and in Argentine, Uruguay and Paraguay corn growing and *alfalfa* may pave the way to a more successful animal farming and industry and support increased population densities. In the more arid grasslands near desert fringes, whether in Asia, Africa, America or Australia, the introduction of proso, barley, rye or Chinese millet (*kaoliang*) may contribute to extend the frontiers of farming. Potato, millet and seeds may pioneer expansion of settlement into the colder and less desirable tracts of Siberia and Canada and into Alaska, while the pasturage of yaks imported from the high region might succeed where cattle raising fails. It is in this manner that ecology may help towards the choice of crops, animals, agricultural practices and peoples for the utilization of the empty lands of the world. Further, vernalization or seed treatment may in future lead to the extension of agriculture into the colder northern and drier savannah lands to an extent which cannot be discerned at present, opening out fresh possibilities of migration and colonization. Mankind has succeeded so far in extending its frontiers of settlement to regions of almost any degree of cold, but its success in pioneering in regions of any degree of dryness, warmth and humidity, and in choosing appropriate varieties of crops and animals here has not been achieved. The keynote of man's further progress in colonization lies in his selection of crops and animals which most closely approach his own optimum and economic and social pattern in the hot and wet lands.

Instances of the Failure of Agriculture

The world's agriculture is too full of instances of setback or failure due to the introduction of inappropriate exotic plants, animals and agricultural practices. Only three instances may be adduced here from the history of modern agricultural colonization. In the United States it is now increasingly realized that the major cause of soil erosion and destruction, which have introduced serious population problems in that country, is the spread of monoculture, which is poles asunder from Nature's variegated natural community. The European colonists as they came to the New World forsook their diversified farming methods which were an adaptation to the climate and which maintained soil fertility in the Old World, but adopted the practice of continuous production of one crop to the exclusion of all other crops in each region. Thus cotton was grown in the South, corn in the Ohio and Upper Mississippi valleys, wheat in the Central and Northern Great Plains and in the Palouse Country of Oregon, Washington and Idaho. Speculative farming rested on the production of "cash crops", and in periods of high agricultural prices even the semi-arid Great Plains were invaded by grain farmers. The prairies of Texas and South-East states suffered rapid destruction due to the cultivation of cotton and tobacco. Many range lands in the centre and the west also lost a good deal of their stockcarrying capacity. "By the thirties," writes Frederick Turner, "the exhaustion of the soil in the South Atlantic states has gone so far that many of the planter class with their slaves moved in great numbers to the cheap and fertile land beyond the mountains." Cotton, tobacco and corn were the major crops that were dangerous soil removers for 100 years in the continent. Thus the United States is faced now with the insistent problem of soil conservation and reorientation of agricultural economy when 100 million acres have been already laid waste, another 100 million acres stripped of one-fourth to three-fourths of its top soil and the way is open for active erosion on a still third 100 million acres.[16] No wonder that this country now leads the world in the knowledge of agricultural ecology and its applications to uses of land, water and vegetation.

Secondly, the white man's advent in the tropical and subtropical lands, whether in Africa or in Malaya, in the East or the West Indies has led to the adoption of exhausting crops and agricultural practices for meeting the ever increasing demands of tropical produce and contributed to devastate vast areas. About Africa, Jacks and Whyte observe:

> From Cape Town to Cairo European influence has been responsible for the rapid and in place now uncontrollable biological deterioration of the land.

Both native cultivations and European plantations have suffered.

> Nearly all countries which have been opened up for any kind of planting afford striking object lessons in what ought *not* to be done.[17]

Wherever crops and agricultural practices do not pay adequate regard to the ecological complex of soil, vegetation and rainfall,

---

16 Bennett, *Soil Conservation*, pp. 57-58.

17 *Empire Cotton Growing Review*, 6, 1929.

tropical soils which are generally of low quality will be irretrievably damaged. To cultivate tropical soils by methods practised in more favoured lands in Europe is to put too great a strain upon "this tender cuticle of the earth". Not merely the soils but the tillage practices of the tropical peoples should not be disregarded if the ecological balance has to be safeguarded. For Bowman aptly observes:

> Each regional environment is a different thing to different groups of people accustomed to distinctive food crops and modes of tillage. Temperate zone analogies are misleading. Nearly 100 per cent of the tropical peoples must make their living by growing crops or raising cattle. Unless we build-up a permanently productive soil, tropical production in the devastated lands will collapse, and all our engineering skill and our control of tropical disease will be memorials of misused power.[18]

The abolition, of the European practices of "mining" the land and monoculture in the tropical world is indissolubly bound up with a new responsibility of the advanced races for the well being of the natives and with economic internationalism.

Thirdly, we may refer to the inadequate agricultural development of the last uninhabited continent of the world, viz. Australia, under European methods of land utilization. In tropical Australia the agriculture of the European temperate crops cannot thrive due to the great heat, but tropical or semi-tropical crops such as rice, maize, manioc, millet, oilseeds and groundnuts might be grown successfully. Manioc has increased the population-supporting capacity of savannah lands in Africa which are too dry for the cultivation of plantains. Here one should think of the future in terms of tropical agriculture. But it is only Asiatic settlers who can introduce such kind of subsistence farming, cultivating seasonal crops and keeping

---

[18] *Scientific Monthly*, April 1949, p. 297.

Indian buffaloes or zebu cattle. European cattle show very heavy mortality in the Northern Territory due to the long and arduous summer when the grass is dry, while the cattle tick communicates an enervating disease that lowers their natural resistance to the dry and difficult period of the year. The zebu cattle are immune from tick-borne disease, and can be used as draught animals and these will certainly thrive and multiply and retain their condition much better than the European cattle during the dry months of the year. The Australian government is now encouraging the breeding of a beast which is a cross between the European cattle and zebu and which can stand the climate better and at the same time will supply good beef especially in its hind parts. The zebu cattle and buffalo from India might introduce successful mixed farming into the Australian tropics just as they revolutionized the agricultural economy of the West Indies where their animals were suffering severely from tick transmitted disease. But the introduction of the Indian cattle or buffalo which will lead to the eradication of the cattle tick from the thinly stocked pastures of the vast tropical north, and can more effectively establish both cattle raising and agriculture on sound lines rests on the encouragement of migration of Indian colonists in the Northern Territory. It is noteworthy that in spite of the White Australia policy, the Payne Commission (1937) recommended that Chinese gardeners and coloured domestic servants on indenture should be admitted to the Northern Territory on a limited scale. There is a growing recognition that a dog-in-the-mangerish policy prevents agricultural reconstruction on right lines in this continent.

Climatic Controls for Domesticated Animals

In the case of man's domesticated animals the present distribution and successful introduction are more rigidly controlled by climate. For the livestock the lower temperature limit is about 30° F, where sheep occur. Cattle are not much in evidence below 35° while pigs and goats begin about 40° F. The optima are somewhat as follows (according to Finch and Baker's charts): pigs at 45°, cattle about 50°, goats at 56°, and sheep at 65° F. The cattle (excluding dairy cattle) range importantly through the tropics, but the other stock are not of much importance above 70° F. As in the case of plants so in the case of animals progress can be achieved largely through utilization of indigenous varieties. We may refer here to the interesting experiment in Canada in domesticating the reindeer or caribou. Reindeer can thrive on lichens and dwarf vegetation in many a place where cattle would starve, and it is in other ways admirably adapted to the conditions of the far north. In parts of Arctic Canada where other forms of agricultural development are out of the question, reindeer raising would materially lessen the severity of the struggle for existence. The Canadian experiment can be said to have passed its initial stage, there being in this country about 1 million deer at present. Hornaday remarks in this connection:

> On the whole, the systematic introduction of reindeer along the north-west coast of Alaska — now almost barren of wild life fit for human food — is one of the most humane and sensible measures ever undertaken for the children of the cold. If this industry is further fostered and diligently pursued, its ultimate value in the promotion of the moral and material welfare of the Eskimo is beyond calculation. The multiplication of the herds in the hands of private owners means a great increase in the animal food supply, less dependence upon the foods of civilization, a greater measure of general prosperity and contentment, and in the end far less expense to the government in the form of animal maintenance for starving natives.[19]

---

[19] Quoted in J.A. Thompson, *Biology for Everyman*, p. 1349.

The Need of a Planned Ecology for Man's Permanence

Man's domestication of animals is now a lost art. He has not added any to his stock of helpful animals which his ancestors made friends with and bequeathed for his exploitation. He has made remarkable advances, however, in selecting and encouraging breeds of cattle, sheep, horses and goats for his own manifold uses and for withstanding pests and diseases in his own climatic optimum. But he has overfattened the pig and often depressed the donkey in his eagerness to reach some utilitarian result and multiplied numbers of cattle to such an extent as to bring about ruthless destruction of other valuable animals and often their own starvation. Man now is the most numerous species of the same size on the earth and the assemblage of human and animal production, which he has deliberately protected as his commensals, is built up on a pyramidal pattern, he being at the apex and vast numbers of his domesticated livestock which formerly much exceeded his population forming the base of the structure. As he himself has increased his numbers, the numbers of his animal dependents and allies have been drastically reduced and the pyramidal pattern of assemblage of populations has been undercut at the base. Until the beginning of the 20th century, human numbers were exceeded by man's domesticated stocks. Overstocking, however, is hardly tolerated in a heavily populated country like China which favours only the hog that converts slop into food, while the industrial nations in the West can easily dispense with animals as beasts of burden and draught animals. It is estimated by Huntington that about four-fifths of the population of the earth still rely exclusively on animals for the supply of their foreign energy, and his map shows that regions with many inhabitants per square mile tend to have many animals per square mile, and that a high animal density per unit-area corresponds with low density per capita. But if heavy human concentration is generally associated with a high density of livestock population, man has ruthlessly exterminated other beasts. Of late years ecology has stressed that an indiscriminate elimination of all species of animals, which compete with man for a place in the sun, affects unfavourably the ecological optimum of human population. "We have numerous examples," observes Bennett,

> of the disastrous results that have followed thoughtless destruction of certain animal populations. Animal life not only is inter-related with plant life, but with the soil itself, and our knowledge of ecology is still insufficient for us to eliminate any species complete from our fauna or flora. It is only the part of commonsense, therefore, to try to maintain the best biological balance that may be attained under agricultural conditions.

The safety of the agricultural structure depends upon a reasonable balance being maintained between soils, animals and plants, both wild and cultivated. Nor should the activities of countless creatures of the soil, centipedes, beetles and earthworms which contribute to soil aeration and renovation be disregarded. Bacteria, protozoa, fungi, and actinomyces also aid in crop production. Soil ecology pits one kind of bacteria or fungi against another or the protozoa against the bacteria so that in the end the balance of their collective activities is tilted in favour of the crops grown in the way either of improvement of fertility or reduction of disease. In its applications to agricultural planning, ecology aims at a balanced condition where soil and cropping, rainfall and runoff, birds, insects and bacteria, crop yield and cattle and human power in the holding are in complete adjustment. Man everywhere consciously or unwillingly depresses Nature's balances of adjustment which establish a maximum interplay and conservation of soils, waters and plant cover and make the evolution and continuance of higher forms of life possible.

Thereby he constantly threatens his own food production and safety. Especially where he has invaded the dry grassland with his deciduous forest culture or has multiplied too fast, he has snapped the threads of the web of life that surrounds and overreaches him and links him with other organisms, and thus his aggregate life which functions within a system of relationships with other organisms is deprived of vitality and renewal which wild Nature or a planned ecology assures him.

The ecological optimum of man's population is accordingly the result of a balance, always a shifting one, with profound effects upon the stability of his civilization between Nature's store of water, inorganic salts and hydrogen ion-concentration and the prodigious expenditure of these by the plants suitable for his own consumption and of the animals he eats and between human exploitation of the cycle of ecologic life processes which interlink man with other organisms and Nature's forces of their renewal. Man's attack on the environment is the outcome of his conscious planning, and its effects are as quick as the workings of his mind. All these make it more easy for man to upset the balance of Nature. If the communities of life grow tardily through gradually accumulating changes in Nature, the growth is through reciprocal adjustments which ensure no void anywhere, no tentatives untried. Man's ascendency has no doubt quickened the rate of change on the earth but such quickness has been bought at the expense of an appalling waste that is not generally true of the superior creations, the super-dominants in Nature's scheme. Soil, water and vegetation have worked together for countless ages through physical, chemical and biological processes, creating and maintaining the region of abundant resources for organic life. As man exhausts soil fertility and moisture and removes the mantle of vegetation of hill and plain, he initiates the processes of destruction which aid and speed up one another until he himself becomes powerless to resist these. By speeding up soil erosion and the destruction of vegetation in both wood and grasslands and the consequent upsetting of the balance of land, water and trees, man thus has brought about his own destruction as an inhabitant and made the conditions of life more and more severe for his cultivated plants and breeds of domesticated animals which are largely forest-margin plants and animals. As man develops industrially and builds towns and cities there is intensification of his interference and dominance. The original plant–animal community is completely destroyed, and even the domesticated types of plants and animals meet with their doom. Organic evolution has meant an increasing specialization in the businesses of appropriation and exploitation. In a progressive chain of appropriation the modes of man's attack and his implements have become increasingly diverse and subtle. The balance has been more difficult to maintain, the more, the circle of his life intersects the circles of other lives. Man's instincts are not infallible guides, and he is unable by the light of Nature to foresee the complex consequences of a onesided exploitation. He often brings about a new disharmony when Nature's subtle system of checks and counter-checks is done away with, bringing him along with other inhabitants of the region to a common doom with the region itself. Man's future in order that his ecological base may not fail him and his culture, will consist in so building up an institutional structure rooted in experimental ecology and supported by law, ethics and tradition that his economic efficiency may not be achieved at the expense of the future generations, and he may not convert the shifting balance of the region against them. Man has superimposed upon the life communities of the earth a dynamic and purposive organization. As this weaves more and more vital threads with the Kingdom of Nature in all its parts, Nature will be always on his side in his unique effort to substitute her clumsy and dilatory devices of evolution by the quick and systematic methods of science.

7

Status: Ecological and Social

The Universality of Stratification

OUR analysis of life organizations, whether of plants, animals or humans, reveals the universality of ranking or a typical pattern of social relations of power and distance. Aggregation, competition, division of labour and specialization are all implicated in this process of social differentiation. Ecologically speaking, all these processes establish successful spatial adjustments of population to the region. Social stratification at the human level corresponds to the divisions of tiers in forest communities and of links in the food chain, niches and "occupations" in animal communities. It subserves the ecological purpose of a most suitable arrangement for the co-operative exploitation of the region's limited resources.

Neither an ecological area nor any society is in stable equilibrium. Resources and modes of exploitation change. So do also fluctuate not merely the aggregate of population but also numbers in the many different tiers, niches or occupations of the life organization. All this ceaselessly realigns the patterns of stratification and the forces that determine statuses and positions. Status and position constantly fluctuate in the dynamic give-and-take between the aggregate population and its units and life's restricted environment.

Status, accordingly, is a fundamental factor in social differentiation which is the community's response to an increase of population or restriction of the habitat. It may be defined as any ecologically, economically or institutionally defined role of individuals or groups in the social structure. The definition of such role or service in the human community implies, in the first place, the participation of the individuals having the same status in certain opportunities, interests and attitudes of life; and, in the second place, a pattern of dominance or subordination of the unit or stratified group as a fundamental part of the social milieu.

Distinction between Status and Position

"Status" and "position" have to be distinguished. Every group or society is a plan or placement of persons or groups of persons, a system of interrelated statuses and positions which comprises its structure. Both "status" and "position" are defined in terms of function with reference to members of a group or society. When this function pertains to a definable category of individuals it is called "status"; when it refers to the individual *per se* without any consideration of the category it is called "position". Status thus must have associated with it certain culturally or institutionally prescribed privilege, dignity and role which are subjected to less variation from generation to generation and from group to group in the same culture. In the case of position, privilege and dignity are achieved and subject to more variation due to differential capacities of individuals, and are less precisely defined and standardized. Status continues even though the personnel is changed. As the saying goes: the king is dead; long live the king! The status of kingship is operative notwithstanding the death and abdication of individual monarchs. The reason why status is ascribed and relatively fixed is that society seeks to establish a rigid framework of relationships between different categories of individuals in order to secure its own stability and continuity amidst the fluidity of the individual's occupancy of position, privilege and power. Incidentally, because the kingly status is reserved for only one individual, there are greater powers, privileges and prestige attached to this than in the case of any other ranking, status or position. A man's "position," on the other hand, is associated with the vicissitudes of individual life and efficiency. Society furnishes the tests or criteria by which one or more persons competing with one another for the same position achieve it. The maintenance of such position is dependent upon the approximation of the individual's role to the norm of conduct culturally prescribed. Even in the family group where statuses and positions are rigidly fixed, a wayward son may be disinherited and in his position a son from another family can be substituted and obtain the former's status and total rights and duties through the principle of adoption. The definition of both status and position, whether relatively fixed or not, subserves the all important social purpose of presenting a norm of behaviour to the individual with reference to individuals of other statuses and positions, and hence in evolving meaningful personality differentiations in society's scheme of competitive and co-operative behaviour.

No society succeeds which, on the one hand, associates all statuses exclusively with heredity or a person's relationship by birth to family, race or class, and shuts the gates of privilege and prestige to open competition, and, on the other hand, depends exclusively upon competition for the accrual of all categories of status. In the same society we find man improving his position and status through his unique achievement, while many statuses are also fixed. With such improvement the individual obtains greater opportunity, privilege and security of position. Thus as positions become stereotyped and fixed these tend to approximate status. Status accordingly is the resultant or emergent arising out of aggregate successes or failures (mobility) of individuals in their specific roles and positions. From another point of view status is mobility slowed down and regularized; mobility is status in movement.

The assignment of status and position governs the roles, behaviours and lifegoals of individuals. It is because an individual has a variety of statuses and positions in the family group, the class, the community and the state that society calls for selection and integration of values in the personality pattern. The modification of status or position in one role alters the whole personal organization. On the other hand, the individual by presenting to society his distinctive behaviour pattern may alter social and institutional norms which prescribe status and thus play his due role in the fixation and assignment of status. Thus both cultural heritage and individual achievement (mobility) are involved in the assignment and maintenance of statuses and positions.

In a society where there is a large variety of statuses and positions which are less defined and relatively subject to variation, freedom of mobility and the competitive spirit, coupled with the impulses of appropriation and possession, dominate. In a society where statuses and positions are rigidly prescribed by institutions and traditions and relatively secure, for instance, through the principle of heredity as by parentage, sex, class or race, caste predominates over the competitive order, and a socialized type of individualism develops. The social type, the personality type-pattern and the scheme of status and power are in keeping with, and contributory to, one another.

Threefold Relationship Involved in Status

Every status or position involves the following constituent factors:

1. An ecological space which an individual occupies and which differentiates his specific role or service from other members of the same group. This indicates different kinds of contact between individuals and between groups and

the possible invasion of the particular position by other individuals singly or *en masse*. Relations of competition, co-operation, accommodation, dominance and subordination; all are implied in the acquisition and maintenance of ecological status.

2. An economic niche, job or occupation, which he performs and in which the group as a whole has a specific common interest and which also binds him to every other individual in the group. Division of labour, specialization and segregation are among the further processes which are implied in the acquisition and maintenance of wealth, power and freedom associated with status.
3. A social space involving associated rights and duties, prestige and distinctions with which the individual is invested by the community. Social consensus, judgement and evaluation are the further processes that inhere in the assignment of status.

The cultural pattern of the community develops a hierarchy of values and normative standards for the acquisition of status and for the specification of a person's total rights (rights to wealth and security, to social distinction, to freedom, power, leisure and recreation) and duties (duties to work according to certain recognized standards and social and moral obligations). In the concrete social world each individual plays different personal roles (such as those of the parent, the employer, the housekeeper, the customer, the man of fashion, the president of a school committee, the director of a commercial company or the local representative in parliament). To each kind of social role a specific status is attached. A person raises his status by expanding his role or service to greater importance; while status is lowered or lost through restriction of his role or activities. The more extended the ecological and social space-time on which the various kinds of a person's role or services impinge, and the greater the significance of these roles, as judged by society, the higher is the person's "total" status. If an individual be displaced from his central position in ecological and social space through the limitations of his ability and achievement, he not only loses status but also his own self-esteem and thus suffers personal maladjustment or disorganization. While the maintenance of status constitutes the core of the personality process, society is a creative synthesis of personal statuses. Culture is a super-individual system of values and norms which underlies the struggle for achievement and recognition of status. Every concrete individual in his social roles and relations brings status into existence and becomes a person and at the same time forms a part of the status system of the community. Status holds the double key for sociological analysis: the key to man's consciousness of his personality and of his role in the community, and to the system of interpersonal relations, ecological, economic and social, that constitute the community.

Status and Mobility, the Primary Data of Sociology

The processes of status and mobility constitute the scope and subject matter of social ecology and sociology. The basic unit of investigation of ecology and sociology is the relationship rather than the individual. All ecological and social interactions take place in a definite framework of social positions and relations of the individuals involved. All persons, individually and collectively, strive to gain and retain position in ecological and social space. What position is in ecological space, status is in social space. All social phenomena can, indeed, be reduced in terms of the existing or wished for norms according to which not merely objects, individuals, groups, functions and institutions but also concepts are assigned status in social space. Each scheme of status, relationship of objects, individuals and groupings is part of a larger configuration of norms and values by which society regulates the activities of all individuals, groups and institutions. It is the task of sociology to determine the nature of the status system, investigate, the nature of the various groupings and institutions where individuals interact in the various dominant, subordinate and co-ordinate relations, and ascertain the value and symbol systems by which rank or any social position (status) is assigned by the community. Sociology sees society as a configuration of interrelated statuses, and studies quantitatively and qualitatively the behaviour of individuals (mobility) within the configuration that has to be viewed as a changing, interdependent whole. It studies not one but diverse types of societies, their institutions, rank patterns and dominant cultural motifs with a view, to reaching adequate generalizations in respect of social interaction and the order and hierarchy of social values. From man's spatial position, niche or occupation to the range of his status and uniqueness of his personality and achievement and the scheme of cultural values, sociology sees the process as one single, integral interaction.

The major function of society is to place status assignment on a definite basis, to offer easy, effective and unequivocal guidance to individuals in their status–deference behaviour. The stability and progress of society require, on the one hand, that all persons should know to whom, when, what and how to submit, and that on the other hand, they should also have opportunity and initiative for independent performance and movement within the framework of the authority–submission system. Mobility is thus as all pervasive and fundamental a process as the fixation of status in a social hierarchy. While status is the outcome of individual desire to conserve the gains of achievement which society selects and upholds, mobility is the outcome of individual variations of efforts and capacities to mould society and appropriate the goals of life in conformity with individual desires and interests. Both status and mobility are, therefore, rooted in the fundamental needs of human nature. Man's desires of self-assertion, achievement and power demand fulfilment in a scheme of social gradation where he may find some individuals, "possessions" and distinctions above others below him as he climbs up the social ladder. He must have some position in the society to look up to, and some to defend with all his mental equipment and resources. Even in the smallest group, the dryad or triad, we find variations of mastery and subservience. Thus ranking or gradation is normally a part of the institutional pattern of any society, which provides the individual with both an opportunity to rise in the social scale and a privilege, monopoly or some effective superiority when he does rise or "achieve" status. In terms of desires and satisfactions, the pattern of social gradation offers their largest fulfilment when it permits a fluid status and mobility so that freedom of choice and competition and elasticity of division of labour and occupations can give free play to differential individual capacities of all kinds.

Status and Personality

In status conscious society mobility is, indeed, to be understood as the universal and basic activity by which status is gained, retained, lost or regained. Status is an incidence of both hierarchy and mobility in the institutional pattern of society. Mobility as represented by spatial and social circulation, by vertical and horizontal movements of the population indicates the rise and fall of individuals in the quest for status. In the spatial distribution of institutions, utilities and services in man's habitation, whether village, town or city, the status of population units improves directly in proportion as the distance from the area of dominance increases. Status and mobility are like matter and motion in ecological and social space. It is through mobility that persons obtain their status which has also to be maintained through constant effort. In this effort of retaining status the individual is guided and helped by the atmosphere of unanimism of the small group which exhibits similarity of both interests (rights and privileges) and attitudes of life. It is for this reason that status maintenance represents the essence of personality expression. On the other hand, the loss of status implies not merely the loss of material interests and prestige but also of self-esteem, which defines the individual's participation in the group pattern.

Ralph Linton has recently developed the concept of "the status personality". In addition to the common factors operative in the culture, there are specific factors related to status — either natural status, determined by age and sex or acquired status, due to prowess in war, wealth or other types of achievement. The position in the community resulting from status determines the habitual experiences and reactions of the individual and has direct effect upon the characteristics of the personality. No feature is more significantly connected, on the other hand, with personal maladjustment than the loss of status or caste.[1] Distribution of status and constant physical movement, which brings about distribution of individuals in natural and social space, are the dual processes which constitute the complex game devised by *Homo sapiens* as he has lived in society. There are biologic rules of this game such as competition, co-operation, migration, division of labour and dominance common to animal and human societies; but *Homo sapiens* has added to these psychological rules in respect of the labelling of status by deference gestures and symbols which express different degrees of status on the one hand, and the sense of self-respect, worth or prestige associated with status maintenance on the other. In animal society, the leader may gain a position of ascendancy, but his is no legitimatized status which is the result of the penetration of the social consciousness into an ecological hierarchy. Men who gain power in society not only gain material possessions and distinctions but also certain symbols of status and power which may be prized for

[1] Linton, *The Study of Man*; also Klienberg, *Social Psychology*, p. 500.

their own sake, and which obtain social recognition and approval. Above all, they enjoy a sense of self-esteem and pride which emerge out of the feeling of conformity to society's moral sentiments and standards that underlie its scale of ranking. If ecology and economy primarily build up an effective system of superiority and inferiority relations in man's limited universe, man's mind and culture weave into these moral values and rewards which raise the struggle for status from an ecological dominance or an economic uplift to an achievement of ideals of the society and of the personality.

Status Determination in Animal and Human Society

In the pecking, biting, bullying and mounting order or ecological stratification of the animal community, status is determined by coercion or by some subtle manipulation which is largely influenced by age, strength and sex of the animals. Any defiance or disobedience is immediately punished by assault or by expulsion of the subordinated individual from the herd. Already among troops of monkeys and anthropoid apes a new factor is introduced. In the first place, dominance behaviour is not always forced, but is solicited. Thus grooming is often begged for as well as insisted upon or commanded in accordance with the dominance–subordination relation of the individuals.[2] Secondly, the subordinated individual develops an inferiority complex and a feeling of guilt and loss of prestige when he or she disobeys the command of the power-holder who is also the overlord of the harem, carefully guarded by him, and to the fringes of which the younger and less dominant males attach themselves. At the human level, the distribution of status largely rests not on the exercise of force or manipulation but on customs, sanctions and norms. Status is something which is often defined by law, custom and norm

2 Yerkes, "The Life-history and Personality of the Chimpanzee", *The American Naturalist*, March-April 1939.

of conduct. That is to say, status depends upon past status. A person who commands deference does not form or initiate the obedience reaction. His role is often pre-determined for him by the social structure. It is the pattern of custom and institutions which casts for him the role of either the master or the slave. The king, the priest, the soldier, the landlord command not because they are the strongest, the most intelligent or the most aggressive, but because they are the king, the priest, the soldier or the landlord. Each individual develops the attitudes, traits of character and modes of conduct required of his special role. But as each plays his specific role he shows a performance that varies from egregious failure to complete success. His failure or success contributes to strengthen or weaken the assignment of status designed for him by the social and institutional pattern. Thus in one sense individual initiative and action contribute to the distribution and recognition of status.

Yet in another sense the role of the individual in social ranking is even more significant. For, in the distribution of status the individual's own judgement of others and ranking them on the basis of his own hierarchy of values are implied. Status assignment is then as much a cultural as an individual product. It is an ethical judgement depending upon the hierarchy of values of different individuals in society. Park aptly observes:

> Status is determined in any single case largely by the extent to which the individual man is able to participate in the common purposes of the community, conform to its standards, submit to its discipline or, through the force or personal prestige and influence, impose his own purposes upon his fellows.[3]

There develops within cultures an integrated system of ends and values. Thus the social stratification reflects the moral

[3] Park, "Sociology" in *Research in the Social Sciences*, p. 34.

evaluation of the community; it can function only so far as the individuals broadly agree to certain moral norms and standards.

Criteria of Status Assignment

In spite of certain inevitable differences in status judgements of individuals it is, however, possible to lay down certain criteria of status assignment and maintenance as under:

1. High social status may be the result of personal qualities, such as sex, age, health, strength, pugnacity and intelligence as in the ecological stratification of the social animals. Animal biologists find the factors governing dominance and deference rather complex. In general, among the animals might makes for right. But in anthropoid life physical prowess may be outmatched by intelligence, courage and self-confidence. Not merely physical and to much less degree mental traits and capacities but also economic factors, such as numbers, limitation of the size of the habitat and territory enter into the position of the higher animals in the social order. All this is extended and amplified in determining the social status assignment of men. Preeminent personal qualities tend to raise some individuals and groups above or at the expense of others, and the superior position obtained is sought to be safeguarded by legal privilege, economic monopoly and social resistance, and becomes hereditary. Their nature and influence depend upon the size of population, the area of occupation and the conditions of community subsistence and economic pressure.
2. Achievement and possession become more significant factors in stratification in the human than in the animal species. The reason is not far to seek. Human individuals show far greater physical and mental energy than other animals. This has been pointed out by Pitkin:

> Man has built up, through the ages, a huge fund

> of physical energy with which to maintain himself against the hostile forces of his environment. He possesses more than three times as much for each pound of his body weight, as any other mammal which has yet been measured. For each pound of flesh in a horse, cow, dog or cat, there is considerably less driving power through adult years than there is in five ounces of human flesh. (The exact ratio seems to be 2 : 7.75, according to Rubner.)[4]

Wealth, learning, attainment of special skill and dexterity, including capacity to control others, or attractiveness of women now become secondary acquisitions which carry with them high status. Most of these are the valued results of individual talent and application and are non-transferable. Thus the persons who possess such talents and special aptitudes become models or leaders whose achievements serve as examples for others to follow. Some, indeed, become sources of inspiration of life principles, symbols of great and cherished values which dominate the goals and efforts of their generation.

3. Birth and kinship become important elements of stratificatory status in human society. This is based on the recognition that since like breeds like, status breeds status. In social differentiation at the human level individuals who are members of kinship units obtain approximately equal status. Societies follow the principle of adoption for the extension of the kinship principle as the basis of the acquisition of status.
4. So far we have referred to the natural causes of individual superiority or inferiority as the basis of graded relationships. But more significant than these are social and political factors of conquest, expropriation and control over resources and means of production which place stocks,

---

[4] Quoted in Wheeler, *Essays in Philosophical Biology*, pp. 258-59.

families and social groups in positions of dominance and power utilized by them in establishing a firmly knit pattern of economic, political and social hierarchy. In the normal division of labour and differentiation of social and economic interests in society, political, cultural and racial factors supervene on the natural personal difference in ability in the determination of the institutional pattern of status and stratification. Ranks or graded relationships are rooted in both the entire ecological and institutional background and personal history and achievement of individuals and groups.

Conquest and Status

From age to age and country to country the criteria of social differentiation have differed. High status is based on physical strength and achievement, or on subtle manipulation of men in savage society, where the more successful huntsman, warrior or medicine man is the leader. As society becomes more organized and differentiated it is the group of soldiers, priests and noblemen who assume the reins of social and political control. In an agricultural community social control rests in the hands of the patriarch or a council of village elders; where it has passed through conquest and expropriation of the feudal landlord, owing his authority to the ownership of land and the protection he affords to the tillers of the soil, occupies the position of dominance which is hereditarily transmitted to posterity.

Both feudalism in medieval Europe and the caste system in ancient India represent rigid systems of hereditary social ranking which prevented the free upward social and economic movement of individuals and classes, separated as these were by rigid barriers. Both developed under similar political and social conditions, viz. the need of a *modus vivendi* by which invading and conquering peoples might stabilize conditions and bring peace and order in new lands. In Europe the continuous wanderings of peoples and shocks of war and conquest brought forth a social system that established the supremacy of the conquerors, both kings and their companions in war and the heads of the great families, viz. the barons or nobles and at the same time rendered defence and collection of armies easy. On the other hand, conditions were absent in medieval Europe for the gradual peaceful assimilation of different tribes and peoples. Both feudalism and the caste system built up accordingly a rigid hierarchy based on conquest and expropriation of land. In feudalism such expropriation had taken place more than once and the holding of land became the basis of all political and social status. Freedom was sacrificed by the free man in order that he might obtain the lord's protection, and thus he became a serf, a villain and a cottar. In this manner the extension of serfdom and manorialism was an indispensable social adaptation to internal anarchy and external invasion in the Middle Ages in Western Europe, which was split up into a vast number of semi-independent principalities ruled by a warlike caste of nobles of many ranks from dukes and counts down to viscounts, barons and chatelains. In India the conquest of the aboriginals by the Aryan peoples was there, and differences of colour and race which did not exist in Europe stressed cleavage. Such cleavage was also fostered by differences of religion and culture and skilfully nourished by a priestly class which was in fact the custodian of the social ranking. But a peaceful society and steady development of agriculture and industry, when conquests were stabilized and the Aryans became themselves sedentary like the rest of the population, ushered into existence in India a workable social system based on the autonomy of each people, tribe or caste, collective discipline and mutual tolerance. Each tribe, community or caste has had within its own limits complete social self-government, while opportunities have existed for the fusion or assimilation of lower into upper social groups and the formation of new castes. Thus feudalism and the caste system have both distinct as well as common features in their formation and development, presenting interesting examples of the origin of the social stratification on almost a similar background.

The Predominance of Stratification over Mobility

In modern capitalism high status and dominance depend upon the possession of capital and capacity of management of machinery, resources and men. In all epochs the processes of status have been challenged by mobility, adventure and enterprise as the result of which individuals from the lower ranks defied or seized power and dominance in some way or the other. Monarchies, aristocracies, priesthoods, hereditary castes and feudal systems have in the course of history been modified or have changed their guise. The authority–deference relationship is a historical and social product which is strengthened by law and custom and by teaching and propaganda of those who are in power and is constantly attacked by those who belong to the lower ranks and yet rebel at the existing authority–deference classification. The growth of population and vast technological changes which introduce a new division of labour and transform the economic base of society as well as new culture patterns bring new classes into ascendancy. But no sooner than they implant themselves in the position of dominance and power they obstruct the forces tending towards equalization and mobility. The chequered course of social history always exhibits the predominance of stratification over mobility. New social groups constantly rise and supersede those which were dominant before, but soon entrenching themselves with exclusive rights, powers and privileges hold back social progress. For social selection is hindered or abolished whenever individuals occupy and maintain high status for reasons other than ability. The complexity and plasticity of the human individual and society demand for the sake of balanced progress a relatively unceasing process of social mobility and selection, as compared with animal societies. Stratification should face fairly and squarely the constant impact of man's physical and social mobility and his individual variation and versatility in order that human societies with their ever increasing specialization may not approximate to insect societies — societies of very low intelligence of the individuals combined with an intense and pugnacious solidarity of the whole.

The Open and Closed Groups: Class and Caste

Alverdes dealing with animal societies distinguishes between open and closed groups. By the former he means those into which strangers are acceptable easily. By the latter he means those into which it is difficult to obtain acceptance. Such an ecological classification is applicable to the differentiations in human society.

As a matter of fact it is the openness or permeability of the social boundary which distinguishes classes from castes. In the caste organization neither personal qualities nor achievements nor wealth can give any individual an entry to social status which is determined solely by heredity. Castes are characterized not only by biological segregation, i.e. endogamy and exogamy, but also by economic and social segregation through the regulation or abolition of contacts. A fixed hierarchy of dominance and subordination operating on the basis of social segregation and distance, which nourishes generally a striking disparity of wealth and culture among the social strata distinguishes the caste system. In contrast free, open groups are classes where birth, kinship or biologically hereditary qualities have nothing to do with an individual's ranking. It must be admitted for the sake of realism that no caste is completely closed nor any class is completely open. Both arise in the maintenance of status and role by individuals and groups. Both, therefore, assume some kind of social distance and discriminatory roles for individuals in the social structure.

In animal social stratification polymorphism or the scheme of hereditary "castes", with attendant physiological atrophy of important functions and interests or their wholesale repression, are Nature's devices for limiting access to values for large numbers of individuals. In human societies a process of stratification which excludes values that bring high status from large masses of individuals cannot succeed easily. Accordingly, we find that in caste-ridden societies where values and goals of life are rigidly fenced off and occupation and rank are prescribed and transmitted from generation to generation, there is a systematic attempt to enlarge the limited occupational values and interests. Caste in India has developed an ideology or philosophy which seeks to reconcile the limited life goals of a rigid social group with the more comprehensive aims in living, and thereby not only maintains discipline and morale but also offers hope and promise for the individual. A tanner's son would be a tanner and his rank would be the lowest in society. Mobility is excluded for him by the social law that he must marry within the same caste and by the conventions of untouchability or unapproachability. Yet even for the tanner the occupation hardly comprehends his entire interest in life. The tanner has to approximate to forms of behaviour and a culture pattern which belong to the caste as a whole and which are linked to the larger purposes of the social aggregate. Village festivals and observances, *panchayat* meetings and caste codes of etiquette and social manners constantly remind them of values and interests which overreach their vocation as offering the road to status. Certain duties, such as those of messengers, drummers and torchbearers in village and temple gatherings or processions of the gods, demand their participation in civic life and elicit the enthusiasm of all caste men, however low in the social scale. The tanner thus finds security and status in harmony with the more comprehensive goals of the society. The caste-ridden society makes him not merely status-minded, but also in some measure conscious of his role in relation to the collective social aims. Though untouchable he lives and moves in his caste and never loses his self-esteem, and sense of participation in community life.

Class Divisions in Industrial Society

This may be an overdrawn picture although necessary to analyse the mechanisms in stratified societies where castes tend to develop specialized values and interests that are sought to be blended and integrated with the significant culturepattern of the group and with larger purposes of the social aggregate. This picture has to be placed side by side with that of the class system in an industrialized society where at least five class divisions may be identified:

1. Capitalists and large entrepreneurs.
2. Smaller entrepreneurs, traders and the professional class.
3. The class of skilled workers.
4. The class of farmers and tenants.
5. The class of unskilled workers and farm hands.

The order of social esteem is almost the same among all industrialized communities, and thus occupations tend to assume a hierarchical arrangement which represents ascending levels of socio-economic status, and which reflects somewhat roughly the varying degrees of esteem assigned to each vocation. But there is little or no correspondence between socio-economic status or prestige and intelligence. A recent survey in the USA has shown that

> no class can be said to skim off the cream, and only the cream, of mental ability as measured by the intelligence tests. The highest score in the entire sample, for example, was made by one classified as an unskilled labourer.[5]

---

[5] Clark and Gist, "Intelligence as a Factor in Occupational Choice", *American Sociological Review*, vol. III, p. 683.

The major causes of the disparity between merit and grades of socio-economic status are not far to seek. In the higher socio-economic strata men develop "vested interests" and want to protect these for themselves and their descendants. Those who occupy the higher ranks aim at personal aggrandisement and subordination of those below them and treat the ambitious as serious would-be competitors; the latter are as far as practicable pushed back to the strata from which individually they seek emancipation. Apart from the direct and overt or indirect and subtle resistance of those in the upper strata, men belonging to the lower strata prefer security even at the barest subsistence level to adventure which may result in the loss of what they have, little as it is. Where there are widespread insecurity and fear of unemployment ambitions in the lower ranks are chilled and frozen. On the other hand, in the intermediate dignified strata, salaried persons who belong to what is designated as the Middle Class become too enamoured of stability and decent domesticity to run any risks which entering into business or politics imply. One result is that instead of getting the best qualified and the most honest citizens in political office only the best of those who cannot make a decent living any other way enter the political area. The risks in a democratic country are grave. "Politics becomes synonymous with crookedness, the object of jibes, people lose faith in the democratic process and loss of our freedom may be the price," observes an American writer.[6] The social efficiency of modern democracies is threatened by the unstability and insecurity of employment which prevent the use of "economic escalators" by men of talent and energy from the lower levels, on the one hand, and the crystallization of "vested interests", jobbery, corruption and mental bankruptcy at the higher levels, on the other. Though there is

---

[6] D.T. McCutchen, "Vertical Mobility in Economic Status", *Journal of Social Philosophy*, July 1940.

no legal barrier of ascent from one class to another, industrial communities vary with regard to the development of such vested interests which are protected at the expense of other groups in the society and are bequeathed to descendants. Wherever, therefore, social differentiation recognizes ancestry in the determination of rank or the vested interests of a group are sought to be ensured for descendants and safeguarded at the expense of the society, the principles of caste or the closed group and of class or the open group formation merge into each other. Besides our custom-bound economic and political hierarchy and occupational stratification and differences based on heredity, such as the caste system represents, the disparity of race, education and culture between the classes and physical and social hindrance to migration and intercourse operate as effective agencies to prevent spatial and social mobility. Where such operation has been persistent, societies approximate to a closed or stratified caste organization. Thus we have castes or castes in embryo in all countries and epochs.

Patterns of Culture and Status

Even in a closed or stratified society, where birth is apparently the primary criterion of status, we find a certain norm of living and achievement enforced by institutional and social control so that other values and realizations besides hereditary qualities become part of the ascribed pattern of conduct to which incumbents of high status have to conform due to social pressure. The caste of brahmins which has had the highest status in Hindu society and enjoyed unusual dignity and prestige has stuck to the basic virtues of plain living and high thinking, abstinence and purity of life demanded of them for the very performance of their special role as ministers and educators of kings, nobles and the masses. Similarly, the senatorial aristocracy of Republican Rome was subjected to severe discipline, military service and office-holding which developed the essential qualities required of the builders and rulers of an empire. On the other hand, in a free or unstratified society where skill, talent and achievement and the wealth which flows from them are criteria of ascribed status, inherited wealth and property and social resistance of the upper classes thwart the economic principle of social stratification, while there is also a large disparity between income and the social value of certain jobs, occupations and achievements, not to speak of the various illegitimate ways now remaining open for money-making and improvement of status.

All societies show a general scale of prestige of jobs and occupations which is supported by an income hierarchy or by social prestige. In many countries of the world, priests and teachers earn less but are recompensated by prestige and authority. Even in industrial employment "the white collar occupations" are paid less than skilled labour but have a superior rank and authority over the latter. It is, therefore, society's scale of preferences and culture pattern which build up the institutional framework into which the scale of prestige of the various jobs, occupations and achievements is dovetailed. Neither birth nor an income hierarchy can adequately explain the assignment of status and position in the concrete social world though for the purposes of analysis birth or income forms a convenient point of reference for closed caste and open class systems respectively.

8

Man's Social and Moral Boundaries

Man's Limited Field of Activity and Goals

MAN in his complex social milieu of today shows only a limited participation in its affairs. He belongs to a job, occupation and position in society, which is his and none else's; he occupies but a small ecological and social niche in the environment which decides for him his aims, efforts and achievements. The personality of any individual is the product of the interaction between his organic and cultural equipment and the limited social space from which he appropriates his quota of satisfactions and values. It is these latter acquisitions which give us the clue to the personality process that consists in resisting the pressures of myriad groups with ends entirely different from one's own, and chalking out one's own field of goals and achievements from the distraction of disharmonious wishes and interests. Accordingly, the classification of the different types or orders of personality depends on the use of certain status criteria. Man achieves his relative status and develops his unique personality in his limited ecological and social space, within the boundaries of his own class, his occupational group or profession. Both space and time are limited to the range of man's possible mobility and contact with his own associates. The uniqueness of the individual personality is rooted in personal ecological space and time. No doubt the field of activity and goal of life of a man of letters, a statesman or a financier extend much beyond the boundaries which confine the aims and pursuits of a village craftsman or farmer. It is the segments or parts of the broad society where man is in regular daily competition with his peers which assign him his exact position and determine his relative vertical and horizontal mobility. These also govern his attitudes, life values and the nature of his personality equilibrium in ecological and social space.

In modern democratic communities all human values are theoretically prized as potential goals equally for all classes of men. But due to the prevailing insecurity large masses of men are denied opportunities for the pursuit of such goals. All demand wealth, all demand status, all demand power. But the majority of the population lacks security on which the pursuit of wealth, status and power rests. The many who lose status lose self-respect, and set out for goals which isolate them from normal society or live a vague goalless sort of life in which the consciousness of the society's goal for them never penetrates. As groups become isolated from a communal reference, they become tinged with passions and feelings which well out from the unconscious as expressions of the repressed desires or life goals.

Social Pathological Features in Caste and Class

Both class and caste are to some extent social caricatures. Caste is the frustration of individual freedom of movement and competition and denial of social mobility and is a superb instance of permanent stratification in society. It is based on the supersession of the factor of competition by the factor of heredity as the road to status, privilege and prestige. Such is the artificiality of the caste arrangement that it can persist only through the aid of institutions that heap economic and social disabilities, prevent free communication and intercourse between man and man, and of myths, creeds and superstitions that implant firmly an inferiority complex and habit pattern.

Thus, even the man of low caste does not feel unhappy in the caste into which he is born and looks down upon his fellow man of a yet lower caste in the social hierarchy. Caste accepts a stereotyped discriminatory pattern and develops defence mechanisms which grow out of the recognition of the social myth that a man is doomed to play a peculiar role in the social regime. He becomes reconciled to that role through a weak kneed religion of grace, pity and compassion and a philosophy in which good and evil deeds of past lives become associated with present high or low birth, occupation or status. For each rank, occupation or birth society decrees a definite code or standard to maintain and safeguard. Caste autonomy flourishes along with the variegation of the interests of life within the small group which seek to enlarge life's goals and prevent both the feeling of being without caste or status and the appreciation of the goals of the *elite* as being within their own reach or compass. Thus rigidity or immobility becomes pathological.

The class accepts, on the other hand, an egalitarian pattern. But society reserves in practice the values of life for selected groups. It is the *elite* who through historical accident or achievement occupy the dominant positions of social control. Thus society is always on the verge of a revolution or some less violent form of revolt. Such revolution or revolt is facilitated by the masses being dominated by fear, greed and resentment due to the contrast between society's acceptance of a creed of equality and of wealth as the road to status, and the insecurity and poverty of the major portion of the population in modern industrial communities. Thus excessive mobility or an aggressive upward movement becomes pathological. Not merely individuals but groups also become pathologically mobile, linking themselves with other groups on the basis of segregated economic interests. Class alignments, economically founded, face the vested interests and challenge the monopoly of the values of life by selected groups or "classes". But the class structure expanding by aggregation and assimilation on the basis of sectional occupational interests for assuring class status to the proletariat soon becomes a *Leviathan* which disregards and even overrides the authority of the state. Social and political unstability is the inevitable consequence in an atmosphere of chronic class antagonisms and struggle for class status and defiance either of the role of the state or of the solidarity of the community. The social consequences of the class structure are much wider and go deeper. The capitalistic structure of society promotes class gradation, while democracy is a great social leveller. Man constantly seeks to climb up to higher social grades and finds a large family a serious handicap in the struggle for status, wealth and power. Mobility which the occupational system of modern industrial society requires, reduces the role and solidarity of the basic kinship group, viz. the family.

The Standard of Living, the Symbol of Status

Dumont, analyzing the causes of the decline of birth rate in France long ago developed his interesting theory of social capillarity. In a democratic society the individual as he rises in the scale of social stratification, like oil in the wick of a lamp, draws himself away further and further from his natural social and ecological space and from the family. As he seeks individual satisfactions and aspires for the standards of living of the social and economic class or grade just above him, he loses interest in the family and in the welfare of the race. "What gravity is to the physical world, capillarity (what sociologists now term 'social mobility') is to the social order", observes Dumont. The effort to emulate the standard of living of the social class just above that to which the individual and the family belong, even at the expense of children, manifests the hard struggle for a higher status. Money, though an infinitely divisible measure of status, is not a visible measure.

A more convenient, as also more conspicuous, measure of status is man's standard of housing, food, clothing, recreation, and "ostentatious" display of luxuries. Thus the standard of living attains a secondary symbolic significance in relation to status. Throughout the medieval world in both Europe and the East, lest the acquisition of wealth might lead the lower orders to imitate those in high rank, custom, tradition and even law intervened prescribing the kind of dwelling, the amount and quality of food, the kind of clothing and equipage and even the dialect for each class so that the privileges permitted showed the exact position of each in the scale of social stratification. Thus the standard of living was a symbol of status, a means of maintaining the distinctions in social ranking. In the contemporary world, not food in general, but the kind of food, not dress in general but the style of clothing, not shelter in general but the special kind of dwelling associated with a particular social class, have become economic though conventional imperatives to win status, even with family limitation. A mere economic notion of the standard of living cannot adequately explain the prevalent connection of family limitation with the improvement of economic position of individuals and classes.

No doubt the standard of living includes not only man's biological and economic needs, but also the entire mode of living, embracing working time and leisure, use of leisure, recreation, display and many other items which cannot be expressed quantitatively. As a matter of fact the display of leisure and of consumption has now become the chief forms of the general display of wealth as the basis of maintaining the distinctions between class and class. Not the standard of living, but the display of the standard of living, in which the major role is played by the women, perpetuates the existing distinctions in rank and status. All these are thus symbolic of status, and hence it is that a car is preferred to a perambulator by hundreds of families involved in the competitive struggle for status and position. This is true not merely of democratic communities with a free open class system but also of aristocracies, in fact of all types of social situations, where a class of high status maintains manners of living strikingly different from the rest of the society. In Imperial Rome both the old senatorial nobility and the new imperial nobility as well as the upper middle class which aimed at equestrian rank adopted a highly artificial standard of living at the altar of which children were sacrificed. Both in Europe and America of the present day for a considerable section of the population the scale of income and material consumption is found incompatible with the duty of raising children; and social mobility or capillarity and associated individualism have now raised serious biological and eugenic problems throughout the West. In the Oriental countries spiritual or ecclesiastical authority and dignified office and profession have been more significant criteria of status than an artificial plane of living and comfort. Thus the conflict between an upward social movement and family life has not been discernible. Contentment in one's lot or station, thrift and obligation to the family and kith and kin are prized social virtues in the Orient. Thus the display of wealth does not here confer rank and status; while as far as possible artificial living and comfort is discouraged among the rich. There is to be found far greater uniformity in food, apparel and conventional necessities among the Oriental peoples than in the West. But here ostentatious display is not discouraged on occasions of domestic ceremonies, expenditure on which is regarded as a social obligation, and accounts for a large proportion of debts of the people. Thus the idea of kinship obligation and philanthropy keeps men from sinking too much below an accepted standard of living. With the increase of population, poverty, however, is aggravated, and this sometimes leads to abortion and infanticide, on the one hand, and incompatibility between fulfilment of social obligations and of indispensable food requirements of the family on the other.

The Conflict between Status and Family Life

In the industrial West the middle- and working-class families, consisting of the adult males and females, are now feverishly engaged in maintaining a newly acquired or relatively insecure status through the contributions of the earnings of both. It is true that the husband and wife do not always come into direct competition for class status with each other as workers in industry do, but the wife is not entirely removed from the kind of occupational status which contributes towards the determination of the status of the family and thus the latter's solidarity is endangered. The working mother or a wife engaged in a professional job does not always find it easy to choose between her desire to maintain her occupational or professional status by her efficiency and her age-old delight in raising and maintaining a pleasant and successful home; or using her personal charm and attractiveness to gain her ends in the competition with her male rival for the same job. Thus the effort for achievement of class status either weakens the desire to bear and rear children or threatens the unity of the family. The serious decline of birth rates and disruption of the family in contemporary Europe and America are functionally related to the extensive mobility necessary for the maintenance of the class structure.

Intermingling of Class and Caste in the East and the West

Closed or stratified and open or unstratified societies have equally failed in harmonizing the special adopted roles and functions of individuals and groups with the unifying goals of the society. As a matter of fact a concrete system of social gradation reveals in all societies a combination of the principles of a class and a caste structure for normal group formation and the attainment of normal personality attitudes. In Hindu social organization, for instance, there is not only a caste system, but there is also a class structure. Even in modern democratic communities we find a class system being maintained together with a caste structure. In Hindu social organization, below the upper castes, viz. the brahmins, the kayasthas and the vaishyas in northern India are arranged above the intermediate castes which are engaged in agriculture and the arts and crafts. The untouchable castes, generally represented by tanners, scavengers and farm hands, occupy the lowest rungs in the economic and social ladder. The spread of education and increase of economic opportunities for all castes, high and low, have brought many "low" caste men at the top, whether as rich merchants and landlords or as holders of public offices. The tendency now is for these successful men to be regarded as superior to the poor men of the intermediate castes. But the upper castes yet look upon them as of inferior status, in spite of their wealth. Even more significant is the process by which a sub-group separates itself from castes of handicraftsmen and other groups of low socio-economic status through invention, modification of the occupation or adoption of the calling of traders in that particular business, and develops into a sub-caste refusing to intermarry and interdine with their former associates. Or, again, the caste of handicraftsmen or agriculturists seeks to obtain the status of the higher castes. There is no attempt to challenge or alter the caste hierarchy as such, but there is a desire to claim equality with the superior castes, the brahmins, the kshatriyas and the vaishyas who have the pride of status in the ancient social tradition. This is indicated in modern caste history by three general tendencies. First, castes which want to climb up the social ladder adopt the social practices of those higher in ranking until these are ultimately assimilated into those of the highest order — the twiceborn of Manu's

Institutes. For instance, they would first give up meat in favour of vegetarianism, and eschew liquor; they would abandon occupations considered unclean or dishonourable; they would adopt infant marriage, forbid widow remarriage and seclude their women; they would then assume the sacred thread worn by the twiceborn castes; and, finally, they would have their domestic ceremonies performed by semi-brahmins or brahmins. Secondly, such castes aiming at advancement endeavour to pass themselves off as superior by adopting new fanged names which are reminiscent of noble descent. Thus the carpenters, blacksmiths and goldsmiths would adopt a common designation, Vishwakarma or Vishwa brahmin; the barbers adopt the designation of *nai* or *kulin* brahmins, the milkmen castes call themselves Jadavas, and the lower agricultural tribes and castes adopt the name of Rajputs, connected with some special clan or locality in the course of their historic migrations. Brahmin priests and teachers or bards and minstrels are requisitioned to support such claims of rank and precedence by the invention of some myths or legends or interpretations of sacred texts. In northern India there are *kayastha-mochi*es, *bania-lohar*s or *lohar-barhai*s, indicating the improvement of status in each case but it is amazing that even scavengers claim themselves as *kastkar*s (cultivators) and have social dealings with them. Thirdly, such castes which assert themselves and endeavour to narrow the gulf with the superior orders yet maintain barriers as against the lower and especially the depressed castes. This movement, whether economic due to change of occupation and consequent material advancement or cultural, due to adoption of the cultural pattern and social usages of the superior orders, is a group process rather than the achievement of individuals. In the dynamics of the caste system, we see, therefore, a constant change in the social hierarchy through the amalgamation of castes and formation of sub-castes, especially among the industrial and agricultural workers. But it is not individuals who move but are rather born into the new-born caste or subcaste or one in the process of making. Thus individuals have not to fight against the caste hierarchy, but rather castes and subcastes which are on the way to a vertical advance. The result seems to be that individuals can adapt themselves more easily and successfully to the changing social situation due to the solidarity of the group.

In social stratification in the southern states in America where the Blacks are dominant, we find that certain class distinctions have evolved within the Black's caste. But there is no intermarriage between the Black and the white population. Thus the poor whites yet look down upon the richer Blacks, and in this attitude they are supported by the socially dominant, yet less numerous white population. A recent study in the United States reveals the social organization of the Deep South as comprising two different kinds of social stratification, viz. class and caste systems, which are in conflict with each other leading to the instability of many individuals who cannot obtain easy, effective guidance from the social arrangement. Certain fairly well marked class groups have developed within the Black's caste, but the supraordinate white caste still maintains the social ascendency and institutions such as the family, schools, associations, cliques and church are utilized to fit the dominant caste social situation of the dominant social caste.[1]

Stratification in Relation to Technology

In all countries where populations show a mixed composition and there is a large disparity of culture between different layers or levels, social classes tend to develop the characteristics of genetic groups and hence approximate to castes. Thus even in democracies heredity can be recognized

1 W. Lloyd Warner, "American Caste and Class", *American Journal of Sociology*.

as a factor in the assignment of the socio-economic status. In systems of social structure, marked especially by the effects of conquest, expropriation and feudal landholding, the hierarchy of ranks is almost caste-like in its inflexible assignment of superiority and inferiority and prevention of marriage outside the social strata and is a hindrance to democratic institutions. On the other hand, in many homogeneous peasant societies there is an assumption of superiority of a portion of the population, based on the ownership of land, a recognition of the higher socio-economic status by the remainder of the population which, however, coexists with a human equality and closeness and active community co-operation in the daily routine of life. In rural communities there are fixed status groups but they live in social amity with other social groups or ranks. Social exclusiveness and distance of castes in rural India are mitigated in large measure by intimate personal ties and community feelings of solidarity. Yet rural status groups are different from classes inasmuch as they do not seek any formal organization to promote their special economic interests. The class denotes a segregation of economic interests and an idea of social struggle which are excluded by the voluntary co-operation of the various status groups in rural society which may yet seek to safeguard their status by keeping the members of other status groups "in their levels". It is with the change from an agricultural to an industrial civilization, from ruralism to urbanism, that we find status groups gradually assimilating the temper and attitude of classes. Such transformation is an incident in the change of ecology and technology of man and his habitation and can be adequately understood only from this synthetic social-ecological viewpoint. With urbanization the organic communal aspects of society and natural modes of association recede into the background and the formal and rational aspects and deliberate and secondary associations become more important. Status now becomes less the assignment of the role and position of individuals by the society and more an outcome of individual effort and achievement; stratification becomes less an articulation and orientation of undeliberate and enduring status groups in amicable equilibrium with one another and more a formal organization of classes struggling with one another for the purpose of safeguarding and improving their special interests and socio-economic status.

The Role of the Individual in Status Acquisition

Status or the institutionally defined position of individuals or groups in social space, their roles or functions in the social milieu and their physical position in ecological space are implied in one another in the same human relationship which, indeed, shows three facets: ecological, economic and social. Status depends on the role the individual plays in society. As he strives after and reaches the goals which society holds dear he raises his status and self-esteem; as he recedes from them he suffers loss of status, prestige and self-respect. The latter involves personality deterioration. The regulation of personality growth consists in giving the aberrant individual a new type of position and status, and thereby altering his attitude and behaviour. Delinquent children placed in appropriate foster homes and disgruntled tradeunion leaders or political opponents supplied with some responsible public role or activity equally illustrate the influence of status on the socially approved conduct of individuals. Whether by raising or lowering status society entrusts the individual with a definite role or activity in the culture pattern. Means to the acquisition of status are also set by the culture pattern. In India and China men who acquire the highest learning or spirituality have obtained the highest status and deference. Age and veneration go together in China. In medieval Europe the martyrs who burnt themselves at the stake or the saints who discerned witches and burnt them without pity or compassion obtained the highest status. In wartime Europe, invaded and conquered by the Nazis, it is not those who show marks of divinity or sainthood or who produce and amass riches, but those who die for political liberty climb up to the highest status. Among some tribes of American Indians the man who achieved the highest status was the man who gave away the most wealth. In modern American society he seems to be the man who can acquire the most wealth, although there have been philanthropists who having built up great riches find a road to recognition in redistribution of a part of it among charitable organizations.[2] Further, status and an adopted or specialized role or function are reflected by the individual's ecological or spatial relations resulting from competitive co-operation. Men and functions segregate themselves in their natural habitats or territories as the outcome of high mobility, keen competition and minute differentiation of rank or status. Individuals and groups who win high status move into the prestige areas or districts of high land and rental values of the region or city; those who do not succeed in the competition move out into the less esteemed quarters, sections or areas. The segregated habitat which is socially acceptable or disreputable and the personality type influence each other. It is thus each "natural" area of the city or region leaves an indelible stamp on its residents and their functions, and takes on something of their character.

Interweaving of Ecological and Social Relationship

The distinction that some sociologists draw between ecological and social interaction does not, therefore, hold good. Park, for instance, speaks of "symbiotic" human relations in the biotic

---

[2] Landis, *Social Control*, p. 119.

or ecologic level maintained by competition and other processes as contrasted with the cultural relations based on communication and consensus. There is, however, no ecological human interaction or relationship *per se*. With reference to human needs and activities governed by limited ecological and social space, which human ecology deals with, it is clear that society or culture defines the kinds of needs, selects the specific resources out of the ecological complex which may be used or manipulated by man, and also provides the mechanical equipment or technology for their use and manipulation. Man, unlike the plant or animal, lives in a derivative environment for his collective subsistence. The natural or biological environment mingles in the case of man with his heritage of culture, of tools and economic procedures, of exchange, communications and transport. Man's needs and satisfactions are culturally defined as his efforts are shaped by forms of technology and regulated by the framework of institutions, law, tradition and public opinion and the standard of social values. Man's ecological interaction or economic relationship is accordingly at once the basis and outcome of human culture. Competition, specialization, division of labour, dominance and distance, these ecological processes which govern phenomena in plant and animal ecology are given a specific meaning and purpose in the cultural milieu. Their products can no longer be described as biologic but are psycho-social; these become part and parcel of the social inheritance, which plays a significant role in shaping the specific forms of social relations and personal organization. The importation of meanings and values into ecological human interaction in the medium of culture makes division of labour, distance and dominance far different from what these are in plant and animal communities. In fact, man's consciousness of similarity and dissimilarity of qualities and functions of fellow men transforms the ecological processes into enduring behaviour patterns, organized habits and culture motifs which guide his ecologic adjustments. His attitudes, values and moral standards as these become interwoven with specific ecologic relations make these a basic, persistent framework of class and occupational stratification that is transmitted through long generations of social life and that selects his behaviour for the exploitation of the limited resources of the habitat in the best interests of the community.

The Dynamic Concourse of Ecology, Mind and Culture

The framework of stratification as well as ecological and social mobility are maintained at once by the limited ecologic factors of the environment, the customs and ideals of the society and the individual's unique definition of his limited tasks and goals of life. The ecological or spatial distribution of man's role, occupation and class obtains a social definition and ratification through the hierarchical arrangement of status, deference and prestige. The spatial segregation of functions and institutions and the differential prestige of localities or their inhabitants aid each other. Man's position and distance can, therefore, be expressed in terms of both ecological and social space. His distribution and movement in ecological space are symbols of his social status and a means of maintaining the existing social hierarchy that is a highly complicated mechanism of adaptation for the co-operative exploitation of his restricted environment and values of life. In the economy of the human social arrangement, competition and selection manifest in mobility; differentiation and co-ordination place different individuals and groups in their appropriate stations where they make the best use of themselves in the community framework. Man's collective consciousness then comes in and refashions the ecological organization into a social hierarchy in order to give it stability. It is society's ordering of values or goals of life which converts division of labour and specialization into social distance which is a symbol of class-standing. Society creates its own symbols of rating and ranking and rewards those who can most successfully achieve the goals it prizes most by offering them the highest status and power. The enforcement of distinctions in rank and power aids society in defining, integrating and selecting its chief goals of life. Man's cultural pattern, his overemphasis on certain values of life as defined by him at a particular time inevitably slips into the ecologic pattern of spatial and functional distribution of individuals and classes. The esteem which the individual wins for himself by playing his due, specific role in his ecological and social station is at once a matter of living up to certain moral standards of his own which he derives from the ethical code of his culture, and of maintaining his status in the hierarchical organization of society that reflects this code. On the other hand, the antisocial individual, whether a confirmed pauper who has lost his morale and incentive for work, or a criminal who has fallen in with a gang, or, again, a prostitute who is an outcaste may be restored to a normal course of life when provided with some useful or esteemed role or occupation that improves his or her status. Man's personality development, his pursuit of values that are in harmony with the culture pattern are intimately associated with his role and status and participation in the normal group life. The phenomenological theory of ethics includes not merely the principle of autonomy as a universal basal law to which a clear expression is given in the Kantian demand to "act from duty" or the Fichtean demand to "act from consciousness of duty". But beyond this general and still formal demand, ethics speaks, still in the ethical field, and with concrete reference to its content, not merely of moral duties, but also of legal duties, political duties, religious duties, duties of the entrepreneur, the scholar, the artist, briefly too, of the duties of one's calling, etc. Conscience, according to the new ethics, is the totality of what individual experience and effort yield in the way of moral insight in man's own particular situation as contrasted with the accumulated products of authority and tradition. "Every individual," observes Scheler, "ought to undertake the culture of the values accessible or applicable to him alone, and this applies also to groups, nations, races or civilizations. To every phase and every moment of development belongs a specific relation to value that will never recur, involving facts and duties that belong in the nexus of the objective order to just this moment, and if unfulfilled, are lost for ever. . . ." Space or territory, mind or the culture pattern and status or a well defined orientation in the social organization in terms of moral sentiments and values accordingly exert reciprocal effects in the dynamic concourse of region, mind and society.

The Ethics of Appropriation and Participation

Differences in race, sex, age and class create unequal opportunities for the appropriation of the limited resources and values of life that society creates. These give rise to an ecological framework which orders man's life within the realm of the limited or selected values that are open to him. It is the primary ecological fact of the limitation of energies and values for certain individuals and groups that creates the organization and mechanism of authority and deference and the notions of status, prestige and self-respect, associated with the appropriation of these limited values, which motivate the conduct of individuals and separate them and their abodes and roles in life. It is the primary sociological fact of the participation of all values by all individuals, irrespective of race, sex or class, which is stressed by religion and morality that helps man in his struggle for appropriating the values which culture emulates. Mobility, adventure and revolt are as much laws of society as the laws of status, prestige and monopoly. Status, the outcome of ecology and economy thwarting man's desires, values, and mobility, the outcome of his self-assertion, versatility and achievement, equally come under the guardianship of law and the state, and the stress of one or the other in a given age or social situation determines the general pattern of life of the masses and their enjoyment of the amenities of life. Such contrasted habit patterns of the people, as competition–success pattern and co–operation-security pattern, characterize the distinctive ethos of different peoples, stable and enduring, and regulate their attitudes and behaviour, having their origin in cultural heritage and historical experience. Thus it is the ethos, national character or cultural compulsive which largely determine the fixation of status, monopoly or privilege or their challenge by the competitive spirit and the sharing of the rewards and acquisitions of life and society. But the ethos and culture are constantly renewed by man's contact with new poverty, his search for new culture values by which he redefines the chief goals of life. That society succeeds better in reaching the goals of life to all which sets before itself such a hierarchy of social aims as learning, religion, family and wealth, which promotes the distributive rather than appropriative impulses or the shared rather than the exclusive satisfactions of individuals, and at the same time places the scheme of values beyond any doubt, confusion and conflict in their minds. These are the four traditional life goals in Hindu ethics: *dharma* (religion), *artha* (wealth), *kama* (family) and *moksha* (learning).

The Apotheosis of Status into a Religion in China and India

In Chinese ethics the goals of life are circumscribed within the family system. Most of man's rules of conduct are related to the ties of the family and the clan. Social space is accordingly very much limited as the following admonition shows: "Sweep off the snow from your own doorsteps, but don't bother yourself about the frost on someone else's roof." The Chinese family is the centre of virtues and beauties, the seat of moral forces that bind people together. It is the family tradition which elicits sacrifice, consideration for other people and refinement of manners, and curbs individualism and the competitive spirit. Most of a person's duties are related to man and woman's role and position in the family, such as the services to parents, husbands, and elder brothers. The duties of the superiors — father, husband, elder brother — are based upon the domination attitude according to the superior's propriety, while those of the inferiors — wife, son and younger brother — are founded upon complete obedience according to the propriety of the inferior. It is the norm of the family which regulates social virtues.

The moral relations of Chinese society are all derived from the primary group of the family system. These are originally classified under (1) three bonds, i.e. those between the sovereign and his subjects, between parents and children and between the husband and wife; (2) six orders which comprise (a) father and uncles, (b) brothers and sisters, (c) clan, (d) mother and aunts, (e) teachers and friends; (3) five relationships which comprise (a) parents and children, (b) sovereign and subjects, (c) husband and wife, (d) brothers and sisters, and (e) friends. What are called *Wu-Chang* or the five eternal ideals: humaneness, uprightness, propriety, insight and faith are based upon the principle of child obedience. *Szi-Hsing* or the four forms of moral obligation are also derived from the same: filial piety, brotherliness, loyalty and faithfulness. In the classic called "The Great Learning" it is stated that filial submission in state matters appears as loyalty to the state and its ruler. The reverence for an elder brother is transmuted into reverence and ready obedience to elders and those in authority. The subordination of personal interests to the needs of others in the family appears as universal courtesy. It not merely transforms the spirit of government in the hands of gentlemen but also converts the violently bad citizens. It must be pointed out here that in the Chinese attitude the system of family relationships is not that of "blood relationships" as these are regarded by other peoples. The father is not a relative; in the sacramental unity of the family his authority proceeds from his quality as the family high priest and possessor of the ancestral virtue. The son is not a son; he is his father's man. There is neither intimacy nor familiarity, nor "tender privacies" between them. Granet observes:

> Their relations do not belong to the domain of affection, but to that of etiquette and honour. It would be still more exact to say that the relations between father and son are relations of honour to honour.[3]

Such is the reign of moral formalism which Chinese mysticism, with a tendency towards the practical, has established. It is neither feeling nor affection nor "ties of blood", but honour, decorum and etiquette which forge the moral bonds of Chinese family and Chinese society. The master says:

> From the loving example of one family a whole state becomes loving, and from its courtesies the whole state becomes courteous.

Again, he asks:

> Filial piety and fraternal submission — are they not the root of all benevolent actions?[4]

Filial piety is, indeed, the very basis of virtue and the origin of culture and religion in China. Confucius explains as follows:

> The reason why the gentleman teaches filial piety is not

---

3 *Chinese Civilisation*, pp. 320, 343.

4 Clarence C. Hahn, "The Chinese Family System", *Sociology and Social Research*, May–June, 1928.

> because it is to be seen in the home and everyday life. He teaches filial piety in order that man may respect all those who are fathers in the world. He teaches brotherliness in the younger brother, in order that man may respect all those who are elder brothers in the world. He teaches the duty of the subject, in order that man may respect all who are rulers in the world.

The whole social ethics of Confucius is based on the theory that if every man knows his *ming* or name in the home which defines his relationships to others and undertakes his duties accordingly, social order is ensured. Training in social obligations begins naturally, therefore, within the family system. Confucianism has been called *mingchiao* or religion of names.[5] Each man is given his name, title or status in any society from which proceeds all his moral obligations. Confucianism is the best example of the apotheosis of social status (*mingfen*) into a specific religion and culture based on the family system.

In India there is less of family mindedness. Here caste and not the family, as in China, is the more important stabilizing factor in her civilization and the seat of moral forces. The exclusiveness of caste in India is, however, mitigated by co-operation between different families, clans and castes within the village system and by the emphasis of other-worldly or spiritual values which promote a sense of commonness of humanity. In China there are no castes, nor fixed social classes. Confucianism stresses the distinction between men and women, between sons and parents, between the elder and the younger brothers, between king and subjects and between the old and the young. But within each station or social stratum absolute equality is pictured. Lin Yutang points out in this connection that the Chinese word for the five cardinal relationships, *lun*, means equality within its class. Further, there

---

5 Lin Yutang, *My Country and My People*, p. 168.

is a chance for each family to send out an able scion who may become a scholar, rise through the imperial examinations and become a member of the privileged class. Chinese society, as contrasted with Indian society, does not maintain a rigid social hierarchy. The inherent differences between man and man receive clear recognition in China. "Men's minds are different just as are their faces." But each man should be given the opportunity to rise in status. That rise of status through talent is assured by the openness of the Chinese examination system. By passing the examination any Chinese, howsoever low in his birth, can prove his knowledge of the rules of government, and thus become entitled to the highest offices.[6] This makes the Chinese state essentially democratic in its constitution and outlook, though it is in the hands of a highly trained *elite*. More than perhaps any other country in the world the *savant* is a leader of thought and action in China. Thus a young man, to whatever status he may be born, may cherish the idea of rising to the top through education and ability. In India the belief in the law of *karma* reconciles the individual to an inferior role or status full of pain and misery. Thus believing in the fruition of consequences of deeds in the past births he finds happiness in his limited social space, in his hard environment. The Hindu dictum is, "Better to die in one's own status than to imitate the ways and functions of the superior", while the Chinese saying is, "Keep your own status and resign yourself to heaven's will". The *Bhagavad-Gita* stresses the need of a person performing the specific duties of his own caste, even if these be sinful or wrong. To turn to the duties fixed for other persons only does him harm. For it is the deity who being everywhere and in everybody incites all action. And one can best realize himself by adoring him and by the performance of duties of his own station or caste (*sva-dharma*) from a pure sense of duty, with a

---

6 Only those whose ancestors had for three generations been actors, barbers, chiropodists, priests, executioners and domestic servants were excluded.

mind devoid of attachment. In China such reconciliation in circumscribed social space that denies to the individual many of the values of life has been due to the Chinese temperament, its sense of duty and impermanence of life and unexampled capacity for leisure and laughter.

The Reconciliation of Limited Social Space or Status with Universalities in the East

Thus the two ancient civilizations have discovered and practised for centuries ways of living which have made people happy, though circumscribed within restricted social roles with settled systems of norms and values and denied many people satisfactions of life. Their ethos and culture seem to have succeeded better than those of Western communities where everybody in the search of all human values, wealth, status and power, the considerable majority of the people lose status, self-esteem and happiness. Where many values are presented to every individual in a complex civilization, it can guide individual conduct better if it selects certain definite life goals for him. Selection of the goals of life is the secret of achievement of planned society in India and China. Personality problems, so common in the urban–industrial West, are accordingly seldom met with in Chinese and Indian society. Unlike the West the individual here is surrounded by homogeneous and unified culture patterns or schemes of life which he accepts and assimilates, and is fully prepared to follow in his family, clan, caste or calling. In both China and India society has, indeed, fashioned a carefully weighed and graded system of relationships which posit the individual in his role or niche in society, assign him duties which he is able to perform, and make him happy in the consciousness of the successful fulfilment of such duties. In all Chinese ethical attitudes George H. Danton finds a sense of the necessary distance between human beings, an unbridgeable gap as expressed in the saying: "You are you and I am I". This is responsible, according to him, for Chinese manners, courtesy, custom, the inevitable *kuei chu*, the criterion of the moral world.[7] Characteristically enough, the mysticism or the asceticism of India as embodied in the contrasted saying, "Thou art that", has engendered a transcendentalism which has merged the personality in the universal and at the same time affirmed and guided social action in the person's own niche and position in society. In the West the individual is always on the move from one role or status, and from one plan or pattern of life to another. Thus he often finds himself maladjusted and unhappy. There is also another consideration. Man's achievement and happiness within a limited social and moral space are possible in India and China because of the preference in these countries for goals of life which may be shared rather than exclusively appropriated and possessed. We have already referred to the hierarchy of values in Hindu ethics, viz. religion, wealth, family and learning. The major occupational groups were accorded a corresponding traditional gradation in India which was as follows:

1. the learned and spiritual-minded;
2. the soldiers;
3. the merchants; and
4. the agriculturists, artisans and labourers.

In China the adherence to the Doctrine of the Mean laid down by the ancient sages has disciplined the people in moderation and temperance and in the control of desires and emotions. Ostentatious display or any kind of excesses is looked upon as a sign of immaturity.

> *Han-yang*, a Chinese term implying the cultivation of personal character, a term used to distinguish maturity from immaturity, experience from inexperience, means, among other things, ability to control one's emotions.[8]

---

[7] Danton, *The Chinese People*, pp. 115-19.

[8] Theodore H.E. Chen, "Racial Characteristics of the Chinese", *Sociology and Social Research*, January–February 1940.

The traditional Chinese social hierarchy definitely indicated like the Indian tradition that society should be dominated by the philosophers educated in the lore and the virtues of civilized humanity. The gradation is as follows:

1. the teachers and scholars;
2. the soldiers;
3. the farmers;
4. the artisans;
5. the merchants; and
6. the *de-classe*, comprising actors, "runners", slaves, etc.

In both India and China the indestructible and universal belief in the transitoriness of life and its satisfactions and in the supremacy of the virtues of moderation and self-regulation have made it much easier for the people to conform to the established community purpose and idea, and to a relatively restricted role or status in life.

In India and China man has been able to obtain his happiness and fulfil his social roles and responsibility in relatively limited social and moral space. Man in the West, with his exaggerated sense of individualism, sharpened by the Renaissance and the Reformation, his immoderation in private enterprise and pursuit of wealth encouraged by the Industrial and the Commercial Revolution, and with all the customary controls of the primary groups disintegrated by modern machine technology, finds himself adrift on chartless seas without any sure social direction and sanctions or guiding sets of values.

Life-Planning in Terms of Definite and Restricted Life-Goals

In modern dynamic society the extensive mobility of peoples, the increased opportunity of contacts with other groups and individuals with different culture patterns and plans of life, the universal desire to rise in the social scale by improvement of the standard of living, and, above all, the orientation of fluid masses of urban dwellers in secondary associations and pecuniary–contractual standards have introduced a confusion of moral sentiments and sets of values underlying the scale of status primarily conditioned for the homogeneous rural *milieu*. Thus there arise serious problems of personality adjustment arising out of the struggle for status. The study of personal maladjustment will be concrete and fruitful if we understand the frustration of the individual's urges and goals of life due to the disharmony or conflict between his various roles or statuses in society. Each individual constantly moves from one role or status to another and faces different social situations. In modern civilization a man's role or status is largely the outcome of his own individual achievement and experience. Thus an individual often finds himself unable to regulate his attitudes and modify his behaviour when his various statuses are not in harmony. In a mobile society the amicable equilibrium between an interdependent system of statuses, which underlies the individual's total integral relations and behaviour, is seldom found, calling for continuous change of attitudes and behaviour with an enormous drain of mental energy. The loss of status in one kind of social space may bring forth serious personality problems although the individual may participate successfully in other roles and maintain his status effectively in that context. Personality development or maladjustment takes place in the constellation of social spaces in which the concrete individual is placed. Not all social roles or values of life are intended for everybody. Man can prevent a good deal of maladjustment and insecurity through a wise choice of roles and plans of life even though it may mean the restriction of the orbit of his social life. The remedy of much of insecurity and frustration in interpersonal relations largely lies in the recognition of the fact that in our complex society individuals cannot participate in the whole of social experience and of the heritage and rewards of life, but in bits of such experience, heritage and reward as represented by their appropriate ecological, mental and social space.

It is well known that man's mental world is largely a limited world selected for him by his group. "For the most part," observes Lippmann, "we do not first see and then define, we define first and then see." Mental sets or stereotypes tend to limit our ways and range of knowledge which is but a limited selection from the whole body of knowledge at the command of the social group. We do not apprehend the world with our original mental equipment. But rather we apprehend it as the social group wishes us to apprehend it. Thus our mental perspective which defines the panorama of our lives and the avenues open to us for self-assertion and achievement of status becomes limited. Similarly for easy adaptation to the world of values and realizations, it is necessary to cast aside a great deal and concentrate definitely and wholeheartedly on some values from which definite aims of life may be chosen. For successful achievement of status, it is better for the individual to recognize that he can reach only a few of the goals of life among those that shine from afar. His moral space in which judgement of status and mobility takes place should be defined and circumscribed as his mental, social and ecological space is limited. The struggle for recognition, status and power threatens less the sanity of the individual and stability of the social order, if human life be planned in terms of fewer promises and less frustrations than in terms of greater promises and more frustrations. Life planning in any complex society with several competing scales of values and stratification means the choice and selection of some categories of values to the exclusion of others for living rationally and steadfastly. From this narrowed but sharpened perspective of values and realizations the individual has to select wisely the cameos of his life goals which may give him sometimes security with or without freedom, sometimes wealth with or without distinction, sometimes learning, with or without recognition and so on. In so far as he aspires after a status in terms of the definite and restricted values of life that lie within his range and acts well his part as a conscious link in a vast, vital social chain, his personality functions fully and maintains its integration. Not only is thus his freedom of mobility subjected to revaluation and restriction in terms of what the personality can tolerate, but also as each individual attains or maintains his status in his specific role, which is morally approved for him by the social order, he at once lives up to his own conscience and keeps up the banner of the society's normative pattern or scale of stratification high above the storms and stresses of life.

9

Mobility: Ecological and Social

STATUS and mobility, as we have seen, are complementary ecological processes that emerge in the give-and-take between the organism and the environment. Status implies the success of man's spatial adjustment to the environment, while mobility implies effective freedom of adjustment within the limits of the environment. Mobility is fundamentally freedom of mobility and of competition and is both ecological or spatial and social.

Movement of organisms through space is an incidence in their selection and survival. Plant ecologists have made us familiar with the methods of mass migration of plant communities as well as of the less spectacular phenomenon of distribution of individual plants from a given ecological area by wind, water and animals. In fact, the present green mantle of the earth amply testifies to the vast migratory movements of plants, especially associated with the climatic oscillations in the past. Smallscale migratory movements are visible everywhere whenever a new bit of the landscape is laid bare, a forest cut down or burnt, a low land or marsh becomes dry, or a seashore is captured for human occupance.

Animals and plants live interlocked lives. Thus, wherever in mountains, sanddunes and marshes, intermittent migrations or mass invasions of vegetable communities take place from a neighbouring or distant area, animals also move and swarm, adjusting their advance to that of the much less mobile plant matrix. There are also the diurnal and seasonal migrations of animals which are equally significant. Striking resemblances are also discernible between human and mammalian migrations which should not escape the attention of students of social ecology. These have been described by me elsewhere. Migration, in the first place, brings about a successful adjustment of numbers to the limited resources of the habitat. Second, both animals and man tend to concentrate in an optimum habitat. Temporary and seasonal shifts are of the nature of gregarious ecological tentatives; these are later on followed by temporary and permanent settlement or colonization, of which the ecological finality is governed by the *ensemble* of factors of successful adaptation and assimilation in new regions. Third, migrations show wavelike movements with centres of dispersal, zones and gradients of dense, medium and meagre colonization. Fourth, the distribution of certain plants, and in the case of human settlements certain crops and animals, definitely restrict both the range and mode of distribution of migrants. This fundamental ecological principle lays down the limits of successful colonization or settlement. Migrations to new regions succeed best when stocks and communities colonize from similar climatic regions, whose crops, agricultural practices and other economic procedures can be more easily adapted and assimilated in the new immigration areas. Fifth, man is much more tied to his vicinal association by kinship and social bonds than any other animal. Yet the introduction of the money economy has, in modern industrial society, made him the most mobile among the animals. On the whole the number of migrants and the proportion of women and children are in inverse proportion to the distance of their original residences. The larger the number of cultural and economic interests a town or city combines, the greater is the size of the town or city and the wider is the hinterland from which it pulls migrants and the greater the average age of the persons participating in the more distant migrations.

The consequences of ecological mobility are far reaching. The role of early migrations in man's primitive history, in the physical and psychical differentiation of races, and in the diffusion of new culture traits can hardly be exaggerated. Man's bodily frame, his economic history and heritage of culture bear the indelible impress of waves of migration of new stocks from neighbouring or distant regions. In later history migratory movements are connected with colonization, conquest and expansion of the peoples who represent the vanguard of humanity. Both historically and in the present, migrations have been the outcome of differential pressure of population and capacity of peoples for acclimatization in new lands where they seek to find out optimum living conditions. Political conquest and extension of trade and of spheres of influence have been incidents in this expansion of people, the major consequence of which is the spread of new culture, technology and institutions all over the globe. With improvement in the means of transportation which have linked the different parts of the earth, overseas migration has considerably increased in volume and significance. Long distance migration is undertaken by the more intelligent and competent individuals of the society. Thus, on the whole, the more distant the migration, the greater are the selection and quality of the migrants, irrespective of their original racial or economic background. Therefore, the abolition of the barriers of space has been contributing towards an improvement of biological selection, and an approximation of the standards of living of the peoples on earth. The process of migration is from lands of limited resources and low standard of living to lands of abundant resources and high standard of living. Given free opportunities of migration and settlement, the world's food supply increases and industrial production expands due to the development of international division of labour and of new markets in pioneer zones, while there is also much needed relief from poverty and population pressure in the overcrowded lands.

There are, of course, strong hindrances to this ecological movement. Migration is now discouraged even in countries of fewer economic opportunities which are interested in manpower, and migrants are more often those who are incompetent and have failed in the country of emigration. The immigration country, threatened with reduction of the standard of living due to competition with low paid migrant labour, stems the migratory currents. While it does not altogether eschew migration, its discriminatory treatment offers an unfavourable social environment for the migrants, who for the sake of self defence are compelled to develop a cultural and social segregation that nullifies the biological and social selectivity of migration. A restrictive migration policy is both biologically and economically wrong. Where peoples regard new lands with vast empty spaces as their exclusive preserve and follow a dog-in-the-manger policy in respect of utilization of their resources, international relations become embittered. Two Europes and two hemispheres with their dual standards of living cannot be welded together into an international economic community. Thus the freedom of mobility of peoples touches fundamental demographic, biological and political issues at both national and international levels.

Within the boundaries of the same political area the same economic causes, viz. differential economic pressure and standards of living stimulate migration. Ecologically speaking, the change of human spatial distribution is brought about as a result of the process of competition and selection brought into operation by differential opportunities of living conditions in the habitats. Change in the nature and distribution of resources, such as the destruction of forests and their animal inhabitants and desiccation or seasonal shrinkage of pastures lead to primitive nomadism. Change in technology and arts of production as, for instance, the supercession of hunting and shepherding by agriculture stimulates migration. The gradual exhaustion of the soil in new lands due to inappropriate farming practices, coupled with increase in population, leads to trek or migration further and further into the pioneer fringes, whether in America, in South Africa or in Australia. In the nineteenth-century the advent of the new technology had a profound effect on the redistribution of population. Rural arts and handicrafts were everywhere disorganized or destroyed and industrial production was concentrated in a few favoured regions. Later on an agrarian revolution followed up the industrial revolution. The introduction of agricultural tools and machinery and mechanized large scale farming have enormously reduced the proportion of population needed to produce the food and raw materials for the entire population. All this has promoted a city-ward drift in most countries which has far reaching effects upon the modes of living, social habits and stratification of peoples all over the world. It is thus the transformation of the ecologic base of society, a shift of occupations and interests by the new technology and improvement of the facilities of transportation during the last century or a century and a half brought about a new spatial distribution of population. Such redistribution will also continue so long as the machine technology persists in industrial production, and as improvements in agricultural techniques and organization continue to create lesser and lesser demand for workers engaged in the farming enterprise. Physical or ecological mobility will thus increase in volume and intensity and it will have profound effects upon man's society and culture.

Types of Ecological Mobility

Various types of physical or ecological mobility are now discernible. First, there is the steady city-ward drift in every country which becomes more intensive in periods of agricultural depression or industrial prosperity, and which gradually transforms the social composition of towns and cities. This trend coexists with industrialization and mechanization. Second, there is the daily ingress and egress of rural dwellers who come to the city for their work or for trade, business and amusement and return to their village homes every evening. The hinterland from which the city draws its "daily passengers" gradually extends with the improvement of transportation and communication. Third, the urban folk also go out of the bounds of the city on weekends and holidays for rest and recreation. Fourth, there is the movement of urban dwellers from one room, flat, hotel or house within the city to another. The change in residence of urban dwellers tends to become more and more frequent in every large city, and associated with many social pathological features. Finally, there are casual movements of urban dwellers within the city who daily or periodically set out in buses, trams or tubes in search of recreation or adventure. Not merely the new technology which brings about improvements in industry, communication, transport and organization but the entire technique of mass propaganda, directed to engender new cravings, amusements and excitements, contribute to intensify physical mobility of the various types. Each type of mobility has its profound reactions on individual and collective patterns of behaviour and values.

Ecological and Social Relationships

It is necessary at this stage to distinguish between ecological and social mobility and interaction. Ecological mobility is movement in space by which individuals come to compete or co-operate with one another for position and status, developing a characteristic type of human relationships. The interaction is dominated by reciprocal accommodation in relation to the limited resources of the ecological space; yet it is a social interaction. In ecological interaction man meets fellowmen not as a person but as a competing or cooperating unit in the context of spatial and sustenance relations; hence it is characterized more by deliberate–contractual and less by instinctive–communal patterns. In the urban dweller's reactions to fellowmen there is the predominance of ecological reaction. In the fast moving cultural stream of the city his contacts are casual, transient and fragmentary so that he does not know the person but only apprehends his role and builds up what Lippmann calls a "stereotype". A stereotype is just a superficial picture of a person, empty of content, but useful in appraising the role he appears to play. It hides his unique individuality but concentrates on the performance which is the basis of immediate contact. The urban dweller reacts to fellowmen as a co-worker, or as a boss or subordinate, a customer or client, even "as a mere address or number", as a stereotype, a symbol or a figure which acquires interest, simply because of its performance which may be objectively evaluated in terms of money. The emotional tone recedes into the background, and thus an anonymous and superficial rather than an intimate and personal relationship finds favour. Ecological relationship may be defined as one of proximity in ecological space but of distance in social space. It actually hinders the development of personal and sympathetic relationship, characteristic of rural contacts and associations that are stable, direct and face-to-face, and in which both personality and performance are apt to be defined and valued reciprocally. It is all the same human relationship, but of the abstract, non-sentimental *Gesellschaft* kind, different from the consensus and communion arising in man's vital modes of association in rural society, such as the family, the neighbourhood, kinship group and the community.

In urban–industrial society the ecological, formal and impersonal relationship increases with the size of the habitation and social group and the frequency and range of mobility.

More and more of contacts necessary for the satisfaction of the daily requirements, amenities and conveniences is mechanized and mediated through the written communication and the phone; the primary relationship being distributed over larger ecological space ceases to elicit emotions, and neighbourliness or kinship feeling breaks down. The ecological relationship fosters and is promoted by money economy. In the network of utilities and services, which are implied in the casual and frequent social contacts in industrial society, attention is given only to the money token ignoring the person who serves or mediates. The human bond becomes the impersonal cash nexus which gradually supersedes the natural and organic familial ties. In money-economy man's physical movement is accelerated as is the circulation of goods and services. Money economy also promotes social mobility. When an individual spends with greater and greater reference to his own status and standard of living and less and less reference to primary group associates, as he releases himself from his traditional obligations to the family or kinship group, he can climb up the social ladder faster. But he may also sink faster if he be not safeguarded in his status by the family or kinship group. It is the new machine technology and impersonal wage economy which furnish the basis of social mobility in any urbanized and industrialized society.

Ecological and Social Mobility in Village and City

Ecological mobility co-exists with social immobility in both tribal and agricultural societies. Primitive peoples show a collective spatial adjustment. As they move out to a new environment, their food being relatively uniform, specialized or limited, they do not develop any new division of labour. Thus savages do not change their social or economic status nor shift their tribal or group afflictions as they follow the wild deer and bison or practise shifting cultivation from forest to forest. In urban–industrial society social mobility accompanies physical mobility, and mobility is both an individual adjustment and a group process. Movement of individuals in space, a complex division of labour and specialization in machine technology with interchangeability of jobs and occupations, an impersonal wage system and change of social and economic status aid one another in the urban–industrial milieu. In the peasant society status groups are rigidly fixed corresponding to the prevailing simple division of labour and specialization. The peasant's life, toil and recreation are adjusted to the balance and rhythm of Nature's processes, which cannot be speeded up. Just as simple routined movements, dominated by Nature's sequence of the distribution of sunshine and rainfall and synchronous human habits and traditions, are true of rural dwellers, their status and position are also relatively persistent and enduring; for hardly have they any opportunity of change of job, vocation or even residence. In rural society it is only the acquisition or loss of land which leads to the change of status. The landlord and the landed farmer are in the highest social level; those who have no land and work out as farmhands or domestic servants are in the lowest social level. Small tenants and artisans occupy an intermediate position. Traders and shopkeepers comprise a more mobile group than cultivators. They usually come from outside the village, and are not firmly attached to the soil. It is only by acquiring land in the village that they obtain social rank. Thus the social hierarchy is closely related to the interest in the land which defines the role of the social group in the collective affairs of the village. Rural stratification bears the indelible stamp of much toil and wealth in cultivation. Although a brahmin, a Rajput, a Samurai, a teacher may be poor they are yet given social recognition. To acquire or destroy landed wealth requires considerable time, while there is neither competition nor change of job, residence and standard which are symbols of rank in urban society. Thus upward or downward movement in the rural social ladder is relatively slow. The new urban occupational classes, such as traders, shopkeepers, school masters and officials, are not as yet assimilated to the village and their loyalties are chiefly to the town. The rural dwellers owe allegiance not merely to their social classes but also to the primary family and neighbourhood groups with which they are bound by a variety of intimate and primal relations that become the seats of higher values underlying the development of personality and the ethical order of the rural community. The latter may be traditional, but it has the merit of defining clearly and specifically the values and life goals of individuals. Man's interests and values are surface rooted and volatile in the city as he constantly changes his role or position in the fluctuating patterns of urban modes of association. In urban society individuals not only jostle with one another as they quickly shift from job to job, association to association, flat to flat and one quarter of the city to another, but they also quickly move up or down the social or economic ladder. The modern town or city has become a highly mobile social situation, where contacts between men are segmental, and their roles fractionalized and the social habits and sentiments moulded by the secondary economic and political rather than by the primary and intimate familial institutions and controls. Individuation is the result of the impersonal machine and wage economy in which a man's income and expenditure, his standard of living and status become no longer matters of familial or collective concern or control. Individuation is connected with what Eucken calls " a economismus". A pecuniary scale of valuation replaces the traditional hierarchy of social values. Money promotes abstract, non-sentimental relations between man and man, and hence both physical and social mobility. It fosters the rational–

contractual standard as the norm of conduct. Since it buys everything and plays the major role in all phases of social life and relations, besides the intimate and the familial, the conviction gains ground that economic values are preferable to values which are intimate, ultimate and non-transferable. It is the pursuit of limited, divisible hedonic values and satisfactions in industrialized society which favours the development of an intensely individualistic rather than socialized personality. This completes the disintegration of primary groups and atomization of society.

In rural society ecologic, social and moral space tends to coincide. Men live in close physical proximity with one another; social distance which exists in rural society is abridged by neighbourly spirit and sympathy and community service; while all participate in a certain well-established set of moral values and social aims, which are integrated with one another and are favourable to personality integration and social and moral order of the village. In urban society culture becomes no longer an organized, integrated pattern of living adequate for the needs of individuals, but rather an agglomeration of individuals, associations and institutions, characterized by the constant conflict between individual achievements and moral values and social objectives. The urban dweller constantly strives to change his ecologic space, drift to jobs, occupations and areas that represent higher levels of economic attainment; he strives to change his social space, attain higher social status and prestige; and he also aims at the realization of maximum goals of life, although he actually secures few of them, and the few he achieves often become incompatible with the wellbeing and progress of society. The urban dweller's ecological position, his social status and his role and station in the network of moral values and social obligations which we call "culture" are constantly fluctuating. The individual is always off his balance in relation to his three levels of space and action, ecological, social and moral. Society is also off its balance, there being a profound discord between its economic and technological acquisition and the lag in its moral organization, between man's freedom of mobility and struggle for status and social order and progress.

Mobility and Civilization

The essence of the sociological method is to interpret the ecological, social and moral interaction in the *Gestalt* of the primitive, intermediate or peasant and modern or industrialized society as an integral whole. In each pattern there is a correspondence between ecological, economic and social relations. A synoptic analysis of social life and relations in the different levels of collective adjustment, so that every sector is seen in relation to the whole, is the crux of modern sociological treatment. In contemporary industrialized society, as contrasted with rural society, the study would naturally stress social deviation and disequilibrium, these having become the chief characteristics of the *Gestalt*.

With this unified approach in mind we can discern mobility in its successive levels or phases, which are mutually interdependent, in social accommodation and relations with a certain social norm emerging at each level.

1. *Mobility has a physical and technical basis:* Modern large-scale production, development of rapid transit and communication and the rise of modern sanitation. Without the rapid turnover in factories, shops and establishments employing millions of persons and the vast technical progress in engineering, communication, organization and industry which promote locomotion of persons, goods and power and communication of the word, the excessive mobility in the modern city is not possible. Speed and convenience of travel and intercourse and mobility help each other. From this phase of collective technological

adjustment contemporary civilization has deduced the norm of increase in the tempo of life as the keynote of progress.

2. *Mobility has its biological basis:* The preponderance of a heterogeneous, foreign-born, adult population, with an excess of single and unattached persons and a deficiency of women and children, a high divorce rate and a low birth rate. Communities characterized by a dominant male sex ratio and a deficiency of children show an increase of competition as is indicated by the brisk, feverish tempo and the rapid rise and fall of individual status and position. Such communities are also characterized by an eat-drink-and-be-merry attitude towards life and by the absence of community controls and traditional obligations which not only quicken mobility but also promote family breakdown and social deviation and disorganization. The characteristic population pyramid underlies economic prosperity since there is a large per capita earning power, which is constantly replenished by new migrants; while trade and business are stimulated by the cumulative demand for housing and for articles of luxury. There is a maximum of physical movement and of social change reflected in the ascent or descent to the different social and economic strata, promoted by the cycle of economic fluctuation and the cycle of demographic movement. The mobility and rapid tempo of contemporary society are biologically rooted in the social composition of groups, especially the age and sex composition. From this phase of biologic adaptation in the throbbing, fluid life of the exuberantly growing and heterogeneous city emerge the norms of sexual freedom and racial admixture, and of amelioration of the urban environmental conditions as providing the clues to progress. Mixed strains exhibit intellectual and emotional plasticity, which favours mobility. Without the stress of nurture or environment, instead of human nature

or heredity, in vast schemes of urban and regional planning and improvement, the breeding of slums by slums and of inferior stocks by slums would have endangered the racial stock. Biologically speaking, the mobile sections of the population perhaps show greater mental and social stimulation, activity and inventive capacity, which promote further mobility and tempo of life. But the fluid mass of persons and objects constantly calls for more numerous and quicker mental adjustments and causes excessive mental strain; while moral adjustments are also rendered difficult by the heterogeneity of mores and cultural patterns of different persons coming to the city with different social backgrounds. The urban dweller is a member of several secondary associations with different patterns of behaviour and scales of values, and oscillates from one pattern and scale to another without necessary loss of status in the anonymity of the city. Moral confusion or chaos of values thus accompanies mental breakdown or inadequacy.

3. *Mobility has its economic basis:* The vast complicated system of mass standardized production cannot be run without an elaborate division and interchangeability of jobs and occupations which demand quick movement of individuals. It is the interchangeability of labour and the process of substitution which are the distinctive characteristics of the modern industrial structure that make high mobility inevitable. From this emerges the economic norm of the freedom of mobility or competition that may permit an easy rise and fall of socio-economic status according to merit as the keynote of progress. Competition or freedom of enterprise has been regarded throughout the nineteenth century as the *sine qua non* of social efficiency, and economists have been prone to regard the primary groups and the social values and conventions they represent as causes of economic friction and backwardness.

In spite of the classical economist's prophecy the movement from one pecuniary group upward has been found arduous, limited and infrequent. In Germany, an earlier investigation found that only one-sixth of the professional people came from middle-income groups, now one-half of the intelligentsia has a middleclass background. The fact, concludes Nothaas, that the number of professionals who rise from the proletariat or the peasantry directly is negligible indicates that it takes a few generations to climb to the highest strata of society. On the whole the range of occupational mobility, according to Sorokin, fluctuates from a minimum of 3 to a maximum of 70 per cent, the average of all occupational groups in Western society being 20 and 60 per cent. In the USA 70 per cent of business leaders have been drawn, according to a study of Taussig and Joslyn, from 10 per cent of the population. The middle occupational classes are more stable than the extremes. Yet there is no doubt that as industrialism has spread there has been a marked decrease in the hereditary transmission of occupations from father to children, and a marked increase of the rise and fall of persons between the different occupational classes and strata of society. Even custom-bound India, China and Japan testify to this social change. In India and Japan many of the premiers and ministers, during the last few decades, came from poor families. In modern industrial society, occupations are more numerous and social levels more pronounced than in peasant society. Man is engaged here in constant struggle for his position with fellowmen. If he climbs up he ousts another, and he must struggle on to retain his position. And, again, he may be brought up or down by the vertical movement of the group to which he belongs. A constant vertical movement of individuals and economic classes is the economic consequence of machine technology, and presents a marked contrast with the rigid social stratification in rural society. In urban society the greater the mobility, the greater are the economic contrasts of wealth and poverty, independence and insecurity.

4. On its characteristic technic biological and economic base, mobility builds up an appropriate mode of group life and relationships. The fluid and heterogeneous mass of people in contemporary industrialized society have numerous group attachments, which develop in each individual numerous social selves. Each social self represents a fraction of the person; each group satisfies some fractional needs and interests. Such a group is far different from the primary group in the rural society which is adequate for the total recurrent needs of the individual from birth to death. Groups in the modern industrialized society are secondary associations, based on a rational consideration of reciprocal convenience, needs and interests of individuals. As the latter blend, integrate or contradict with one another, groups also coalesce or split up. With increase of mobility in modern urban–industrial society, we see a greater variety, complexity and instability of groups, and a greater predominance of the abstract, superficial, complex and intensive system of contacts in secondary groups and associations over simple, enduring and face-to-face primary group relations. From this complex and dynamic process of shifting group affiliations and individual relations emerges the norm of deliberate agreement or contract rather than consensus rapport and an established status or position of the individual in a traditional scheme of rights and obligations as the clue to progress. If the folk and the peasant society, the small kinship and neighbourhood groups and the village community have been superseded today by the larger impersonal territorial group in the Great Society, election appears not as a mere political contrivance but a

universal formal procedure underlying modern secular and deliberate forms of control.

5. Finally, mobility develops its characteristic pattern of personal and moral relations and values. Mobility cannot be understood without reference to a characteristic background of ideology and sentiment, moral ideal and cultural goal that stimulate and regulate the freedom of mobility and competition in economic and social adjustments. Contemporary industrial society is marked by a formal, objective, pecuniary standard which fits well into the machine technology, rapid tempo of life, interdependence of labour and freedom of mobility. The complex and interdependent Great Society in which man lives requires not only an appropriate mechanism of communication, organization and industry but also an appropriate value mechanism which may express and measure the widest range of human values. But the money token used in measuring and energizing various individual and social goals ends in subordinating to itself the ultimate values. Money is associated with man's health, comfort and leisure, and gives access to many cultural, personal and spiritual values. There is, in modern life an intermingling of economic with aesthetic and moral values. But as pecuniary value enlarges its scope, society slides into the acceptance of the principle that everything has its price. Pecuniary value becomes a real end rather than a means, and is used to manipulate a great number of social activities and values which should be outside the pecuniary domain. Thus, the hegemony that belongs to the ultimate, underivative values ends. The cult of the hedonic and the useful supersedes the ancient adoration of truth, love and goodness.

The norms of the rapid tempo of life, the fluidity of social relations, the freedom of competition and contract, and the deliberate–pecuniary standard that emerge in the successive levels of social accommodation — all these are reciprocally interdependent and express the *Gestalt* of modern industrialized civilization of which physical and social mobility is the fundamental process. The contemporary social scene cannot be understood without placing mobility in the centre of the perspective, nor can mobility be adequately interpreted without adopting an integrated and synthetic viewpoint in this regard. No significant feature of modern civilization can be delineated without introducing mobility as one of its causal factors operative in the levels of ecology, economy and morality.

Social ecology contributes to make the study of human culture exact and quantitative through the establishment of ecological indices for the measurement of the types and trends of community life in respect of human aggregation (density of population), technology (horsepower), social stratification (social proximity and distance), social mobility (including the tempo of life) and pecuniary valuation. Culture can be expressed quantitatively only partially. But by the separate and combined use of such ecological indices as density, technology, mobility, distance, tempo of life and the cash nexus we can precisely express and measure certain deep and subtle forces which move persons in a society but which otherwise sociology cannot lay hold of. The change from tribal to peasant culture and from peasant to modern urban–industrial culture is roughly measurable according to the increase of density, machine system, mobility and money valuation, indices which will be increasingly used by social ecology in the study of the spatial adaptation and arrangement of the human community. No doubt a fixed quantitative relation between a measurable ecological index like density, mobility, distance and use of money and a non-measurable social one like urbanism cannot be posited, but that the combination of the several ecological indices indicate the degree of approximation towards a definite social type and trend can be demonstrated. Thus studies of the movements of density, machine-power, mobility, distance, tempo of life and money economy should supplement one another, and if the trends all indicate an increase over a period of time, the presumption is strong that the community is moving towards the artificial, impersonal and contractual urban pattern of living.

Of all the ecological indices the index of mobility (both physical and social) for the measurement of cultural types and trends is of the greatest significance, mobility being the central causal trend subsuming many other social forces and trends. To give sociological analysis a mathematical presentation in terms of the three principal co-ordinates, density, mobility and technology, we have the formula as follows:

$$C_{(T)} = F(DM),$$

where C = modern urban–industrial culture

T = machine technology

D = density of population

M = mobility

Now mobility has several measurable components such as migration, change of employment and income, cash valuation, fluidity of social relations and tempo of life as well as certain non-mensurable components. Thus the complete formula will be somewhat as follows:

$$C_{(T)} = F\{D\,M(m\,e\,c\,f\,t\,p)\},$$

where m = migration

e = change of employment and income

c = cash nexus and valuation

f = fluidity of social relations

t = tempo of life

p = non-mensurable factors

Similarly,

$C_{(A)} = F(D\ S)$

where C = rural culture

A = agriculture

D = dispersal of population

S = status

Like mobility status has also several measurable components such as fixation of habitation, fixation and specialization of role and occupation, hereditary acquisition of privilege, power and prestige, social distance and non-pecuniary valuation as well as certain non-measurable factors.

Thus the formula will be

$C_{(A)} = F\{D\ S(f\ r\ h\ d\ n\ p)\}$

where f = fixation of habitation

r = fixation and specialization of role or occupation

h = hereditary acquisition of privilege prestige and power

n = non-pecuniary valuation

p = non-measurable factors

The concept of ecological indices should, indeed, prove of great significance in the future development of sociology on a quantitative basis.

10

Time, Technics and Society

Ecological and Personal Time

THE concept of mobility presupposes the categories of space and time. Man's ecological and moral space is limited by society. He plays the role selected for him by society, and appropriates his limited categories of values from a niche that society carves out for him. Both his status and mobility are incidents in a dynamic social process of which he is an active partner in the limited universe that niggardly Nature and social destiny have chosen for him. This dynamic process embraces both social continuity and social change and involves the concept of time. Now, time in life and society is something very different from time in the starry heaven. Astronomical time is postulated as uniform and homogeneous, as ceaselessly flowing at a constant rate, but this is a myth of the mathematician. Einstein and others have stressed the limitations of Newtonian absolute time, and the dependence of time on space and its essential relation to velocities as part of a four-dimensional continuum. The time which is real, concrete and objective in man's world is related to his experience; experience, first, of the rhythm of life-processes in their relations to the environment, and second experience, of the rhythm of activities of the group with which his own activities synchronize in the process of social adaptation. It is a law in the living world that physico-chemical and biological processes in organisms, within favourable temperature limits, are increased by an approximate constant (two to three times usually) for each 10° F rise in temperature. This is the well known Van't Hoff's formula, which underlies the universal variation of the metabolic rate in response to environmental changes. The rate of metabolism measures biological time, which accordingly varies with age. To the old, time appears to pass rapidly, since the solar time envelope is relatively constant while physiological rates are less and physiological times, proportional to reciprocal rates, faster. According to Lecomte du Nouy, for example, for parents of forty and a child of ten, one year for the child represents the same amount of physiological time as three years for the parents.[1] Man's experience of the rhythm of his own internal activities such as the heartbeat, inhalation and exhalation, the woman's menstrual cycle, the recurrence of hunger, relaxation and sleep and of the cycle of the phenomena of Nature is built up into the consciousness of time. He feels hungry and wants rest and sleep at regular intervals, and thus the major physiological needs and their recurrent experience and satisfaction at stated intervals give clues to the passage of time. More significant than the mental construct of duration is the formation of regular habits. Such ever recurrent habits of individuals as those of seeking food, work, relaxation and sleep weave into the consciousness automatic patterns of activities which not only express man's time sense but also aid him in his inner and outer adaptation. Biological time is manifest in man's most stable and generic habits in respect of bodily functions.

Psychologists also have discerned rhythms of growth in mental life and crises of adolescence and senescence. The psycho-physical state or maturation of the body–mind and the content of time being crowded and interesting or simple and tame underlie differences of time estimate by individuals. The perception of events in successive order due to the fading of one image and the dawning of another and the capacity for

[1] Lecomte du Nouy, *Biological Time*.

grouping successive images into a whole measure psychological time. A strongly felt emotion or a stirring experience shorten duration as a mental construct. "One crowded hour of a glorious life is worth an age without a name." This has been explained by William James thus:

> In general, a time filled with varied and interesting experiences seems short in passing, but long as we look back. On the other hand, a tract of time empty of experiences seems long in passing, but in retrospect short.

Laboratory experiments demonstrate that when there is greater need-tension, accompanied by strain and sometimes emotional excitement, time-intervals Hare estimated as shorter than periods in which there is less. It is well known that man loses the sense of time in sleep, and in the waking stage while day-dreaming or using his imagination. In the thrill of sexual activities, aesthetic delights or mystical experiences or through the use of drugs time loses its precision for the individual. Time-sense is considered to depend on basic cell metabolism. *Hasheesh* and quinine make time intervals seem longer than they really are, and thyroxin shortens the interval. Alcohol lengthens the interval. Caffeine shortens it. These are laboratory findings, time estimation apparently depending upon the metabolic rate of the individual. Time-perspective varies not only according to a state of tension or ennui, but also according to the differences of intelligence, learning capacity and foresight, and between youth and age and the boundaries of social space of individuals. Individuals are found to differ in respect of the estimate of immediate or deferred needs and consequences of action, of the thought and discounting for the future, and of precision and computability of time. Thus one may speak of personal time.

The Genesis of Social Time

Social time is yet different. Superposed upon the unique

individual experiences of biological and psychological duration is the rhythm of recurring social events and activities which determines time reckoning in society. For social adaptation requires that time should not be the unreliable time experience of individuals but must be invariable and common time for all individuals on the basis of which alone co-operation in economic and social activity is possible. Even man's physiological needs and satisfactions are determined by the social milieu. Malinowski observes,

> Man does not depend on the physiological rhythm of hunger and satiety alone; his digestive processes are timed and trained by the daily routine of his tribe, nation or class.[2]

Early man's time reckoning had its source in the seasonal course of organized economic activities. Hunting folks whose activities were intermittent hardly develop a calendar in the fashion of pastoral and agricultural folks. In the jungles of the Andamans the jungle dwellers have adopted an original method of marking the different periods of the year by means of the odoriferous flowers that are in bloom in different times. "Their calendar", observes Radcliffe-Brown, "is a calendar of scents which play an important role connected with magic in their life." The shepherds were the world's first star-gazers and astronomers; they are known to reckon time according to the life-round of flocks and herds which they control, seasonal migration to distant pastures being imperative for their collective existence and welfare. It was in the agricultural stage, however, that man's timetable was for the first time systematically drawn up; it was determined by the routine of agricultural practice, at first collectively regulated, which became a powerfully entrenched social habit. In the formative stages of civilization it was this agricultural routine which saved the children of the soil from misery and starvation. Indeed, with the advent of

---

[2] "The Group and the Individual in Functional Analysis", *American Journal of Sociology*, 1939, 44.

agriculture man acquired regular habits of work, recreation, rest, play and sleep for the first time. This was perhaps the single most momentous phase in his psychology that contributed to his advance. The agricultural routine in its turn was governed by the rhythm and cycle of Nature's activities, by the sequence of the agricultural seasons with their distribution of sunshine, humidity and rainfall, and the ecologic cycle of soil recuperation and vegetative growth. Not the rutting season of animals or the time when the young are born, as among the shepherds, but the sprouting and falling of leaves, the ripening of crops and fruits, snow and rainfall, became a means of time reckoning of the agriculturists.

Primitive agriculturists in India such as the Khasis of Assam designate the months according to the agricultural operations that are undertaken in each, the month for weeding the ground, the month when cultivators fry the produce of their fields, etc. In Chota Nagpur the tribal peoples reckon spring as the beginning of the New Year inaugurated by the auspicious marriage between Sing Bonga and the Earth, when the latter is resplendent and fragrant with the *mahua* (*Madhuca Indica*) flowers in the forests. The Hopis in the American desert divide the calendar according to the precise time of various agricultural operations which is forecasted by their religious official, the sun watcher, who examines the daily shift in the position of sunrise on the horizon. Dates of the various operations in the fields and of ceremonies also punctuate the horizon calendar of the Pueblos.[3] The Bontoc Igorot, a rice cultivating people, reckon eight seasons, varying from four to seven weeks according to the nature of the agricultural operations in the fields, e.g. seed sowing, seeds planted out, first harvest, etc.[4] In various parts

---

3 See the sketch of native drawing given in C. Daryll Forde, *Habitat, Economy and Society*, p. 227.

4 Sturt, *The Psychology of Time*, p. 32.

of the world vegetation years reckoned from sowing to harvest make up the calendar, and moon months are organized as units. Concrete phases of vegetable and animal life in which the rhythm of man's economic life is harmoniously set are even now of supreme importance in respect of time reckoning. Sturt observes that in modern life we still use such indications and have the general feeling that spring really begins with the cuckoo or the return of the swallow, that winter is breaking when the catkins come out, that the spider's webs, characteristic of November, mean that autumn is well here, and that the song of the robin heralds winter.

Such designations are concrete, and one would expect that many primitive peoples would show not only unwillingness to substitute numbers for the descriptive names of the months but would also express the times of the day according to concrete events in the rhythm of their life in the forest and the field. The Maria Gonds of Bastar designate different times of the day as follows:

1. About 2 or 3 p.m., when the king-crow calls, "Thakurji, Thakurji !" in the forest.
2. 5 a.m., when the yoke is put on the oxen.
3. 7 a.m., when the women go to fetch water.
4. 4 p.m., when flocks of green parrots invade the fields and the women return from the fields.
5. About 7-30 p.m., when the flowers shed their greatest fragrance.

Coincidence of Agricultural and Social Rhythms

Even advanced agricultural peoples who have a regular calendar find it hard to discard the concrete point reckoning of time and indicate days and months with reference to changes in the seasons and weather which recur annually, and to the phase of the moon which, governing as it does the supply of light at night, provides another measure which has been almost universally used from primitive times.[5] In China and India the lunar system is largely used for religious sacrifices and festivals. Thus among the Chinese the offerings to the kitchen god are made on the first and fifteenth day of each month. Pilgrimages to temples and the observance of the vegetarian rituals are also carried out on these days. In India, the new and full moon days, the eleventh day of the moon and the nine nights (*navarātri*) in autumn are especially significant for fasts and festivals and for ceremonies of ancestral worship. But along with the lunar system both the Chinese and Hindus adopt the traditional solar system of seasonal climatic changes for remembering and predicting the sequence of agricultural operations. In fact, it will be more precise to state that both solar and lunar calendars regulate the sequence of work of the Chinese and Indian peasantry. In China the unit of the solar system (*chieh*) is described definitely in terms of climatic, vegetative and biological cycles. Here are some of the names of the *chieh*, beginning of spring; rain water; waking of insects; grain full; gram in the ear; autumn equinox; frost's descent; winter solstice; Great Snow.[6] In India the equinoxes and solstices are well recognized in the calendar for the traditional, agricultural and social activities or, again, all agricultural peoples mark days with reference to marketing which is held periodically twice or thrice a week and sometimes according to the places where the principal markets are held in the region. Throughout the central parts of Africa there are numerous market places where neighbouring communities meet regularly to exchange their produce. Usually every fourth day is a market day, observed with the cessation of ordinary occupations. With the regular market is inseparably connected

---

5 See the article on Calendar in *Encyclopaedia of Religion and Ethics*.

6 Hsiao-Tung Fei, *Peasant Life in China*, chapter. IX.

the market week, the length of which varies from three to ten days.[7] Not merely in Africa but also in Asia it is the market days which come in regular sequence that punctuate the calendar of the agricultural peoples. In fact, throughout the world among the agriculturists the periodicity of agricultural life and operations is used as the standard for time reckoning, governing the rhythm of their fasts and festivals, marriages and pilgrimages. The earlier form of the world's present calendar was introduced from Egypt where, according to the historian Meyer, the new year was fixed by the coincidence of the spring overflow of the Nile and the heliacal rising of the star Sirius. The annual inundation of the Nile was the most striking natural phenomenon associated with the origins of cultivation, and it is no wonder that this was used for the fixation of the 365-day calendar in lower Egypt as early as 4241 BCE. It appears that at first the lunar calendar was invented which was later on succeeded by the solar or sothic calendar. Both Elliot Smith and Perry suggest that kingship and priesthood in early Egypt originated in the control of observation connected with the calendar and the maintenance of the irrigation system. In other climatic zones it was the sequence of the seasons and seasonal points governing the commencement of agricultural operations and their end which measured the year that was in reality the vegetation "year", often left incomplete, the idle or vacant interval being passed over without counting. "Fairly common", observes Nilsson,[8]

> are New Year festivals at sowing and especially harvest times; in the far north, winter during which labour rests is the time of festivals, hence the popularity of yule tide; and half Africa assembles to dance on the nights of full moon.

The round of seasonal rites, ceremonies, and festivals in rural society is fixed according to the position of the sun in the

---

7 Webster, *Rest Days*.

8 See Nilsson, *Primitive Time Reckoning*.

meridian, the phase of the moon and the sequence of the vegetative or agricultural cycle. In fact, the agricultural, social and religious rhythms coincide in peasant societies as the common source of differentiation of time intervals. Fasts are usually associated with the period of anxious expectancy for the rainfall during the course of agricultural operations, and festivities with the maturation and harvesting of crops. The big fairs and pilgrimages which draw thousands of persons from different tracts, whether in the mountains or in the plains, are also eternally fixed from time immemorial, linked with the procession of the stars. Thus the time systems of different peoples are adapted to the rhythm of their economic and social activities, which they seek to synchronize and co-ordinate. Durkheim observes that a calendar expresses the rhythm of collective activities, while at the same time its function is to assure their regularity.[9] Sorokin and Merton also have pointed out that systems of time reckoning arise from the round of group life that are largely determined by the routine of religious activity and the occupational order of the day and are perpetuated by the need for social co-ordination. These are essentially a product of social interaction.[10]

Time is an inevitable element in the pattern of social behaviour. All social contacts involve co-ordination of time. Since a given amount of time has to be distributed by a large number of participating individuals between work, leisure and social relationships, it is the rigidities of time distribution which limit the tempo and interval of social contacts and govern the habits of work and rest of the people. The system of time reckoning sets the pattern for the personality and the collective social activities, leisure and recreations of the people. In rural

9 *Elementary Forms of Religious Life*, p. 11.

10 "Social Time", *American Journal of Sociology*, March, 1937; Cottrell, "Of Time and the Railroader", *American Sociological Review*, April, 1939.

India, not merely the round of workdays but also rest days, market days, holidays and days of religious celebrations follow the routine of agriculture.[11] Aphorisms and proverbs are current in the country indicating the schedule of farming operations, crop by crop and week by week, according to the variations of climate and weather, and in this schedule agricultural experience has mingled with the social rhythm of popular religion and recreation. The little red almanac in India also lays down the auspicious and forbidden days for sowing, ploughing and harvesting, for journeying, for wearing new apparel, for making repairs in the house, and even for eating the vegetables and fruits of the season. It is remarkable that the Chinese peasantry have a similar little red booklet in which each day has a column indicating those things which are "lucky" or "unlucky", and certain recurrent natural phenomena such as flood, blossoming of plants and beginning of thunder. As in India this almanac (whose publication is now prohibited by the Chinese government) is consulted for arranging various agricultural operations and personal and social affairs. A comparison of the Chinese and Hindu timetable of agricultural operations and social and religious activities shows how religious festivals, ancestral sacrifices and family ceremonies follow the harvesting of the major crops of the region, and visits, weddings and other distractions are avoided as far as possible in the busiest agricultural seasons. In rural society not merely are the workdays sanctioned by religion and custom in which idleness is censured, but the intervening weeks and even months of rest from fieldwork are also cherished since the peasant knows that without these breaks he cannot show his marvellous achievement. These must wait for nature's own cycles of climate, soil and vegetation. In these idle weeks or months of agriculture men show an indifference to the passage

---

[11] *Man and His Habitation*, pp. 132-33.

of time which is not met with in other seasons. The peasant's tempo is largely governed by the slow maturation of crops in his field, and of animals in his cattleyard, and by the slow movement of the animals as they draw his plough in the field and drive his cart from the village to the nearest market. The slow tempo of Nature's processes and the flexibility of human time distribution which it implies also give abundant opportunities of the festal dance and rhythmical movement of labour, of collective leisure and communal revel elicited by the deep lying emotions of toil and feasting, love and religion, which tend to humanize and socialize the rural dweller. The latter, therefore, can enjoy leisure or endure idleness, whether in the night or midday, in midsummer or winter, according to climate, in a manner impossible for the city dweller. It is the peasant's leisure and idle time, and his moderate speed of living which govern his characteristic mental attitudes, his deep religiosity, piety, sensitiveness to Nature and deep poise.

The Imperatives of Mechanical Time and Rhythm

The social and economic rhythm of urban industrial society is far different. In industrial society the occupational order, day by day, has nothing to do with the phenomena of Nature; it is largely governed by the speed of the machine system whose rhythm does not follow the rhythm of life. The vast, intricate and elaborate division of labour, spatially distributed in both space and time, which characterizes industrialism, demands a meticulous co-ordination of activities according to anticipated and scheduled time intervals, and imposes upon the people closer and closer limits of mechanical time reckoned in seconds and split seconds. Even the least delay or deviation from the scheduled time throws the system of transportation and technology out of gear, and may lead to general misunderstanding and even accident and disaster. Thus people's work and movement, leisure and social contacts are governed not by the rhythm of man's organic impulses and needs, but by that of mechanical time as time marches on. In industrial society mechanical time that differentiates the intervals of work, food, recreation and rest, becomes second Nature; the acceleration of the tempo is accepted as the corner-stone of progress for a million horse power civilization supported on the wheels of the machine. Lewis Mumford observes:

> Human pregnancy still lasted nine months but the tempo of almost everything was speeded, the span was contracted and the limits were arbitrarily clipped, not in terms of the function and activity, but in terms of a mechanical system of time accountancy. Mechanical periodicity took the place of organic and functional periodicity in every department of life where the usurpation was possible.[12]

The alteration of the tempo from organic to the mechanical period implies everywhere its acceleration since timesaving in the machine system is a part of labour saving, and acquires a pecuniary significance; time like a capital good being accumulated, saved and reinvested in the process of industrial production.

The synchronization of social activities in different fields goes with acceleration of the tempo, and this makes industrial society adopt for its temporal frame of reference mechanical and astronomical time, which is uniform, homogeneous and divisible into minute fractions. It is the dial of the clock that not only regulates the vast quick and variegated contacts, activities and movements of fluid masses of men, but also often measures them in money tokens in industrial civilization. Newtonian time becomes socially imperative with industrial progress.

---

12 *Technics and Civilisation*, p. 198.

Punctuality as a Social Habit

Industrialization, to be sure, implies the co-ordination of a vast, complex series of activities ranging over an increasingly larger area and number of social fields. Man's multidimensional social space expands continuously. This calls for a meticulously divisible and uniform astronomical time system which synchronizes and orients the social functions of different and distant groups in the Great Society. As mobility increases and with this the tempo of social functions and economic transactions no virtue is prized more in industrial civilization than punctuality. Georg Simmel observes that

> the conditions of the large cities are such and the relationships of the typical urban resident so manifold and so complicated, and above all so interwoven into an organism of so many through the agglomeration of so many persons with such differentiated interests, that the whole would breakdown into an inextricable chaos without the most exact punctuality in promises and performances, without an unambiguity in appointments and agreements, similar to that which is mediated externally through the general diffusion of watches.

It is of course true that industrial communities vary in their degrees of mobility, tempo and institutionalized punctuality. Many industrial cities in the world are yet ruled by the agricultural routine which permits an elastic timetable and leisurely disengagement at intervals, and punctuality is not entrenched as a social habit. But as mobility and tempo increase with the dominance of machine technology the individual has to modify his habits to keep pace with the fast tempo maintained within the community, and to conform to its rigid time schedule. The latter exercises its social hegemony in the large city everywhere through the ubiquitous clock, the whistle of the factory, the operation of the train, bus, tube and tram on accurate time schedules and the traffic signal on the road. It is man's economic status which defines his freedom of activity within the limits of the rigid timetable of the city, which holds together and directs the flowing myriads from the distant villages that come to it for work and business of a thousand sort.

A large number of local trains carrying daily passengers to Calcutta arrive at Howrah and Sealdah stations from 8 to 11 a.m. The petty clerks in the offices and establishments in Calcutta arrive earliest, and the later the arrival of the train the higher is the economic status of its daily passengers, who have to adjust their hours of meal and rest accordingly. Similarly, Anderson and Lindeman observe:

> If the train which will land the worker at his place of business leaves at 8.45, he must be at the station on the minute even though he runs with breakfast uneaten, for the next train is scheduled to meet the requirements of a group of a different economic status. Being founded upon mechanisms, the transportation system is unelastic, and its users must make adjustments to its rigidities.

The transportation system that operates in urban–industrial communities at tremendously high speed and with meticulous punctuality forms the backbone of industrialism. It brings passengers and goods from thousands of miles to the towns, factories and establishments exactly according to the scheduled time, while the speed of traffic is also accelerated markedly all over the world. It is the train timings which govern the tempo of industrial operations and the intervals of most social contracts in modern urban–industrial life. As a matter of fact the introduction of the train and the steamer with their scheduled timings is the first step of education in precision and punctuality in rural society. Such change of habits is as much necessary for the urban individual's survival as for the efficiency of the mechanized urban–industrial society. The rural dweller who remains unadjusted to the tempo of the urban environment is a misfit. He is a danger both to himself and to the community, for the lapse of a single individual may throw the entire mechanized system of the city out of gear. Modern industrial society lays down, therefore, a number of laws and regulations to check the aberrant and unpunctual individual, whose behaviour that was stereotyped in the rural milieu is now a menace to the social wheel.

Effects of Machine and Speed upon Human Body and Mind

Can mobility and tempo be increased infinitely? Different industrial societies show different rates of mobility. Mobility is a process which still remains incomplete in modern industrial society. It is yet in progress. The appropriate measure of its progress is the tempo which is being continuously accelerated. Vast masses of men move in quick tempo, neither spasmodically nor chaotically; rather the movements of different groups and regions in a highly differentiated society fit into one another harmoniously. The punctuality, computability and precision which the complicated and expanded nature of modern industrial society forces upon the people reduce their life largely to a meticulously accurate and unelastic routine process. In such a mechanical routine the fast tempos of functions in the different parts of society slide into one another harmoniously on the basis of time. This makes man's contacts transitory, fractional and impersonal, even measurable in terms of time. The agriculturist has his regular hours but there is hardly any fixity about these. In the monsoon season in East Asia he toils in the field from early dawn to nightfall. Sudden outbursts of rain or a few weeks of drought change the timetable of everybody connected with agriculture. In industrial society no worker is expected to work beyond the six or eight hour day, and if he does work he gets "overtime". Not merely, the hours of work but also those of food, travel, recreation and rest are precisely determined according to the rigid requirements of the urban schedule. The clock, the calendar and the timetable regulate, punctualize and quantitatively evaluate most of the organized activities of a highly mechanized civilization. The results are both the acceleration of the tempo of human life and functions that must make adjustments to the rigidities of a mechanical system, on the one hand, and the dominance of pecuniary values, which have combined to make human interaction largely ecological, i.e. impersonal, anonymous and calculating, on the other. To quote Simmel again:

> these also colour the content of life and favour the exclusion of those irrational, instinctive, sovereign traits and impulses, which want to determine the form of life from within rather than to receive it from an external source as a general schematically precise form.

Since mobility and tempo are profoundly transforming man's ecological, economic and social relations, and through these the family and other primary groups, the economic organization and the state, it is not easy to see to what extent the norms of mobility that, as we have seen, emerge in the successive levels of social accommodation will be modified in response to the needs of human nature or man's social habits and patterns of group relations and individual behaviour transformed in consonance with these norms. Can the mechanical rhythm supersede with impunity the rhythm of life and growth? Can the tempo be quickened infinitely without injury to man, his contacts, relations and values?

It is remarkable that man's tolerance of speed has greatly extended even within living memory. Sir Josiah Stamp refers in this connection to the Greevey Papers where it is recorded that the Knowsley party accomplished 23 miles per hour on the railway and recorded it as,

> frightful — impossible to divest yourself of the notion of instant death — it gave me a headache which has not left

> me yet — some damnable thing must come of it. I am glad to have seen this miracle, but quite satisfied with my first achievement being my last.

In the British Association meeting for 1836, an address on "Railway speeds" prophesied that some day 50 miles an hour might be possible. Forty years ago we may remember that a cyclist doing 15 to 18 miles an hour was a "scorcher" and a public danger. Twentyfive years ago, 30 miles an hour in motoring was an almost unhealthy and hardly bearable pace. Today the fifties and sixties are easily borne, both by passengers and onlookers. Aeroplane speeds are differently judged, but at any rate present an extension of the tolerance.[13] In industrialized society the tempo is adjusted to the rhythm of the impersonal machine and complicated technology, and its acceleration accepted as a new imperative for industry and progress. There is, however, a growing recognition that the chaining of the human worker to the swiftly revolving factory wheels and the excessive tempo are overtaxing his physique and mental endurance and alertness, resulting in an increase of degenerative wear and tear, accidents and occupational mortality. In what measure the tempo of work for the machine tenders should be reduced and hazardous and exacting machines which overstep the limits of reasonable caution and control excluded are, however, by no means clear. Significant in industrial production are the intensive splitting up and specialization of work and the serialization of machines. Thus the relative tempos of the different parts of the machine system are co-ordinated with one another. A reduction of the tempo in one part would involve diminution in all others and decrease in the general rate of production which may imply bad economics in a system of giant, mechanical power production. On the other hand, the issue in which the health, joy and

[13] Josiah Stamp, "The Impact of Science upon Society", *Science*, 1936, p. 237.

creativeness of millions of workers are involved should not be decided by a narrow technicism. Stuart Chase has stressed the tendency in technology for the machine to do the drudgery that was once performed by human hands.[14] The application of this principle to the different branches of mass standardized production is by no means definite and clean cut. But that repetitive work in machine technology reduces the mental level of workers has now been proved by psychological investigations. Case studies of industrial workers, compelled to do unskilled and uncreative labour, show that morons often welcome repetitive industrial tasks, but that the intelligent workmen especially feel dissatisfied and frustrated and are keyed to the emotional and intellectual level of morons.[15] No doubt, machine and speed in many branches of production and departments of life have proved beyond the capacity of man and his social habits to adopt, and this has increased the incidence of nervous instability and breakdowns and of social disintegration. To decrease the speed of the machine system and industrial organization, and to subordinate the machine to human elements are the major insistent problems of modern technology.

Disintegration of the Rhythm of Life

Perhaps the most significant success in mass standardized production has been obtained in automobile manufacturing which by about 1910 reached a high level of mechanical efficiency through the adoption of a series of inventions in the USA. At the same time the continuous flow-production method, applied by means of conveyors, which was introduced by Henry Ford in 1908, and the adoption of Taylor's system of scientific management, have completely disintegrated the old rhythm of life of the workers. The mass regimentation of

14 Chase, *Man and Machines*.

15 Elliott and Merill, *Social Disorganisation*, p. 269.

the behaviour patterns of the workers, brought into conformity with the rhythm of the machine, has often resulted in unbeatable mental and physical strain with the loss of many essential values. This was the natural consequence of unremittent and uniform production on a gigantic scale which was aided by serialization of the machines, use of conveyors and development of the perfect interchangeability of parts in the manufacture of automobiles. Alice Davis in a study of development of "technicways", a phrase used by Odum with reference to the ways of human adjustment to technology, points out that the year 1918 marks the point of inflection on a logistic curve locating the origin of technicways of automobile patent inventions and standardization of automobile parts.[16] Since then there has been a decline of innovations. Similarly, the points of inflection on the logistic curve fitted into the data of farm motorization also fall in 1918, which marks the start of the steady declining trend in the number of horses and mules. For the technicways of motorization in five series of data covering material and social invention, consumer use and displacement of the folkways, she finds the point of inflection located within the narrow limits of the postwar period 1918 to 1921. Her conclusion is significant in this connection:

> The decline of the patent rate, which some sociologists regard as a symptom of failing inventive capacity in the race, may prove under our assumption to be a hopeful sign that inventive effort is already being channelled off from industrial invention to the field of constructive social invention, designed to restore values and establish the rhythm of human growth in an artificial civilization.

It is possible that a satisfying rhythm of life of the workers cannot be obtained in many cases without restricting the scope

---

[16] "Technicways in American Civilisation", *Social Forces*, March, 1940.

of a feverish colossal machine system and slowing down the feverish tempo of work. Much may also be expected from the distribution of electricity to little towns, villages and homes, and the use of prime movers, light metals and precious elements which may make it increasingly possible to fabricate small things in small habitations. Many engineers and technicians, indeed, believe that we need not accept the accelerated tempo of the new technicways of modern industrial civilization, which has been conditioned by past technical methods, as a settled fact. There is a greater possibility of small rural–industrial habitations contributing a larger and larger quota to the total industrial production, while where mass standardized production is inevitable, mechanical inventions may be concentrated towards re-establishing the rhythm of human life and growth in the field of industry.

We have found the biologic basis of mobility in the heterogeneity of its population and its characteristic age and sex composition. The fluid immigrant population of a large city in which middle aged or adult males or females predominate keeps up the feverish tempo of mechanized industrial society. It is they who are physically and psychically better fitted to keep pace with the fast movement in the city with the minimum of energy. Social pathological features are largely the result of the peculiar age and sex structure of urban populations. Much of the unstability and deviations in the social life of the urban milieu are due to the predominance of a single sex. The proportion of men to women is governed by economic opportunities in different regions and habitations. In the hybrid industrial centres of the Orient, which may be described as the "maginal" or "liminal" habitations, the proportion of females to males is exceedingly small. Calcutta, for instance, has only 469 females per 1000 males. An average industrial town in Bengal has only 526 females, an average country town 787 females per 1000 males (Census data of 1941). In the Western countries it is only coal, iron, railway, steel or timber cities and towns which attract men for heavy work and show a preponderance of the male population, with a proportionately larger percentage in the adult age group. Most cities and towns in Europe and America show an unusually high percentage of women. The "men's cities" show great laxity of social controls, drunkenness, lawlessness, gambling, vice and prostitution. Accompanying these social deviations are an excessive mobility of the workers who move from tenement to tenement, and from job to job, and whose anonymity easily provides an escape from traditional social disciplinary forces and institutions. Wherever women instead of men preponderate in numbers, the effects are not dissimilar. Sorokin and Zimmerman in their studies of rural–urban migrations have referred to the "feminization" of cities. The latter increases the per capita incomes, decreases the proportions of dependent persons per 100 wage earners, adds to the mobility and life of the cities, reduces marriage, increases vice and prostitution, and gives cities the appearance of greater vitality than they really possess.[17]

While such sociological consequences are directly the outcome of the extension of industry as it segregates the sexes in man's or woman's towns, it is impossible to separate industry and city with reference to the biological consequences: increase of mortality, especially infant mortality among the wage earning classes, increase of incidence of tuberculosis and heart diseases, occupational and nervous diseases and suicide among the adults and a higher mortality rate than in rural society. Some observations indicate that modern industrial society has now become dysgenically

---

[17] *Principles of Rural-Urban Sociology*, p. 557.

selective, tending to breed a biologic type, which in becoming adjusted to industry is as socially abnormal in this adjustment as are the criminal and migratory non-workers. The rejection of recruits from industrial areas by Army examiners during the last war in the USA was a particular eyeopener.

The Need of a Planned Technology

Here, again, the remedy lies in planned city, industry, and technology: ecological planning and redistribution of industry and population in the new power age which would follow the machine age, and institutional change in respect of owning and operating giant machinery, natural resources and power resources, which would make industry reflect the needs of the entire nation rather than of particular economic groups or classes. All such trends as the dispersion of industry from the great city into its adjacent suburban peripheries, into satellite cities and satellite areas, the co-ordination between urban and regional planning, and restoration of the equilibrium between agriculture and industry demand an alliance between technology and industrial distribution and planning, without which the biological and social deterioration of the urbanized peoples of the modern world cannot be counteracted. Excessive industrialization and urban concentration, with their associated factors of mobility and stress of personal scale of living and expenditure and status, are also responsible for the spread of family limitation through contraception. The disparity between personal values and the values of perpetuation of the race and culture which threatens Western urban communities with decay also calls for a revolutionary transformation of industrialism which has had such profound deleterious effects upon the institution of the family in respect of its economic status, its unstability and its small size. Sociologists, however, seem to depend more upon new family mores for the rehabilitation of the urban family which may make up for the loss of its economic and social bonds by affection or by a new civic sense. The technics of industry can, however, accomplish more in this regard than the psychology of personality. It would, on the whole, be easier to check family disorganization through the replanning of the city and the region which may provide more adequate opportunities of family life in a congenial and wholesome environment. More than ethics and religion we have to depend upon a planned ecology, technology and engineering for the integration of the family. It is the industrial engineer and city planner who can replan the artificialized and mechanized compact habitation of which the beehive city of competitive and capitalistic industrialism is the extreme type. On the cramped and uncongenial physical base in the beehive city neither the family nor any other primary groups so essential for building up the stable behaviour patterns of individuals can thrive. Technology has been the major factor in the growth of the beehive city with its slums and tenements, its family disorganization and criminal behaviour patterns; and it is to a new technology with its ecological redistribution of men, utilities and institutions we have to look for new social habits, organizations and ethics. In this dynamic technological age social science should give a more adequate consideration to the social effects of machines and techniques so that the present lag between mechanical change and change in social habits and institutions may not only be avoided, but the discovery of inventions directed towards building up a better society and a higher scale of values which overreach the values of mere mechanical and technical efficiency.

The diminution of the machine system, the reduction of mobility and tempo of life, and the breaking up of the large city into great numbers of rural–industrial habitations which is stimulated by the spread of the network of electricity and motor transport, by the diversity of prime movers, by the employment of light metals and precious elements, and by the use of modern electronic media are thus seen to be in accord with a new scale of human values which redefines industrial and technological efficiency in terms of health, happiness and serenity of life. Excessive mobility and excessive tempo show the irresponsibility and extravagance of the colossal machine system; an excessively big city also oversteps the dimension necessary to keep alive those subtle and deep joys and intimate personal loyalties that living in communities of small size can inspire. As necessary as the slowing of tempo in the machine system is the regulation of the size of a town or city on the basis of both social coherence and industrial efficiency. The city of the future cannot be permitted to overstep a certain density of population and a certain size in the interests of social efficiency and collective participation of the citizens in its functions and activities.

Technological Idleness

There is another aspect of machine technology which has a tremendous psychological and sociological significance. In rural society work is intermittent and less strenuous and the tempo is slow, but there is some task, some job for each rural dweller which absorbs his energies and interests. Slack seasons in agriculture, when work in the field is periodically reduced, are filled up by subsidiary employment in cottage handicrafts and industries, by a round of marriages and family visits or by collective festivals, plays, pageants and recreations. There are, of course, the cycles of heavy rainfall and drought which dislocate the agricultural routine and cause widespread unemployment and famine. But the peasant builds up not merely his economic defences of irrigation and appropriate agricultural practice, but also adaptive social habits against the normally enforced idle time and the catastrophes of famine and unemployment. The machine system in modern industrial society is, however, responsible for unemployment on a scale unprecedented in its magnitude. It is estimated that in the United States alone during the period 1920-31, over 3 million wage earners were displaced in manufacturing industries because of increases in technological and managerial efficiency. In spite of the rapid growth of the physical volume of production there were 841,000 fewer workers employed in 1928 than in 1920. It is true that there is redistribution or shifting of employment but the latter depends largely on new opportunities in industries characterized by an elastic demand, and such opportunities are not always present. This implies that millions of men are permanently removed from industry.

More significant than the economic loss are the demoralization, uncertainty and despair associated with unemployment. Many workers also drift into habits of vagrancy and delinquency. The poignancy of the situation is revealed by the fact that during the depth of the depression in the USA 2 to 3 lakh children, among them many girls wandered homeless over the nation. In industrial society sooner or later the right of every individual to work for securing minimum security becomes a social imperative. The evolution of a highly complex and mechanized society makes it impossible to rely upon the traditional personal ideals of resourcefulness and enterprise as adequate for provision of sustenance and security. Different industrial countries, according to their social and historical conditions, are refashioning their social and economic structure to safeguard regularity of work and income. Some countries, have, indeed, curtailed various economic freedoms that have grown in the wake of the freedom of mobility and competition in the liberal democratic tradition in order to safeguard minimum security and standard of living.

Both with reference to the demand it makes for adjustment of the tempo and mentality of the individual, and for the collective process of maintaining a technologically efficient and continuous flow of production, the machine system has proved too inexorable, and resulted in profound individual maladjustment and disorganization, which offset its marvelous mechanical gains. The remedy lies in fresh inventions which may restore the rhythm of human life and growth in the field of mechanized industry, in a new technology which relocalizes industry and population, and reorients rural–urban employment, and in the transformation of the economic organization so that it may safeguard the standard of living and assure reasonable stability for the mass of the workers. Excessive mobility and tempo at the cost of individual health and poise and of social integration and security have been the outcome of technics. It is technics, again, that will cure the present maladjustment in the sphere of human habits, relations and values and usher in the new society and culture. But this it can do only when sociology yields a more adequate understanding of the relations between technics and human nature and relationships, and discovers new social controls and regulative devices for dealing with the human misfits and maladjustments that arise out of the necessities of quick adaptation in a technological age. Personality is much less flexible than the machine system. We have, therefore, to look more towards changes in technology for reducing the inevitable lag between man's progress in the material sphere and progress in his personal and moral relationships. Science and technics, controlled and manipulated by the minority, have proved heedless of individual and social disorganization. Planned science and technics, guided by a sociology of inventions, may direct these latter for the recovery of human values and the continuance of cultural evolution on the basis of greater mastery over the physical environment and larger and more wholesome and socially directed leisure.

11

Freedom of Social Mobility

The Modern Stratified Class System

MOBILITY as a universal social–ecological process has its physical base in machine technology and improvement of communication and transportation, and its biological base in the heterogeneity of population with an excess of adults in modern towns or cities. The norms of acceleration of tempo, and fluid domestic and social relationship which arise out of mobility in the physical and biological levels of social accommodation need revision in the light of disintegration of human rhythm and values that excessive mobility promotes. Some of the major problems of contemporary civilization have accordingly arisen out of the need of restricting the scope of the machine system, the tempo of life and the size of the city or metropolis so that the physical and technological conditions of the urban speed and mobility might not sweep mankind along the stream of life at a more and more astounding rate. Without a technological readjustment or even revolution, many urban pathological features cannot, indeed, be eliminated.

Mobility has, as we have seen, its characteristic economic basis in the interchangeability of jobs in the machine system which facilitates both horizontal as well as vertical movement of individuals. Classical economists have postulated the efficiency of the individualistic economic system on the basis of freedom of competition and enterprise which assures each man his economic position and status according to his native ability or acquired merit. But Marshall lamented that in England, where the privileges of the special classes were being given up and entrepreneurs of the big industry were coming up from the ranks, more than half of society's productive genius, born in working class homes cannot become manifest due to lack of opportunity. While technology encourages the vertical movement of individuals, property and stratified class system account for a hierarchy of social levels with rich dynasties or oligarchical groups at the top who wield control over the political and social machinery and the proletariat or the have-nots at the bottom with the bourgeoise occupying a social and economic status in between. Industrial insecurity and widespread unemployment aggravate the social injustice of a considerable proportion of the population occupying lower economic and social status than they deserve according to their merit and ability. Apart from the redistribution of wealth, the organization of the national social schemes, unemployment and social security schemes, it is now realized that an industrial democracy should provide "moving-stairs" on the economic system on which the able and energetic can stand and be securely moved up to proper rewards. In the United States, one type that has been suggested as an example of possible institutions, involves coalescing the cry for industrial democracy, the minimum wage principle, the child labour movement and the Federal employment bureaus into a labour law by which the courts might treat labour grievances on an individual basis and guarantee equitable advancement on the basis of social productivity consistent with the employer's own equitable rights, a sort of judicial civil service commission.

> Such an advancement of equitable jurisdiction would bring about industrial democracy without breaking down individual dignity or sovereignty or hazarding the system of American individualism.[1]

---

[1] McCutchen, "Technique for Democracy, and Vocational →

Dangers to Democracy and Culture

Contemporary industrial society will break down in a series of social upheavals unless it, in Cooley's pregnant phrase, socializes and equalizes the opportunity for opportunity. In rural society in the West freedom of competition and mobility mean freedom of choice and the vertical movement of individuals according to ability as measured in terms of social productivity. In urban industrial society as the social structure has become more complex and there are greater specialization and gains of specialization, opportunity must receive corresponding stress. In its absence the vaunted freedom of competition of Anglo-Saxon individualism becomes a waste and causes social injustice. Even in a political democracy great inequalities of power and status have accrued due to the different utilization of equal rights, and this has now tended to become hereditary. Rich industrial entrepreneurs and financial magnats can now accumulate vast fortunes which they transmit to posterity to whom they bequeath not merely economic power but also some control over the political machinery which they utilize for increasing the gulf between the propertied and the propertyless. A jobless and propertyless worker cannot effectively exercise his rights of citizenship in a democracy. With insecurity and unstability there develops a conspicuous difference of standards of living, interests and attitudes between different social groups. As they live in different social worlds far removed from one another the democratic process ceases to inspire, and the symbols of democracy themselves become shields for exploitation. The symbols were created and expressed by the mobile, urban intelligentsia in the liberal society of Europe after the French Revolution. For several decades as a sprinkling among the small peasants, artisans, rentiers and traders in Europe rose

→ Mobility in Economic States", *Journal of Social Philosophy*, July 1940, p. 342.

to higher social status and cultural leadership and rubbed shoulders with the scions of noble families or those of the higher officialdom and the liberal professions. Such mobility overcame older class prejudices and reacted very favourably on the intellectual and cultural life of the nation as a whole. But now there is a glut of intellectuals, which, as Mannheim aptly observes, has decreased the value of the intellectuals and of intellectual culture itself.[2] Thus the outlook of contemporary democratic society is being moulded by the disillusion of the elite who have been less fortunate in life, and the latter becomes assimilated to the resentment and despair of the urban industrial proletariat. Too often, however, the socialistic theory has expressed the class interest of the proletarized intellectual workers and not that of the manual workers. The mental workers are a rising privileged class struggling for a place in the sun against the older landlord and entrepreneur classes. Learning was their capital, and political democracy or revolutionary dictatorship, according to circumstances, were the steps in their advance towards power. They won over the manual workers by helping them in their early struggles for better wages and by dangling before them the social ideal of equality, while they would have most of the desirable posts in the administrative organization.[3] The lack of personal security has, indeed, been the greatest hindrance to both intellectual life and culture and harmony in economic and social life.

Contrasted Methods in Democratic and Dictator States

As a matter of fact, the present contrast between the economic structure of democratic and dictator states rests on the latter sacrificing personal rights in many respects for assuring to

2 Mannheim, *Man and Society*, p. 100.

3 This interpretation was put forward by A. Wolski. See Lasswell, *World Polities and Personal Insecurity*, p. 112.

every citizen work, security and a minimum standard of living. In democratic states, in spite of the theory of social and political equality in a mobile and open class system, social aristocracies have emerged, based on wealth and political prestige, and individual justice has been denied when a large section of the population is without work and cannot maintain and safeguard the standard of living. Democracy in the West-European tradition can only be preserved on the threefold basis of (a) industrial security, (b) the provision of economic "moving-stairs" enabling persons to rise into higher social and economic status, and (c) industrial self-government. Many democracies are now coming to recognize the rights to work, to education and to opportunity as the foundations of the cultivation and preservation of many other rights. As against the totalitarian countries the democracies must now safeguard the basic rights which have been obliterated by the former, and a restatement, fuller and more jealously conceived, of the personal rights of individuals might reassert the frontiers beyond which the human person is inviolable, and help to refashion society on liberty, equality, fraternity, reason and law. In the first phase of liberal and democratic society the principles of individualism and freedom of competition proclaimed equality for all, but could not guarantee either security or free competition for the majority of the population. The totalitarian countries now establish the racial superiority myth engendering in the masses the sense of being an elite or privileged group without the counteracting responsibility for individual achievement. No doubt the state must guarantee protection to every citizen of his job and minimum standard of living, but it should not arrogate the criterion of achievement and be just a principle of social selection which underlay the growth of democracy itself. Accordingly the principle of personal security rather than the principle of freedom should receive greater stress in the liberal method of organization without abandoning the principle of achievement or selection in the struggle of individuals and groups for position and power, if contemporary society may not degenerate into totalitarianism. Modern industrial system, as it has increased the opportunities of individuals, has aggravated both the hazards of life and the risks of failures. The scheme of political and economic rights has, therefore, to be redrawn in order to safeguard the principles of social mobility and selection. Thus the formulation of the rights to physical care, to work, to minimum wages and standard of living, to education, leisure and recreation is necessary to correct the natural inequality of man and safeguard social mobility and selection, on the one hand, and to promote a collective sharing of the opportunities and hazards of the industrial system on the other.

Contrasted Means of Social Control in the Primary and Secondary Group Environment

We have seen that mobility fosters and is fostered by secondary groups and relationships. In the highly mechanized, mobile and contractual life of modern industrial society, secondary groups have become most numerous and complex, as these have also become unstable and lax in control. Industrial society, therefore, has brought into marked prominence the problem of social control. In rural society dominated by primary groups and personal contacts, social control is effective, exercised by social expectancy with its reward of approbation and penalty of ostracism and local gossip. In secondary groups, man's contacts have become impersonal, and he has less regard for what his fellowmen think about him, while at the same time not merely are there vast differences of behaviour patterns of individuals coming from different social backgrounds but few also have opportunities to scrutinize them in the moving, motley crowd. Thus the Great Society depends less on social censure or approbation and more on formal laws which are multiplying, and yet these fail to regulate anti-social action in the secondary group environment of the modern world.

The morality developed in the family, neighbourhood groups and rural community has now proved inadequate for a regime of vast massive and invisible organizations, introducing what Dewey has called "a new social age", "a new age of human relationships". In the primary groups, man's behaviour patterns are rigidly controlled by praise or dispraise and by clearcut standards understood and participated in by everybody; on the basis of these latter approbation or ridicule, public esteem or humiliation, going to the limit of social ostracism, are meted out impartially after search and scrutiny which local gossip represents. In the vast invisible secondary associations, publicity takes the place of gossip, local opinion and social expectation in influencing behaviour and in bringing it in conformity with social attitudes. Powerful industrial and financial groups, politicians, men in the different professions, whom primary group gossip cannot reach conform to the standards of group in order to avoid exposure and publicity. Nepotism, bribery, corruption, the misuse of public office and unconscionable methods in the professions thrive in the secrecies of coteries and cliques, and are destroyed by the rays of relentless publicity. In the village or the small town, gossip ruins the life and career of a person who might have been a first offender or has extenuating circumstances to condone his offence. Similarly, publicity in newspapers may do a great wrong to administrators and statesmen through insiduous and false suggestion, and even stimulate divorce, suicide and crime against property through the flaunting of sensational news about sex and crime. It is essential that those who control the dissemination of news should themselves be guided by unimpeachable motives and social objectives in order that publicity may be a constructive social control device in the modern world of invisible group relations and organizations. In very few countries the newspaper profession, however, has risen to the expected standards of social responsibility.

In the primary groups, bonds of kinship loyalty and personal affection have been social binders. The king, the territorial chief, the feudal landlord or the village elder ruled man's social etiquette and conduct and such rule was established and consolidated by both example and precept which were accessible to rural society. The ethics of Confucius and the code of Manu, simple direct and admonitory, are intended for the prince and the peasant whom the elders can meet face-to-face, and over whom the ancestral spirits of the village graveyard and family homestead still exercise their silent invisible control. In the modern world of invisible groups their place is taken by the editor, writer, preacher, teacher and politician who use the press, the pulpit and the platform for the control and manipulation of opinions and attitudes of people. Vast masses of men who have obtained a release from primary group controls are today volatile in their opinions, and are full of whims and caprices. Behaviour patterns can be made uniform, and the people can be unified and co-ordinated only by the subtle lure and illusive technique of propaganda. As Lasswell observes:

> Propaganda is a reflex to the immensity, the rationality and wilfulness of the modern world. It is the new dynamic of society, for power is subdivided and diffused, and more can be won by illusion than by coercion. If the mass will be free of chains of iron, it must accept its chains of silver. If it will not love, honour and obey, it must not expect to escape seduction.[4]

The more powerful the implements of mass impression and suggestion, the greater is the social responsibility of the agencies which use and control them. In the dictator countries,

---

[4] *Propaganda Technique in the World War.*

however, such agencies are now used to protect the interests of the dictators or their political party and their cause, and the press, the newspaper and the radio are rigidly censored in the presentation of both opinions and news. In democratic countries where there is greater freedom of expression of opinion, the newspaper and the radio have proved powerful weapons of democratic control and the moulding of governmental policy by popular sentiment.

Full of passions, whims and caprices, the individual of the Great Society is bombarded by conflicting mass suggestions and pressures which, though they may help him to make decisions this way or that, often keeps him struggling between a choice of values, and even makes him impervious to a sense of values itself. The problem of the modern mobile, anonymous world of the city and the nation is to restore and re-invigorate the evaluation process, characteristic of man's primary group relations and experience. Herein lies the crux of the problem of bridging the present gulf between man's technology and economic organization and his moral and personal relations.

The Need of Revaluation and of a New Ethical Personality

How can contemporary industrial society recover mankind's ancient and essential ordering of values or the subordination of instrumental to intrinsic values, and of economic to moral and cultural values? In rural society, the definitions of the social situation are simple and participated in by all individuals securely stabilized in the primary groups which evolve common integrated behaviour patterns and schemes of values. Society's and individual's scale of values coincide in the village. The entire scheme of life and goals of the individual fit into the moral standard of the community, which brooks neither lapse nor overreaching by the individual. Finally, each individual in the small social space himself participates in the group opinion, law, cultural motif and gossip which mould individual behaviour and value patterns to a uniform model. Individuals living in a homogeneous social world and participating in similar experience have, indeed, very few value problems of their own to solve. Their social attitudes and moral standards are fashioned in a common mould by the culture pattern which serves as an excellent nursery and school for human nature. Nor do we find in rural society the ends and means far removed from one another as machine technology and division of labour have accomplished in modern industrial society. Specialization of jobs and tasks and proliferation of occupations in modern industrial society not merely contribute to remove the means farther and farther from the ends, but also leads to the formation and supremacy of man's secondary groups and associations which are the means of realization of other values, and which are inferior to intrinsic values. The latter are ends in themselves and are expressed by man's primary and intimate groups.

In an age in which secondary groups and associations will become more numerous and complex, and instrumental values will be largely sought, the necessity of maintaining the order of superiority of intrinsic to instrumental values, and of cultural and personal, intellectual and aesthetic to economic values is imperative both for personality integration and social order. In several countries, laws have been passed regulating the preference of, say, aesthetic to economic values, e.g. the forbidding of ugly looking structures and vulgar advertisements, and of social and moral to economic values as the entire scheme of legislation in respect of minimum wages, regulation of hours of work and of leave with pay, housing, social security and the establishment of farm ownership. Much of modern legislation is, indeed, a guidance to the vacillating individual of the secondary group environment to choose the appropriate values. But the multiplication of formal laws cannot offer an adequate solution. Diverse and conflicting norms and values characterize the present social situation. The individual receives countless suggestions from sources visible and invisible. He is not presented with readymade alternatives in which values arrange themselves in a hierarchy to be picked out by his judgement; often the values and ends underlying a social situation have to be discovered and old values weighed in the new setting. He has to define anew the "good", the "just", the "social" and the "human" through intelligent and precise analysis and rational deliberation of the concrete situation. The age of instrumental values, of the secondary group environment and of new and relatively impersonal and mechanical relationships and modes of combined human behaviour today calls for a new ethical personality. No magic solution of an essentially ethical issue for the individual is ready at hand. To cast aside a few old values, to accept some new ones and to fashion a new ordering or hierarchy of values is a much more difficult and hazardous task than to conform to a single set of values in the static rural society.

Old Primary Group Mores as Misfits

This can be well illustrated by a consideration of the conflict of values that every individual in the modern world, which is fast being industrialized and urbanized faces in respect of the family, economic life, social relations and religion. The family ideal or rural society as expressed in the aphorism, "Multiply and replenish the earth", is entirely out of place in the social world of today where the individual treats marriage more as an individual affair intended to promote romantic love and happiness and less as a social obligation for the transmission of the heritage of the race and culture. While his economic struggle and insecurity reduce for him the delights in family life, birth control fosters the desire for maintaining or improving the scale of living through celebacy or spinsterhood and reduction of the size of the family. The usual solution of population pressure in China and India is abortion or infanticide. In family groups which are imprisoned in 5-10 acre holdings the birth of children implies the sub-division of the holding, and consequently poverty and crime. Girls especially are unwelcome in the social system. Only in 131 families or 37 per cent of the total investigated by Hsiao Tung Fei are girls under sixteen, and in only fourteen families is there more than one girl.[5] Infanticide is less prevalent in India than in China, but abortion is widespread. In both China and India as well as in the industrial West, the rural family norm has broken down due to economic pressure. But while in the East the richer peasantry are proud of their numerous progeny which is regarded as a sign of their wealth and status, in the West the desire for posterity has largely dwindled among the upper classes. The family ideal of the future must cherish the obligation to society rendered by the bearing and raising of children by an ethical family, but this has by no means gained acceptance from the majority of the population, which sacrifices children to the maintenance of status and standard of living.

Rural society everywhere prizes work as a virtue and regards leisure and amusement as evil. It accepts the axiom, "The labourer is worthy of his meat." In a simple economic community where division of labour has not developed far enough, man's individual capacity for work can be measured and appraised — what is the yield of his acre of wheat land, or the production of the looms in his cottage. The specific quota of an individual to the complicated machine system cannot be easily ascertained. While man works at the behest of machinery which is owned and operated invisibly, a series of automatic labour serving devices make the workman a mere

---

[5] *Peasant Life in China*, p. 34.

machine tender and a robot. The conviction gains ground that the individual's economic position and status centre not in work, but in leisure and idleness. Man's standard of living, which is an index of status, is largely measured by the hours the individual spends in recreation and amusement. A new social ideal of the dignity and obligation of work for everybody is, however, emerging, and conspicuous idleness among the rich is condemned.

Rural society lays down the axiom of "Love thy neighbour as thyself" for ethical guidance in respect of all dealings with fellowmen. The ideal of good neighbourliness falls, however, far short of the moral demands of the new age with its invisible social bonds in big associations such as the industrial corporation, the trade union or the political constituency. A good neighbour now may be a bad citizen, and thus the virtues of our complex, secondary group environment must include civic sense, capacity for weighing the pros and cons of a national issue and civic honesty which is proof against nepotism, bribery and corruption. In China the primary group virtues, extolled by Confucius, have not prevented the Chinese from being bad citizens. The Chinese literati, though tender and humane, have often proved worst sinners in respect of the use of public funds or the filling in of government offices from their own clan or brotherhood irrespective of merit. Man's social habits and morality, shaped and selected by his primary group world, are inadequate or inappropriate for the complex, modern world of secondary group relations. The virtues of thrift, homespun producer, neighbourliness and sympathy for kith and kin have lost their old usefulness. The colossal nature of the modern problems of unemployment and destitution as well as man's new insight into the causes of vagrancy, pauperism and crime, which are now regarded as connected more with social and economic maladjustments than with individual aberrations traceable to physical and psychical heredity now make a demand for new ethical values and social idealism. There is a shift of emphasis from charity to philanthropy, from direct individual succour or amelioration to organized and institutional help and guidance to individuals who are physically and socially inadequate or handicapped. Secondary group charity is based on a new technique of social diagnosis, instead of non-discriminative support of the undeserving, on institutional care, treatment and guidance in hospitals, "homes", "colonies" and curative workshops, instead of haphazard aid to the handicapped or the unfortunate, and on a new sense of social justice instead of the old ideal of customarily governed legal justice. Man's new understanding of the defects of his fellowman's mental and social heritage has engendered humanized attitudes towards delinquency and crime which places upon the society its due share of the responsibility and burden of support of the social misfits and failures.

Ethical Demands of the Secondary Group Environment

In the static rural society, man's social ideal centres round the promotion of collective subsistence, and the major virtues and life goals are focused towards the preservation and persistence of the culture pattern expressed in the network of primary groups. The individual's aims are integrated with those of the society as a whole for the major purpose of guaranteeing a collective subsistence for the small and spatially isolated community. In the new urban–industrial age, man's social ideal centres round social security. As individuals are torn apart from their primary groups and change their allegiances to diverse and shifting secondary groups and associations with their conflicting mores, adjustment becomes more difficult, and the penalties of failures graver. Failures are by no means confined merely to the economic plane; social and personal disorganization is also the outcome of the dissimilarity between the primary group ideals and secondary group needs and realities. With wholesale rural exodus which is a means of economic adjustment, rural behaviour patterns and moral standards are discarded as misfits in the urban milieu, but the process sometimes ends in complete demoralization and the individual's breaking off from the restraints of any normal group. Man has, first, to regain his moral and social stability in the urban–industrialized milieu. Secondly, he has to redefine his behaviour and norms in terms of general social welfare in the anonymous world of the city and in the deliberate–contractual secondary group environment, where he should be as much conscious of community surveillance and control as in the primary groups which he has left. Thirdly, in the urban–industrialized milieu man's penalties of failure are as condign as the rewards of his success are alluring. Thus his next and crucial task is the development of a new social idealism in respect of social security and socialization of opportunity for opportunity so that the community as a whole may share both the amenities and hazards of progress.

This ethical demand of the complex, secondary group environment of civilized mankind can be met effectively only by a reorientation of spiritual attitudes. In the primary group environment man has devised a personal religion, and woven the pattern of his spiritual consciousness in terms of the emotionally charged relationships in the family and other primary groups which have become the symbols of worship and communion. He has sought the deity first as totem, animal guardian or tribal ancestor and at a later stage as a friend and a companion, as father and mother and even in the tenderest man–woman relation. It is in this manner that the various intimate and ardent loyalties of the primary group environment have become religiously fashioned and organized. The different primary group relationships, allegiances and symbols that the religious attitude seizes and utilizes for its own purpose has played a significant role in the personality integration and development of sociality. Man's religious symbols have woven through the ages the pattern of social bonds and brought about social integration. Mysticism of the personal type has been an indispensable aid to the social process and the integration and fixation of social values.

Mystical Religion as the Inspiration of Social Idealism

In the present age of indirect human contacts and invisible social relationships, an ethical, socialized type of individualism can be emotionally charged and directed by the mysticism of an impersonal type which will function effectively in the complex changing social situation. A religion which stresses a limited personal idealism cannot adequately protect the individual against his own deviation in the anonymous social world of today. The support of a new social idealism, adequate to promote those adjustments made necessary by our expanded, secondary and anonymous social environment, can come only from a universal, impersonal, acosmic mysticism. Primitive and narrow social control devices of the primary group environment fail in the Great Society. Laws and other external compulsives, again, are inadequate devices of social control for these do not work from within. The inner realization of the individual-in-the-community and of the community-in-the-individual in the anonymous world of the city or over the expanse of a modern nation or over international relations can come from an impersonal, cosmic humanism. This is the core of the mystical consciousness and will make man as solid with the Great Community as he was emotionally and morally firmly knit into the primary groups. Some kind of religious development like this, the significance of which is as yet scarcely recognized in modern society, is necessary for inducing that social idealism which is the modern complement of primitive affective attitudes in the system of social control. Such idealism will no doubt use modern implements of social control like the press, publicity and social work for mitigating the present social distance between the classes, and socializing opportunities for all without which the vast progress in technology and industrial organization will accompany misery and deterioration in man's personal and social relations. Excessive mobility in the urban–industrialized world as it has brought to light unheard of possibilities of man's capacity and plasticity and differences of individual personality coexists today with acute social cleavage and adoption of goals of life by considerable sections of population entirely outside of the social code. This social distance now corrodes the values and virtues of the previous social age of primary groups and direct relations. Freedom of social mobility and economic security for all can alone abridge social distance, and guarantee the sharing of the benefits of modern science and technology by the entire community. Such sharing cannot follow from a scientific diagnosis of social conditions or a mere ideology. It awaits a new form of social idealism, directed and inspired by a non-theistic, acosmic mysticism which may find in man's social relations in the vast, secondary associations the seats of the ultimate values that will demand from him the same continuous and ardent devotion and sacrifice for the invisible fellowman of the modern city, nation or super-state as he has shown at the earlier social stage within the bounds of his family, kindred and the rural community. Without this social idealism motivated by religion the gap between man's evolution of his tools and organization and that of his personal and social relations cannot be reduced, and his profound lack of adaptation to his secondary group environment will bring about moral chaos and undermine his cultural heritage.

12

Ecological and Cultural Patterns of Social Organization

The Contrast between Ecological and Cultural Behaviour

MAN'S ecological reaction, taking place as it does indirectly and externally through the limited factors of the environment, is a fractional and impersonal reaction. His cultural reaction, taking place in the medium of social consensus and tradition, is an integral and intimate reaction. The former represents man's segmental role which stresses the individuality of his action, status and lifepattern. The latter represents the persistence and continuity of his collective role, and its products which are transmitted from person to person, and from generation to generation. Both sets of reactions are equally significant as formative factors of group life and organization.

Man's social organization reveals numerous groups that owe their formation and persistence to either ecological and selective or cultural and integral reactions. The predominance of one or other set of reactions governs the type and individuality of the community, whether a cluster of isolated homesteads, a regular rural community, a town or a city. In the early history of man the kinship group, modified by adoption and other factions, and comprising either the nomadic tribes of the grasslands or the settled agriculturist tribes of the plains, provided the basis of social integration and an integral individual behaviour and complete community life, and came to be distinguished from urban society based on neighbourhood with kinship as a subordinate principle of group formation. In the towns and cities of early civilization there was a mingling of various ethnic elements, and economic rather than kinship factors were stressed in social life and relations. Secondary, formal and impersonal rather than ethnic, intimate and primary groups asserted themselves. The authority of tribal chiefs, patriarchs and village elders and the sway of custom and tradition declined. Here both peasants and herdsmen brought their commodities for sale, and the scribe, the trader and the moneylender exerted vast influence. It was here that writing was also discovered and legalism and contact were first manifest as contrasted with the word of mouth and oath of loyalty in the tribal societies of both the mobile shepherds and the sedentary farmers. From time immemorial urbanism stood out in marked contrast with the tribalism of the nomad folks of the grasslands and the settled clan and caste men of the villages who both sold their surplus goods and products — woollen and leather goods of the former, and crops, fuel and timber of the latter — to townsmen and coveted their luxuries as well as their softly reared daughters. The contrasted social groups came into intimate contact with one another from the dawn of history, the shepherd folks often dominating both cities and villages, plundering the riches of the former and exacting their tribute of grain from the latter. In Mesopotamia and in the Indus Valley community life seemed to have centred round cities rather than villages, but in Egypt due to the length of the narrow belt of floodland the villages were more important. In spacious and fertile river valleys the principle of kinship as the dominant idea established compact "nucleated" villages. And these early stabilized themselves as persistent organized communities with increase of population and development of intensive farming, exhibiting a mental outlook sharply different from the urban centres which arose by their side.

Ecological and cultural factors and processes aid one another in developing social cohesiveness and an exuberant variety of both primary and secondary associations. Ecological reaction builds up man's fractional modes of behaviour and secondary groups fulfilling parts of his changeful personality. Cultural reaction builds up the primary groups and community on a super individual plane with a reality and personality that overreach individual lives and actions.

But sometimes ecology and economy, instead of stressing individualistic and impersonal elements develop community life on a broad and stable basis. The agriculture of the rice lands in India, Siam, China and Japan necessitates collective management of water supply and regulation of pastures. Rice farming cannot thrive without the co-operation of many farmers, families and villages in the distribution and utilization of water. Such co-operation is instanced by the collective building of dams and irrigation channels for the storage and distribution of monsoon rains and the construction of tanks owned and managed by the rural community. It is an ecological necessity connected with the exigencies of rice culture in the monsoon zone which accounts for the formation and development of village communities in the rice tracts of South-East Asia. Rainfall is neither deficient nor precarious but water supply has to be collectively managed and distributed across the levelled fields or terraced slopes in the growing and maturing seasons of rice plantation, and this factor becomes decisive in bringing about the clustered type of rural distribution. Where rainfall is inadequate and illdistributed but a perennial spring is found in an oasis in the desert, compact villages and even small towns also crop up round it as in Central Asia, North Africa and south-western Punjab. Water management makes the community *solidare*. On the whole it is the poverty of soil and water resources which controls the type and distribution of man's habitations, and the adequacy or inadequacy of his community life.

But while ecological factors such as the need of collective water management, agriculture and control of pastures originate the compact village type of human settlement, man has forged cultural bonds that support the co-operation in agriculture and irrigation. Sometimes a tribe, a clan or a group of families has cleared the jungle and settled the village; a consciousness of kith and kin finds expression in various tribal-communal institutions such as the panchayat (tribal council) and *hamasayia* (guest house of the clan or tribe), and strengthens the economic solidarity. Where villages are occupied by more than one clan, tribe or caste, co-operation in the field of agriculture and irrigation paves the way to a community life organization on a much broader and surer basis than its economic relations and social institutions develop in which different economic classes or social groups participate as cogs in the moving wheel of corporate life. The compact rice-growing village in the East generally exhibits the scattered field system, which in the evolution of agriculture equalizes opportunities for all in an agricultural community. But all paths and tracks across the fields, which for each farmer lie scattered in the area of settlement like autumn leaves, lead to the village that is the meeting ground of all. Threshing floors, wells, temples, houses for the council of the five, guesthalls, and social facilities which are subject to community use are all concentrated here. There is collective employment of village artisans and functionaries, supervised by the council of the five which takes charge also of irrigation and the settlement of rural disputes. The council of the five breaks down the rigid division of economic classes and castes, and is the guardian of rural co-operative services extending from economic to diverse fields of social life. The landlord, the tenant and the farmhand take part in the rural economic management and in the whole host of village ceremonies and observances, recreations and amusements, and, economically and culturally, a complete, rounded rural community develops. Social and economic stratification and individual differences do not obscure the mutually shared traditions and rewards requisite to the persistence of the rural community.

Types of Habitation and Community Life

Ecologic factors such as the broken topography of a mountain region and the difficulty of cultivation and settlement in the forest, desert and marshland also originate the contrasted type of human occupation, viz. isolated homesteads and scattered hamlets. These are to be found wherever man ascends the terraced hillslopes up to the top of the mountain or fights the aridity of the desert, or, again, implants himself, however temporarily, amidst the wilderness of the jungle or across the sweeping tides of the active delta. Isolated and dispersed huts and hamlets are like pioneer plants which stand interspersed among one another in a new zone of colonization. Man is here under the grips of ecologic forces, and his effort to win subsistence for himself in the precarious life in the forest clearing, marsh or desert gets the better of social intercourse and active community life. Pioneer agricultural communities with their sporadic groups of dwellings are too absorbed in the struggle with the unfavourable ecologic conditions such as inclement climate, drought, excessive rainfall or infertile soil to develop feelings of localism and community life. Insecurity of life, landlordism and the leasehold system and exploitative agricultural finance contribute to the inefficient and unorganized type of community life, while the development of cultivation of a cash crop, like cotton in the Egyptian and jute in the Bengal delta, also nurtures an impersonal and ecological grouping of the population which reaches neither the density nor the social coherence of compact villages of the alluvial plains.

The scattered or compact pattern of human occupation accordingly focuses the dominance of one or the other constant factor in social organization, viz. the ecological, fractional and impersonal or the cultural, integral and intimate grouping which meets the variant needs of men living in a single limited area. Both these kinds of grouping are met with in all human communities. When the ecological reaction dominates we have a strong individualism or development of secondary groups, impersonal in nature tending towards formal, contractual and rational calculating ways of living. Formalism and impersonalism are associated with an increase of freedom of movement of individuals and the wave like expansion of social contacts and relationships much beyond the boundaries of neighbourhoods and regions. When the cultural reaction dominates we have primary, intimate neighbourhood groups with a marked development of localism and community organization which subordinate the individualistic needs of the members to the needs of the aggregate. The zones of wheat farming in the pioneer fringes of the world, which are inhabited by machines rather than by men living far apart from one another in their ranches or farms, are the homes of sturdy individualism and wideminded cosmopolitanism. The ancient zones of rice culture in Asia, dotted with thousands of regular congested villages are in contrast the zones *par excellence* of a zealous localism and well organized and integrated group life, the men irrespective of class or individual differences appearing to merge themselves in the individuality of their communities. In the monsoon region in Asia a few cities which developed over decades, grew from villages slowly, and in an organic manner, and these remained largely half rural in their character, composition and outlook. In America or Australia cities originated and expanded within a brief period, and their secondary impersonal group environment and anonymous monetary social relationship stand in marked contrast with the primary groups and community organizations of the Asiatic country-or-farmer-towns.

Contrasted Types of Institutions

The ecological, economic and impersonal principle of grouping and the cultural, intimate and non-rational principle build up distinctive types of social institutions. With the former are associated the market, the granary, the shop, the store, the warehouse, the bank, the school, the club and other interest groups; with the latter are associated the clan, the caste, the temple, the ancestral hall, the council of village elders, the co-operative, the guild and neighbourhood groups. It is characteristic that while in Europe, and especially America, village names often indicate significant features of the landscape or refer to families who were prominent in early settlements or colonization. In India place names more often describe homogeneous groups of caste or clan people inhabiting a locality and refer to deities which express the community ideals and morale. The deity often gives the village place and community name in different parts of India, and expresses the "personality" of the habitation, orienting the behaviour of the people in relation to a central or dominant spiritual motif over successive generations. The rural community, adequately integrated and organized, maintains a consistency of social behaviour, and is creative and immortal in this consistency in its relation to the eternal, extra-individual ideal that the village deity symbolizes. Every village as the medium of expression of real-group culture develops a "community personality" of its own which works itself out into an integrated pattern of social and moral norms through devotion to the local guardian deity. The deities in the Indian pantheon are numerous; rural communities in India exhibit almost innumerable "personality" types. Vishnu (God as

Preserver), Shiva (God as Destroyer) and the Mother Goddess (as symbolizing the almost innumerable phases of human behaviour and destiny), installed and worshipped in millions of village temples in India, play a significant role in integrating people's behaviour and social relationships by a beyond-human framework, and organizing the community into a "personality", a group system of great significance.

It is significant that just as in the Western type of industrial city the structural centre corresponds to the ecological centre of a market, business and prestige area, in many oriental villages this corresponds to the ecological centre of spiritual and intellectual guidance and prestige area. The ecological centre is the temple of the tutelary deity of the village or little town, the focus of civic attention and pride, and of the major directive activities of the community. The temple in rural India is not merely a place of the gods but also a nerve centre of activities. In south Indian villages the temple has its assembly hall where the meetings of the village assembly are held, and temple dances, theatricals and religious and philosophical discussion attract men from the entire countryside. Occupying the dominant site in the hill range, lake face or river bend, the temple and its influences serve to build up the culture, social manners and mode of living, the community personality of the whole region. The Western type of industrial town or city is complex, diversified and inchoate in structure. The rural community is relatively homogeneous both in its ecological centre and in its hinterland.

The Intermingling of Ecological and Cultural Principles

Yet even villages with an integral community personality of their own satisfy the insistent and purely economic demands of their inhabitants through large, impersonal and more or less secondary groups and institutions. Each large village has its merchant, warehouse, and moneylending groups, and institutions such as the market, the fair, the store, and the bank. Even rural dwellers carry on their trade, business or banking wherever profitable. They are connected with the fair and the bank by purely economic and impersonal bonds, though they may be tied to the village grocer and moneylender by social and economic ties. Cultural, intimate and emotionally charged or ecologic, economic and impersonal groups represent contrasted types of association which are found in the rural community, operating to fulfil the variant demands of rural dwellers. It is from out of the merchant group and out of the ubiquitous rural institutions, viz. the daily market or the periodical fair that the village gives rise to the town which at the beginning serves rural ends. The daily market in the village is a town in embryo which may develop and enlarge itself under favourable conditions. The impersonal, fractional urban ways of living lie dormant in every large village.

Both the cultural, primary and integral and the ecological, secondary and selective forces and relations are accordingly revealed as major factors in social organization whether in the rural or in the urban community. In most rural communities the bulk of social action is based on primary face-to-face, integral and intimate relations as discernible in the family, the clan, the caste and neighbourhood groups. The norm of social action is derived from the familial and cultural types of grouping, characterized by mutual sharing of resources, risks and rewards, and this regulates and "humanizes" fractional, rational and contractual phases of behaviour and relations associated with ecologic, economic, or mechanical types of grouping.

It is important to consider under what social conditions the village exhibits an emphasis of movements towards the ecological, impersonal and selective type of grouping which eliminates or overrides feelings of community solidarity, localism and order. We have already seen that the scattered patterning of rural occupation is unfavourable to the development of a strong, firmly knit community life. Most of the new countries of the world such as the United States, Canada and South Africa have made their progress towards the clearance of the prairie, veldt or forest and agricultural colonization by adopting the dispersed type of rural settlement. In the new world the combination of large scale agriculture and animal industry, which is facilitated by the use of power driven machinery, has been the main support of farmers and homesteaders building on their farms which are separated from other farms and homesteads by long distances. Thus neighbourhood groups cannot be developed, and in the USA recent social trends have called for the establishment of schools, co-operatives and various other community centres that represent correctives of extreme dispersal and lack of social integration. Even in regions of mature settlement where feudalism, absentee landlordism or unprotected tenancy promote differentiation and antagonism between the economic classes dependent on the land (landlord, tenant, metayer, hired farmhand), and disparity in their standards of living, the community established predominantly on the basis of economic relations and interests cannot attain stability and coherence. A mobile population of tenants, croppers and farmhands drifting from holding to holding, chronic poverty and exploitation by the landlord's agents, grain-dealers and moneylenders and sharp social distance between the agricultural classes, which prevents participation in community work and recreation, give the picture of an unsatisfactory and inadequately organized type of community life.

Misfits of Old Mores in the Community Framework

Social and economic conflict between different interests in the land, rise of big landed estates, unprotected tenancy and exploitative metayage as well as the presence in the village of a large floating agricultural labour population are clamouring for land disrupt community solidarity in many compact villages in India and elsewhere. Rural class cleavage based on divergent interests in the land cuts across kinship, occupational or religious groups, and corrodes the structure and solidarity of the community. Family and clan feuds were formerly there. These were sometime-deep seated and persistent because of social memory which cannot be erased in an unchanging social situation. But the modern class conflicts though less deep seated are more widespread, and embrace a larger and larger number of the landless tenants and labourers from the countryside. Rural folks thus come to depend more and more for their unity and cohesion on the articulation of specific and segregated class interests. Grouping arrangements accordingly take new lines. Kolb and Wileden observe:

> Locality groups have lateral or geographic dimension. Interest groups have psycho-cultural or perpendicular dimension. Locality groups depend upon proximity, common life, and residence in a recognized physical area. Interest groups depend upon polarity, promotion, special concerns, leadership, and deliberate effort. The polarity implies the fields of magnetic influence, when thus released from locality restrictions people are attracted to certain places of interest.[1]

Interest groups, by bringing together people from different localities organize and sharpen class cleavages in the rural world. Social distance accordingly is not merely the product of machine technology in the urban–industrial world; it is also the outcome of capitalistic farming, absentee ownership, rack renting, free subletting and mortgage of land and usurious moneylending in rural society. The latter social phenomena are in fact older, and wherever these have brought about an excessive social distance between the upper classes and the

---

1 J.H. Kolb and A.F. Wileden, "Special Interest Groups in Rural Society, 2", *University of Wisconsin AES Bulletin*, 84, 1929.

actual tillers of the soil, the derivative "interest" type of social grouping has dominated, and the impersonal, economic and ecologic ways of living of the city have established themselves at the expense of primary relations, neighbourliness and cultural unity and solidarity of the members. Thus even in rural society the nature of community solidarity changes from spontaneous neighbourly and mutual aid practices of the primary groups to deliberate and contractual co-operation of the secondary groups and associations, whether tenant or agricultural labourers unions, marketing syndicates, credit unions or federations of co-operative stores.

Adjustment of the rural mores to the new deliberate, contractual types of co-operation is neither smooth nor efficient. Too often, with the spread of the network of urban capitalism and finance the countryside has become the battleground of sharply divided political parties, focusing on agrarian differences and with the political struggle drawn up along rural–urban lines there emerges the struggle for status of the rural proletariat who become altogether misfits in the former community framework. The deliberate contractual type of co-operation takes the longest time to take roots in rural society. It is fostered directly by increased social stratification which, however, destroys more of cohesion and solidarity than it can build up, with the result that the transitional social stage is marked by sudden peasant mob risings and outbursts even in peaceful rural India and Japan.

Causes of the Present Cultural Crisis

Both the cultural and primary as well as the ecological, economic and contractual phases of social life and behaviour appear essential to the changing community. Every village or city thus has to face and solve the intimate problem of establishing a harmonious working balance between the contrasted attitudes and ways of living. The contrasts are characterized, according to the familiar dichotomy of the sociologists, as between Gemeinschaft relations (Tönnies), *solidarité organique* (Durkheim), *Vergesellschaftung* (Max Weber), Status (Maine), primary groups (Cooley) and localism (Zimmerman) and Gesellschaft relations, solidarité mécanique, Vergemeinschaftung, contract, secondary groups and centralization that mark distinctive social relations, processes and forms of behaviour in the human community. An exaggerated stress of one or other of these relations, processes and forms of behaviour threatens the existence of the community and indicates personality imbalance and disorganization. It is not the contemporary urban civilization alone which faces the *impasse* due to stress of the ecological, fractional, impersonal and derivative as contrasted with cultural, integral, intimate and primary relations and groups. Phases of the cultural vs. ecological process, the Gemeinschaft vs. Gesellschaft relations, status vs. contract *impasse* are as old as the dawn of human society. Man's social habits, personality traits and standard of social values were moulded and deeply ingrained by the integral primary–cultural group relationships and experience in rural society. Thus the modern trend towards ecology, secondary groups, contract and centralization in the urban–industrial world has meant a chaos in social adjustment and morals. Man will lose a good part of his humanity if the tried and preserved variations of human traits and lifepatterns selected by a particular primary group or groups in rural society and his sense of reality of these and of his community life be overwhelmed and disintegrated.

Recovery of Small Communities

The key to the prevention of this social and moral crisis which faces mankind throughout the world in the new social and industrial age of indirect contacts and secondary associations is not one but many; for various ecologic, industrial and centralizing trends and institutions mutually support and strengthen one another in socially conditioning and selecting formal, fractional and impersonal social relationships and behaviour. Briefly speaking, the sense of reality of community life has to be restored in the new milieu through the organization of associations, neighbourhoods and community activities that differ in species but belong to the same genus as those which humanized mankind in the horde, tribe, family or village. Social nuclei have to be found out for urban dwellers so that many basic needs of human nature which are not fulfilled and are repressed might be adequately satisfied; and the processes of social integration, active intercourse and culture which have been interrupted in the present social transition might be renewed. The renewal of the community personality might be deliberately planned through social work, publicity, education and the fine arts.

There is also need of a new institutional outlook. Social planning appears now to rest on the worldwide conviction that centralization is indispensable in implementing deliberate social and economic policies. This belief is itself the product of the present mechanical and industrial age. As Zimmerman observes:

> The industrial system with its emphasis on centralization, whether through chain stores, branch factories or advertized goods has brought about a similarity of communities. The development of the concept of "parity" between regions, and between rural and urban districts whether in the nature of rewards or grants, of minimum wage laws and industrial regimentation or of propaganda itself, means standardization — one of the primary factors aiding centralization. Finally, the belief that the day of the local community has passed, and that the country, the state and the federal government should take over the functions

> formerly handled by the local community is gradually reducing self-government.[2]

Instead of centralization and bureaucracy, inspection and inspectors, there is need of more regionalism, localism and community realism, more of local and functional self-government, more of local and regional initiative and control in administration, taxation, education, sanitation, land and water utilization and social services.

Politically speaking, democracy can be nurtured best by political pluralism which is a corrective of class struggle, and promotes an alert, active citizenship devoted to the management of local and regional affairs. Centralization, on the contrary, ranges the classes in strong opposition to each other, and stresses class conflict and the paralysing desire of the people to expect everything from the government at a distance. In the East and especially in India where political life began and evolved in small groups, lending a significant richness to the local communal and vocational (of professional) life and interests hardly to be seen elsewhere, democracy will be more adaptive and vital if it can grow from within using and renewing the local and non-local groups and assemblies, region by region, in the framework of the new polity. In Eastern communities local affairs in villages differ only in degree from affairs in the national or central government; thus there will be a great increase of initiative, if the smaller units are entrusted with real powers of self-government, not those limited and qualified powers delegated to them from above — a half measure which is at once discouraging and demoralizing. At the same time the interfusion of diverse and conflicting religious and caste elements in the local and functional bodies, if made really self-governing, will prevent class consciousness and party strife from being developed.

---

2 Carle C. Zimmerman, *The Changing Community*, p. 645.

Such local and functional bodies will correspond to the natural regions of the country, with some diversity of resources wherever possible, but homogeneous in social composition and in all cases with a well defined, central historical town and some connected cultural tradition.[3] Nations that are being fast urbanized and industrialized are becoming shallow rooted. Small towns, villages and "regions" are as necessary to fulfil certain basic needs of human nature and group life, and implement certain essential cultural demands as big towns and cities. Even now the world still very largely lives in the small rural community; while regionalism, in its industrial and administrative aspects, the development of modern suburbs and garden cities, "urbanization", and the co-operative organization, all seek to promote the technical and social efficiency of little towns, villages and hamlets. Only a restoration of the immediacy of relationship and of community life and personality through neighbourhood, primary or cultural groups can bring about balance and normality in urban culture. Perhaps even this may not succeed under the present regime of capitalism in weaving together the snapped threads of community life. In the planned society of the future the distribution of population, industry and institutions will be far different from what these are in capitalistic urban communities. It is possible that the logical sequel of the modern schemes of redistribution of industry and dispersal of population, and regional and social planning will be the regulation of the size of cities and towns on the basis of cultural and industrial efficiency. This will imply such institutional reconditioning of populations that their present citified habits and hectic, abnormal and mercenary living in the social void will be largely transformed.

Civilized man will sooner or later turn to the deeper and stabler joys and intimate personal loyalties that living in

[3] For political reform in India see my *Democracies of the East*, chapter XXI.

communities of small size and participation in functional groups and neighbourhood activities can inspire, and subordinate the impersonal, rational–contractual standards to organic, communal and cultural ties. The latter will weld together individuals and groups in communities which may exhibit a life organization and a personality of their own, and may be something more than their mere place names or addresses. The sense of community life and personality working in and through the press, publicity, social work or some other tool in our modern towns or cities can alone prevent the relative mental and moral isolation of civilized mankind, which is the root cause of its major social and economic diseases. From this will spring a new humanism and social and civic idealism, which will be adequate to control civilized man's myriad indirect contacts and formal, secondary group relationships in the same manner as primary group sympathy in the family, the neighbourhood groups and the village controlled social relationships in the earlier age. Not before man's consciousness becomes expanded to cover different classes, races and nations with whom his life has become interlinked in the anonymous world of the big city, industry and commerce can he redefine what is the human and the right, and secure moral stability for himself in the ecological, impersonal and secondary group environment of today.

13

The Ecology Behind Economics

The Concept of a National Economic Region

TYPES and stages of social and economic development, like those of organic evolution, cannot be regarded as either general or universal. These vary in different natural regions and culture areas, due to the accumulated force of ecology and social heritage in working out human selection and survival. The diversity of ecological features and inequality of natural resources are responsible for the division of the earth into floral and faunal regions and a complicated regional history and distribution of population. A distinguished ecologist, Adams, observes:

> The results of this multiple diversity are far-reaching, indeed, as these differences tend to produce relatively independent units or systems of action and permit and reinforce the development of a certain amount of individuality and distinctness of both race and culture. Between these centres of individuality there develop pressure, competition or friction of some degree (cf. Bankroft's law). Thus with physical, plant, animal and human diversity the stage is set for all degrees of pressure and stress. The broad features of this have seldom been studied in a thoroughly comprehensive manner.

The earth can accordingly be mapped into distinct natural economic regions and cultural zones for the purpose of a comparative study of economic institutions. Ecological or natural resource patterns, economic systems, racial characteristics and cultural motifs are organically interrelated much in the manner of the correlated traits of a living body. There is, accordingly, an organization and correlation of economic, social and legal systems so that the different phases of the social system inhere in a definite culture pattern. Culture patterns in general are thus adapted to the resource pattern of economic systems. Civilization can be compared and classified in various ways. In ecological economics we stress distinctive economic regions and systems. From the comparative point of view, civilization is to be pictured as a tapestry of diverse culture patterns of various hues woven by distinctive threads of social evolution for particular zones rather than a single homogeneous pattern of uniform culture. Throughout this analysis suggestion and comparison rather than exact measurement and statistical treatment are to be employed. The division of the world into clearcut and distinct culture areas aned economic regions is, after all, an abstraction but such a method of analysis, provided that the basic limitations are understood, will be useful in an appreciation of the basic economic contrasts which divide the major categories.

The historical school of economics had a clear conception of the relativity of economic laws and institutions, yet there was an attempt to mark off stages in economic development too rigidly. The stages of economic development given by the economic historians are, first, collection, second, hunting, third, pastoralism, fourth, agriculture, and fifth, manufacturing enterprise, and they held that mankind had passed or was passing through these identical stages of culture in all regions. Later intensive studies in cultural ethnology have revealed that these stages are by no means universal, nor do these follow the logical sequence which the economic historians regard as universally or generally valid.

The Culture Area among the Primitive Peoples

The plant and animal communities of a region are closely correlated with the food supply and the main cultural activities of a people, and with the raw materials necessary for housing and clothing and for the manufacture of tools and implements. The tribal cultures of the great plains of North America were based on bison hunting and the whole social and economic life bore the impress of the bison and of the nomadic hunting life. Similarly, the Eskimo culture extending through the tundra from Greenland to Bering Strait, exhibits a striking appearance of unity. Anthropologists have worked out the conception of a culture area in considerable detail also in Africa and New Zealand. Sayce points out that a culture area is not always or even often a sharply defined region, but is somewhat analogous with the optimum zone of the plant ecologists. Some tribes may be regarded as typical of the culture area, and these will often be those living in the region of most marked ecological characterization, while the cultures of the marginal tribes grade towards those of the next geographical or culture area.[1] The regional evolution of culture does not go as far, as suggested by Baron Nordenskiöld, viz. that "peoples may nourish, and in time pass away, but for a given area there will persist a culture, which, within certain limits is much the same". But no doubt it is the ecological make up of the region which fashions the raw materials of culture, and this is true even of those advanced peoples, which mainly depend upon agriculture. It is in this manner that selected plants and animals of a region such as the bison of the great plains, the acorn of California, the salmon of the north-west coast of North America and the reindeer of the Arctic tundra determined the economic and cultural traits of various tribal groups even as the culture of the more advanced civilized communities have been wedded to rice in the Ganges

---

1 Sayce, *Primitive Arts and Crafts*, chapter. II.

valley, the wine and olive in the Mediterranean counting or the datepalm in the Saharan oases.

Under favourable ecological conditions primitive peoples exhibit the same stages of economic development as are familiar in economic history. Thus in South Africa the Bushmen tribes had formerly represented a hunting and gathering culture which entirely occupied the region. Later on, with the immigration of the Hottentots, a pastoral culture was introduced while at a still later stage the Bantu tribes which now occupy a considerable area, followed agriculture. The varying proportion of highland and lowland, of forest and grassland, however influence the distribution of occupations, nor can there be any fixed sequence of economic stages. In South Africa wars of extermination were waged among neighbouring tribes representing competing methods of economic exploitation. But in the same region the relations between hunting, pastoralism and agriculture followed by different tribal groups may be peaceful and complementary. Thus in the Congo forests pigmies who lead a hunting and gathering life are surrounded by agricultural Bantu tribes from whose gardens they obtain fruits in exchange of deposits of meat.

As in the animal community, there are niches or occupations of particular species of animals, which are interdependent, similarly in the structure of the human population different economic phases may be mutually helpful. Thus these different stages may continue side by side, some representing adaptation to forest conditions, others to grasslands and still others to old clearings and settlements, and the full exploitation of the resources of the region is divided between the various tribal groups and classes. Again, culture borrowings, through diffusion or through migration, enable various peoples to skip over certain previous stages of material culture, while even a small but significant difference in the environment will thwart the economic succession.

Considerable areas in Africa, for instance, otherwise suitable for organized pastoralism are devoid of cattle due to the presence of the Tse-tse fly. In the flybelts a kind of nomadic agriculture becomes the mainstay of the people, as in the case of the Lambas whose culture therefore contrasts very strongly with that of neighbouring cattle keeping peoples.[2]

Mixture of Economic Stages and Types

The order of economic development depends upon economic resources, on the one hand, and the development of the utilization of resources and social history on the other; and the social and economic type need not pass through all the major categories in an immutable logical succession. We have to assume not a straight line and uniform development but a multiform and divergent development of institutions. Further, the limitations of economic resources often leads to a combination of the major economic pursuits into which the evolutionists divided economic history, as amply evidenced by the recent studies of economic life of primitive peoples in South Asia and Africa by the school of cultural anthropologists. We thus meet with hybrid economic types and systems in which hunting and some type of intermittent cultivation, nomadism and oasis farming, agricultural life and a veneer of industrial civilization and commerce are found in adaptive combinations that defy schematization. Nor can we forget that there are sudden changes in modes of economic life brought about by culture contrasts, inventions, diseases and wars. A sudden economic progress may be achieved by a race through a change of environment, when it emigrates to a new region which offers far more favourable conditions of living and of the arts of utilization than the old habitat and enables it to pass to a more developed economic stage and organization by skipping over an intermediate stage. Economic historians

2 Doke, *The Lambas of Northern Rhodesia.*

by conceiving the stages of economic development as gradual, and envisaging the history of man as consisting of slight, slowly accumulating changes has hardly done justice to the world's mighty recurrent pulses of social and technological change and revolution.

The political superiority of the Euro–American people has also perhaps stood in the way of a right appraisal of the economic institutions and organizations of people outside the pale of Western civilization. In recent decades the achievements of the West in industrial efficiency and their political dominance in the world tend to create a certain bias which sometimes has led to the characterization of social and economic organizations of the less advanced peoples and cultures as pre-economic, communal, gentile and theocratic. The primary consideration of a social science is to understand the process of adaptation and the norm or value is to be judged by the capacity of the customs, social arrangements and institutions of a people to subserve the purpose of such adaptation. Neither the variety of ecological conditions and opportunities, nor the divergence of human motives, social arrangements and culture standards are given adequate consideration in economics. The result is that economic principles hardly fit in with the data of the Eastern life and labour, for instance, and there is an unfortunate divorce between economic theory and economic history.

Cultural Type and the Ecological Resource Pattern

The study of the characteristic resource patterns of different climatic zones is accordingly fundamental in the analysis and interpretation of divergent lines of economic development.

Climatic conditions and other ecological features, agricultural resources, occupational distribution of population and patterns of group organizations are linked with one another. Such an organic interrelation is the outcome of centuries of ecological and social adaptation and survival and expresses itself in more or less stable culture types.

Economic types and systems including the distribution of population, occupational balance, legal arrangement of property and employment of labour and habits of thrift and enterprise are parts of culture patterns representing those features which are specially concerned with the material arts of living.

Ecological or natural resource patterns may consist, for instance, of a heavy precipitation, fertile soil, abundant manpower and their corollaries, as in the monsoon lands, or, again, of coal, iron and electricity, mechanical agriculture and industry, manufacture and commerce and their corollaries, as in the industrial West. Culture types are adapted to ecological or natural resource patterns in the diverse zones of the world's distribution.

In a monograph about Europe, industrial and agricultural, Delaisi has distinguished between the new nationalistic, capitalistic, and mechanized Europe and the old feudal vegetable Europe. The former zone would include Great Britain, France, Northern Italy, Lower Austria, Germany, Belgium, Holland, Denmark and southern Sweden. Outside this zone the old feudal agricultural civilization still persists. The great central area which represents the kernel of the whole capitalistic industrial system rests on three basic resources:

A. An abundant supply of iron and coal.
B. A disciplined and skilled labour directed and supported by science and capitalistic finance and enterprise.
C. Colonies, dependencies and spheres of influence which provide raw materials for manufactures as well as markets for finished products.

In striking contrast with the capitalistic industrial zone in western Europe we have the zone of agricultural–communal civilization in the monsoon lands which are now inhabited by more than half the population of the earth. Although divided by racial and institutional differences a certain unity is established in South-East Asia by important common economic features among which rice culture, co-operative irrigation and agriculture, omission of animal raising and the development of rural arts and handicrafts are the most important.

It is easy to find a contrast between northern China which has colder and drier climate and utilizes draught animals and southern China with its predominant rice and mulberry cultivation, its omission of animal labour, and its handloom weaving or between the large sized wheat fields of the Punjab and the western Uttar Pradesh (UP) and the intensive farming of rice, rotating with legumes in eastern UP, Bihar and Bengal. Tribal and village solidarity, small farming and the large sized family are to be found more along the major rivers in the Punjab and UP which directed the course of settlement of agricultural tribes and castes. Where the frontiers of cultivation have recently extended towards the Himalayan forests and swamps, the uplands of the Vindhyas and the lagoons of the delta, we have great feudal and semifeudal estates resembling those of Eastern Europe till recent years in which poor tenants eke out their living with difficulty. In spite of such contrasts, however, there is an underlying unity established by sudden common basic geographical factors which differentiate what Delaisi calls the vegetable civilization from the machine civilization of Western Europe.

With reference to land utilization even a more marked contrast is discernible as between the standard in Eastern Europe and that adopted in South-East Asia. The South-East Asiatic or the monsoon standard is based on rice cultivation, hand labour, omission of animal raising, small fields and peasant ownership. The European standard is based upon wheat cultivation, large estates, work animals, agricultural machinery and industries. The former can with difficulty maintain a dense population, which presses against the means of subsistence. India's and China's population density accounts for almost one third of the world's population. Such heavy human concentration is possible only because of the meticulous hand labour in the fields and rotation of leguminous crops which are the chief features of rice growing. It is important to note that the legumes and pulses which rotate with rice not only renovate the land but also balance the excessive starch consumption of Indian and Chinese diets.

Social Contrasts between Rice and Wheat Cultures

Rice among other cereals is very poor in protein. Thus the rice eater is poor in stamina and small in bulk and there is an adaptation of race and food. Wheat, on the other hand, is the richest in protein suiting best pioneering people, pushing the farm line into the cold climate. Rice among the natural races in the monsoon lands is not cultivated but is merely gathered in large quantities after the rains. Rice, in fact, requires no perfected agricultural tools and little fertilizing manure but demands abundant water. Hence rich river valleys in monsoon areas that obtain the benefits of flood or flush irrigation periodically, are exhibiting today the world's highest records of rural aggregation, such as Bangladesh and Shantung. Rice may be grown successfully in areas unsuited to any other crop. The cultivation of rice makes possible the utilization of marshes and swamps where other cereals would not grow. In Sri Lanka, Phillipines and China the population has ascended the mountains due to the pressure from the lower valleys, and the hillsides are full of productive terraced plots and cleverly contrived dams and irrigation channels. The yield of rice per acre in these areas is higher than in most countries. Wheat is essentially a cereal of a pioneering people in regions of scant population. It is associated with hay growing and pastoral industry. In newly developed areas wheat growing and cattle breeding on a large scale are supplementary to each other. Cattle are raised not for milk but for meat which is exported to other countries. Wheat cultivation thrives with investments of a large agricultural capital, the use of farm machinery and a close approximation to factory methods and regulation. The great fields of Canada and Argentina are described as being inhabited by machines rather than by men. Kansas in the USA has a number of 2,000 to 6,000-acre family holdings, highly mechanized as to operation. Some of the operators of these holdings are called "suitcase" farmers because they can use motors to transport their farm machinery many miles from their homes.[3] The success of wheat cultivation denotes an advanced and elaborate agriculture. Wheat cultivation easily evolves into commercial farming while rice cultivation has been associated with subsistence farming among sedentary non-trading peoples. The cultivation of rice can only thrive under careful supervision of the inflow and outflow of water in fields under collective management. Rice thus encourages communal habits and instincts due to the collectivism for the utilization of water. Among many tribes and races in monsoon areas rice cultivation co-existed with a periodical distribution of holdings while the compact village communities and panchayats which are ubiquitous in South-East Asia probably originated from the exigencies of water supply and the drainage of rice fields at certain fixed periods under common management.

The cultivation of wheat, on the other hand, tends to be individualistic. Wheat cultivation prospers on a large scale basis with the application of capital, use of perfected machinery and employment of a large force of labour particularly at harvest times. Thus wheat cultivation develops into a

---

3 Kolb and Brunner, *A Study of Rural Society*, p. 326.

capitalistic agriculture soon exhibiting a marked disparity of wealth and economic status among the different classes engaged in agriculture. The big estate with its complement of peasants not far removed from serfdom and a floating mass of agricultural labourers and the leasehold system has persisted for a long time in the wheat producing regions of Europe. Social and economic stratification bears the indelible stamp of the type of land utilization.

Rice culture with its family co-operation in fields, its further co-operation in village and beyond for water and water level has worked to produce associated family life in India, the patriarchal life in China and Japan and the joint family and co-operative village in northern India. Rice cultivation also promotes thrift and industry. In rice agriculture the peasant cannot go away and leave the field, for a week's carelessness will ruin the entire crop. Moreover, the work of one year in the rice field gives the peasant considerable benefit in the next year. Such conditions make the rice-growers of India, China and Indonesia more thrifty, industrious, and reliable than tropical peoples. Again, rice cultivation supplemented by the rotation of leguminous crops prevents soil exhaustion. Further, the use of cattle which supply organic manure to the soil also contributes to a sort of permanent agriculture. Rice culture, therefore, promotes a permanent attachment to the land in contrast with wheat which is often a single crop cultivated year in and year out without an arranged rotation, exhausting the soil and keeping the people always in search for fresh fields and pastures new, and promoting the atavism of nomadic habits and the resuscitation of pastoral institutions in the backwood clearings and frontier settlements.

Not merely the major staple crops of the world such as rice, wheat and maize, but also produce such as potatoes, oilseeds, and garden crops and the domesticated animals such as horses, cattle and buffaloes used in agriculture determine the different possibilities of division and co-operation of labour, distribution of population, dietary and economic efficiency. These underlie many contrasts in racial characteristics and forms of social and economic organization, in one word, culture patterns.

Economic regions and systems and culture patterns form together the *ensemble* which is the basis of classification of social types as studied by social ecology. Social morphology forms the indispensable basic foundation of all comparative social sciences, and social morphology leads up to genetic or developmental studies.

The Development of the Rural Community

A scientific study of human culture includes not only a survey of the various economic regions and ecological or natural resource patterns in the world but also an examination of the forms of landholding and property which govern the various socio-economic types and patterns of rural distribution and social gradation. Different social and economic types are rooted in the clustered or scattered pattern of rural settlement and the social and economic differentiation of interests in the land. The latter originate in their turn from climate, soil and topography which determine the natural flora and fauna, crops and modes of land utilization, and from a people's social history.

Agrarian historians, like Meitzen, Seebohm, Gomme and Vinogradoff, in tracing the development of village communities have stressed racial elements and attributed differences in the agrarian organization largely to anthropological formations. A study of small ownership and village communities, as these exist in different parts of the world, shows on the other hand, that these are institutions which have arisen on account of the operation of similar economic forces and agricultural conditions. These include the ecological necessities of a closely compacted population, cultivation of certain cereals demanding a communal routine of farming and collective management of irrigation courses and pasture grounds. More than racial elements and political forces it is ecological and economic conditions and changes which have governed the historical evolution of forms of property and agrarian organizations, and a convergence of institutions in different agricultural systems can be explained much in the same manner by the operation of similar economic forces as convergence in biology.

The change from nomadic and intermittent to intensive farming everywhere, stabilizes the population and introduces a permanent relationship between different economic groups in rural society. Such stability of population is typified by the fact that land becomes the predominant cohesive force in the agricultural community; while social gradation comes to be crystalized into rigid and inelastic groups, clans or castes. Land not only becomes the chief source of wealth and prestige but also the main social binder. This explains the formation of village communities all over the world, with the common lands binding together the agrarian group. Where water rather than land is the limiting agent in production, the necessity of collective management of water supply elicits village co-operation. Peasants must combine where water is scarce, and we find compact, self-governing village communities cemented by common relationship to water rather than to land. Interesting systems of communal tenure are met with in the more arid south-western districts of the Punjab and in Sind where wells and water courses are owned by quite a large number of persons, while a large number of cultivators have acquired the right to irrigate from these wells. Similarly, Brunhes has noted instances of collective irrigation enterprise welding together semi-nomadic tribes into stable village communities in the oases of Central Asia.

But in the villages of the well watered alluvial plains where agricultural communities multiply in population, collective regulation of grazing and pasture as well as collective distribution of water from rivers, tanks or irrigation channels easily emerge in the course of agricultural development. As land becomes fully occupied and cultivated and few plots are left fallow, the need of village common lands arises because of the all important necessity of the grazing of village cattle. Moreover, as Simkovitch points out, the provision of village commons permits a better utilization of organic manure and keeps the soil from exhaustion or impoverishment. With a dense population intensive agriculture develops, and all available arable lands are owned and operated individually, unhampered by the rigid communal routine of agriculture which is associated with the earlier stage of agricultural life. As population further multiplies, the very necessities of agriculture, however, demand that there should be some lands which should be owned and managed collectively in the interests of animal husbandry as common wastes, pastures or meadows. Thus the village community lays down rules of control and management of such common lands.

The rural community usually secures the following equalizing arrangements:

1. Distribution of common lands giving equal opportunities for cattle grazing for all peasant families.
2. Collective management of water supply giving equal opportunities for irrigation.
3. Distribution of land over various soil blocks assuring equal opportunities in farming.
4. Collective employment of village menials who along with the village officers are given rentfree land or remunerated by shares of grain at each harvest. Some of these features

are discernible in the village communities of Europe.

Further, village lands are distributed by standard lots at the beginning of the rural settlement. The village territory is divided out in plough lands, a number being assigned to each family in proportion to its strength. In India, and China and in parts of South-East Asia the distribution of scattered fields in the different soil blocks of the rural settlement was determined largely by the necessities of irrigation so that each peasant family could obtain slices of good, middling or bad land, the quality of the plots being governed by fertility and nearness to the rivers and water courses. In Europe the scattered field distribution found from England across north-eastern France to the Danube basin is associated, according to Bloch, with the use of the wheeled plough introduced from the latter region. The European village community showed, however, characteristics of transition from or back to nomadism and pastoral institutions. Agricultural technique was low, the rural community was still bound together by the idea of blood relationships and the land was distributed roughly in proportion to the need and power of each family.[4] In Russia the Mir * emerged in the process of transition from pastoral nomadism to a semi-permanent agricultural settlement. The rural community whose members are held to their land by feudal laws are in effect restricted in their use of land. In fact, the Mir developed in response to an excessive supply of land. The steppe offered a change of escape from onerous tributes and exacting masters and from social restrictions in general. The coming of the Mir meant the closing of that avenue of escape though each household of the Mir received one strip of every kind of land in the settlement.[5] Tschuprow describes the

---

[4] Nussbaun, *Economic Institutions of Modern Europe*, an introduction to Sombart's Modern Capitalism.

* Village community (K.S.)

[5] Zimmermann, *World Resources and Industries*, p. 78.

characteristics of the organization of the Mir:

> The individual member has no right to dispose of the portion of land allotted to him; he can neither sell it nor bequeath it. Even the freedom of its use is considerably limited by the existence of obligatory regulations.

The emancipation of the serfs led to great misery among the Russian peasants who lost a large portion of their land and had to pay considerable sums as compensation to their landlords; while the disintegration of the Mir, promoted by the agrarian reform of Stolypin left them at the mercy of the village moneylenders or *kulak*s. The latter got hold of more and more of the land. In addition to their share in the village land they purchased more from the landlords while they employed ruined peasants as labourers. A few took advantage of the law permitting them to withdraw from the Mir and went out to the land and established farms after the style of the American farmers. But the great majority of the farmers remained poor members of essentially the same type of village commune which had existed in the past, still landhungry, burdened with taxes and debt and still compelled by economic pressure to work for the landlords at a pittance. Such was, briefly speaking, the agrarian situation in Russia when the Soviets came into power.[6] The New Economic Policy (NEP) of the Soviet government furthered the disruption of the Mir, and in fact promoted the power of the *kulak* class over the Soviet village through the effects of moneypower and market. Later on the government abandoned the NEP and ultimately brought about the expropriation and destruction of the *kulak*s. Now small-scale peasant farming is well nigh eliminated, and the Collective Farm of the village has reconciled the deeprooted individualism of the peasants with the needs of mechanized large scale agriculture under Russian conditions. Whether the

---

6 Karl Borders, *Village Life under the Soviets;* also Strauss, *Soviet Russia.*

replacement of the primitive agrarian organization of the past, on kinship and neighbourhood basis, by a formal purposive organization directed by the state renews village solidarity and community life among the new peasantry is yet to be seen; but there is no doubt that the technical advances associated with collective farming and the consolidation of the minute peasant farms into collective farms are offset by the loss of scope of individual energies and initiatives peculiar to a free peasantry. The Soviet government, however, was sure that the liquidation of the *kulaks* has sapped the roots of capitalism in agriculture, and paved the way for the victory of socialism in the countryside.

In India and China the vestigial remains of pastoral institutions had long ago disappeared while the substitution of strangers for kinsmen began long ago. In the Indian villages several agricultural castes and tribes are now represented, and both the original as well as new settlers have equal rights in village meadows, pastures and irrigation courses. Thus the economic interests of centralized agricultural activity has been superimposed upon the bond of kinship; similarly in China two or more clans are found in the villages and the commons are generally classed as communal lands. As in India so in China, no family could alienate the land in the village community without the consent of the clan or village. It thus appears that as the outcome of the growing pressure of population which leads to a diminution in the size of holdings, decline of animal husbandry and more intensive agriculture, the village community emerged to co-ordinate agricultural activity and the management of pasture lands and irrigation courses as the indispensable support of small farming. Sometimes there were joint ownership and common cultivation and sometimes the periodical redistribution of holdings. There were, again, limitations as to the amount of holding as well as about the routine of agriculture. All such measures, adopted for the advantage of the small agriculturists, differ according to the stage of development of intensive farming. But there are always discernible co-operation of the village community in the maintenance of the common pastures, water courses, wood and any other lands that are used by the peasant families as a whole without division into individual lots; in the regulation and control of water; in repairing and maintaining irrigation channels and wells; in the maintenance of a complement of artisans and workers as functionaries of the community and the upkeep of certain public works such as temples, churches, watermills and smithies.

The Autonomous vs. Feudal type of Agrarian Organization

Political and social history has always checked the natural development of agrarian organization. Political authority has always tended everywhere to become proprietary connection with land by a process of attrition or degradation through the stages of feudal superior, seigneur or overlord, assignee of land revenue, farmer of the state revenue and such like. This has originated and maintained the contrasted type of rural aggregate, the latifundian or feudal, which is quite different from the village community. Here the rural aggregate consists of tenants and owners and the social gradation is well marked. Even in India due to political and social circumstances a feudal order was superimposed upon a primitive republican system from very early times. Similarly in England and France, the old Teutonic village communities gave place to the medieval manor as a result of Norman conquest or of Frankish occupation. But this was the outcome of a long and bitter conflict. In other countries the superimposition of Roman feudality disintegrated the long established and natural communalism. Thus grew up throughout Europe extensive overlordships of emperors, senatorial magnates, feudal knights, bishops and even central cities which by the steam roller of centralisation levelled down village communities beyond recognition. The proprietor of the manor was a court or a duke, a bishop or even a king. From the proprietors upwards relations were feudal, i.e. they involved obligations and rights pertaining to lords and vassals. The king who was at the head of the superstructure of feudalism established his claim of ownership of all land. Yet under the cover of extensive lordships of the king and feudal nobles, a crop of communal usages as distinct from the manor or the private estate grew up. Even today in parts of Europe the relics of communal ownership are traceable, but as a general rule the development of feudalism has eclipsed the rights of village communities and perpetuated many compulsory services, dues and vexatious interferences with the peasantry. Generally speaking, the inevitable reaction of the theory of the crown ownership of land and of feudalism in Europe was that the landlords with a status similar to that of their ancestors in the earlier centuries consolidated the scattered holdings into large farms and estates and turned certain parcels of their territories as leasehold, while the masses of the peasantry were reduced to hired labourers. Feudal society was marked by sharp class distinctions based on an unequal distribution of land, which also carried with it differences in the privileges granted to members of the different estates or classes in various countries.

In Europe migration, conquest and expropriation worked havoc with the autonomous type of village organization. Where the sovereign powers of the state were delegated to the territorial magnate, the overthrow of the liberties of the peasants was carried out, at least in the name of law, by enforcing excessive military services which ruined the peasants, but which were required to meet the insatiable ambitions of the dynasty of territorial lords to acquire new lands and new peasants. Thus the abuse of the rights to compulsory labour or the conversion of the administration of justice into a military operation were the chief methods by which the status of the peasantry was lowered throughout Central Europe. The common freeman, however, received the final blow by the formal delegation or by usurpation of a most important power of the crown, the disposition of unoccupied land or commons which originally belonged to all the peasant folk (i.e. freeman) for common use.

In England in spite of the theory of crown ownership of land which led to a delegation of such ownership to the barons, the king through jealousy of the great nobles took care by means of judges to protect the customary rights of the freeman and the villein. Both of them so long as they performed their services were entitled to hold the enclosed land and what was equally important to enjoy the use of the open land or the waste. The right to use the waste was interfered with only when the great landowners became dominant in England. The Enclosure Acts had much the same effect in England as the emancipation of the serfs in Russia. They made the lord the actual owner of the lands hitherto enjoyed in common by his tenants. One effect of the enclosure movement was to kill out the small freeholders. Similarly the appropriation of the pasture land in Russia by the lords was a bitter grievance of the Russian peasantry and did much to render his emancipation a nullity. The spoliation of the lord's estates by the peasants in Russia at the time of the first revolution was according to the view of the peasants a resumption by the peasants of their old stolen property.

Thus landlordism often became the prevailing element. As Miss Irvin observed:

> Even in the middle ages the landlord of west Europe had the position of the owner of common lands and of such conveniences as the well and wine-press. The tenants were

> regarded only as usufructuaries of the wood and the waste and paid him fees for the compulsory use of the well or bakeries.

And in some countries and districts he was later so able to strengthen himself to their detriment that he appropriated most of the profits of cultivation, and they were either squeezed out of existence or debased towards slavery. The community life receives a deathblow due to the monopolization and abuse of the land by a particular class, buttressed by unequal political disabilities, special prerogatives and rules of social distance. Social *anomie,* to use a term of Durkheim, is the result not merely of a sharp social and economic cleavage in the rural population, but also of an exaggerated individualism and of the disintegration of various local and functional groups and associations which gave expression to the community life and culture in their different aspects. The trends of class opposition, individualism, formalism and centralization support one another, defacing and deforming community life and personality.

The Rural Community in Transition

The history of village communities and the transformation these undergo as a result of the rise of money economy in different parts of the world indicate the similarity of economic forces operating under the stress of population pressure and the development of better types of farming based on money power and commerce, evident in the East and in the West, in advanced and backward communities. The disintegration of the primitive collective agrarian organization on a kindred basis under a chief, headman or village elders, the power of merchants and moneylenders and the expropriation of the peasantry seen in different lands portray both an agrarian and a cultural revolution. New social relationships and norms emerge in this transition, and alter the trend of community life. The rise of big estates, split up among isolated groups of tenantry, and of scattered and feudal as contrasted with the compact and autonomous village organization, whether in Asia or Europe, due to political subordination and expropriation of agricultural folks, also indicates the operation of other familiar social and economic forces and shows the same results in respect of the imbalance and disintegration of free communities. Agricultural conditions like the advantages of enclosures, and extension of the pasture and field grass system, economic conditions like the competition with large scale mechanized farming and animal industry in pioneer countries, and political conditions like inadequate protection of the peasantry by the king, lord, or noble or excessive taxation have led to the dispossession of the peasantry, introduced big agricultural estates and sharpened class opposition in many agricultural lands. Other contributory factors have been the increase of rural population beyond the adequate support for handicrafts and the rigid communal routine of agriculture, the decline of handicrafts, and the emancipation of serfs. Many of these have been found in operation almost universally through different epochs and stages of economic evolution, causing the increase of the proletariat, wholesale migration and breakdown of peasant economy and tradition. Thus peasant ethos and tradition which antedated feudal society, lived through feudalism and has lingered under capitalism and money power can no longer safeguard the community against disintegration, threatened as a result of excessive urbanization and industrialization.

For 38 per cent (2010,K.S.) of the world's population agriculture is the dominant occupation; and thus such agricultural features as the development of the village community, its compromise with money economy, the rise of landlordism, the splitting of estates into farms dealt with on the metayage system, the change from peasant owner to peasant proletariat, subdivision and sub-letting of proprietary or tenancy status, and persistence or lapse of the traditional village communalism, all these are determining factors in community organization whether in the East or in the West, in Asia, Europe or America. From these one can easily rise to broad categories of economic development, which will be applicable to all agricultural countries, and then the present divorce between economic history and theoretical economics will disappear. Such survey is of great significance, for the student of sociology. For the transition from the primary and intimate neighbourhood groups of the village community to the impersonal and economic grouping of the rural population not only manifests the exploitative character of agrarian capitalism and finance but also the imbalance and inadequacy of community organization. The rural community, which is simple, homogeneous, co-operative and intolerant of divergent types, thus develops an extreme individualism. Individualism as a system of life is as much a rural as an urban product. In a country like the USA and Canada where the peasant tradition is weak and the farmer as production and business manager lives shallow rooted on his isolated farm unit, the profit motive and individualism are pretty strong, and the farmer's business, employing outside capital and wage labour, approximates to a capitalistic enterprise on a competitive basis. The farmer disposes of his old farm as and when he chooses to take up another elsewhere, and does not develop firm face-to-face primary group loyalties. Farm tenancy now increases rapidly in the prosperous agricultural areas of the USA due to foreclosures on mortgages. Community organizations which used to be supported by owner–operators languish as a result, the tenants being far more mobile and very loosely tied to the organized social life. The unfavourable social consequences of farm tenancy are particularly marked in the deep South where the cotton sharecroppers are insecure in their position due to absence of a written contract, and have been displaced in large numbers as the result of the introduction of the mechanical cotton-picker. A South Carolina survey shows that white owner-operators move out once in eleven years, and white tenants about once in every four years; Black owners every twelve years and Black tenants every five or six years. "If tenancy," observe Kolb and Brunner, "is a function of industrialism and therefore an inevitable phenomenon of the present state of development of the Western world, those who maintain that landownership is one of the strongest bulwarks of national safety face inevitable defeat". The wandering and adventurous habit, born of the epoch of the open frontier, and the conception of agriculture not as a profession but as a field of monetary investment and returns hold owners and tenants alike in tenacious grip, and militate against their attachment to the homestead, the land and the neighbourhood. In a country like India where the peasant ethos is firmly established but where in the present agricultural stage peasant proprietorship declines, due to disuse of essential co-operative habits in farming, usury, rackrenting, and excessive subdivision of holdings, and the class of rentreceivers, intermediaries and agricultural proletariat multiplies, we similarly find the emergence of secondary group relations, contract and individualism at the expense of the integrated primary groups of the rural community. With the rise of landlordism and creation of grades of proprietors between the tillers of the soil and the state has spread economic individualism resulting in free mortgage and sale of land to the middle and moneylending classes. The new centralization has also superseded the communal employment of village artisans and functionaries, and the authority of the panchayat. All this along with the appropriation of village woods and pasture lands and the obliteration of customary rights of the peasantry to pasturage, irrigation and the supply of fuel and timber has contributed towards the disorganization of agriculture. Such has been the agrarian change in many other Eastern countries like Java, Indo-China and Japan leading to a transformation of the ancient peasant ethos and tradition. Peasant economy in many lands in the West also is now forced into the pattern of a business economy, the farmer producing for the market according to the principle of costing which gradually alters his sentiments and attitudes towards his soil, profession and community. In the Scandinavian countries, in Germany, Poland, Czechoslovakia, the homestead and attached agricultural lands are, however, largely bequeathed undivided from generation to generation and the peasant develops a strong attachment to his own soil and neighbourhood, and subordinates individualism to family and communal interests. In England, the USA, Canada and other areas of Anglo-Saxon culture, the farmer moves from farm to farm and from one settlement to another, although the farm unit may not be disturbed by the passing of the generations and thus snaps ties easily with neighbourhood, family and soil. Farmers are as much torn between organic–communal and deliberate–individualistic standards as urbanities in such a social situation.

Social Anomie

The exaggerated development of individualism makes for the distortion and dissolution of man's social heritage and culture. It is the symptom of a profound lack of balance between ecology, economy and the state. Sometimes ecological conditions such as isolation in machine operated farm units in pioneer lands or in scattered homesteads in virgin forests and sand dunes impose individualism; sometimes economic conditions such as commercial agriculture favour the economic man of money power and bring the agrarian organization prematurely into the vortex of cosmopolitanism; sometimes it is political conditions such as conquest and overcentralization that obliterate the vestiges of localism and functionalism and leave the individual without an adequate social organization and means of social control. Individualism receives accordingly an undue emphasis as a principle of group organization due to a variety of factors and circumstances which introduce a disequilibrium between ecological, economic and political sectors of life. It is such inner disharmony which explains the contrasts between such present irreconcilable opposites as parochialism and cosmopolitanism, individualism and totalitarianism, the cultural or primary and the ecological or contractual phase of behaviour. Individualism, centralization, formalism, contract and cosmopolitanism are reciprocally interdependent. These revolutionize the social structure of the village introducing a chronic struggle between the economic classes and disintegrating the primary groups and local and functional self-government. The decline of the middle class and the peasantry and multiplication of the proletariat go hand in hand with the extended scope of centralized, bureaucratic authority of the state, which distorts and destroys a balanced localism and regionalism, and ethical framework and alters the entire course of cultural evolution. On the other hand, where peasant ownership and tradition are safeguarded, there exists a strong attachment to the soil and neighbourhood, family solidarity, localism, functionalism and regionalism, which check mobility, class struggle and stress of non-humanistic values. The community thus finds in localism, functionalism and regionalism appropriate and wholesome defences against the dangers of cosmopolitanism, formalism and standardization of modern technological society.

The elemental economics and politics of the field differ among different regions and peoples, governing not merely economic and social stratification, but also the basis and evolution of community life. Whether the rural community succeeds or fails depends upon the resource pattern, mode of land utilization and ownership and the "proper" behaviour of one social class to another, the latter being rooted in the economic and social history of the people. No characterization of human culture is possible without an understanding, therefore, of its ecological or natural resource and utilization patterns and the economics and politics of ownership and distribution of the land.

14

The Ecology Behind Politics

Needs of Economic Diversity and Orientation

FOR the unity and health of a nation there is needed diversity of resources and technics. Agriculture should supplement industry and trade and vice versa. For the development of agriculture are needed forests in the mountains, pastures in the mountain slopes and market towns on the rivers. For urban ways of living are necessary the rural. Above all, there is needed a rational balance of the different economic procedures and their developments. There is an organic interconnection between the various economical uses of land in a given country. Scientific agriculture in the fertile plains, forestry in the hills and pasture-farming in poor and cheap lands help one another. On the other hand, the ascent of agriculture to the hillsides and depletion of forests, excessive or indiscriminate grazing in pasture lands, and continuous encroachment on marshes and streams spell the economic decline of the nation as much as the development of a few giant cities or metropolises. Between the different economic procedures in the various regions or sections of a region a definite orientation and organization are essential. The economic planning movement aims at achieving this integration through the rational direction of all the available resources distributed among the various sections of a country. The interarticulation of a country according to agricultural regions, cereal zones, raw produce zones; stock raising zones, forest zones or mineral regions and manufacturing regions underlies a farsighted agricultural planning, as that of Russia. In countries like Russia, the United States or India with their vast expanses of territory, unmarked by political boundaries or tariff lines, the locality or natural region is free to develop in a manner quite impossible in Western and Central Europe. In a considerable part of Europe political boundaries thwart the orientation and development of economic regions. This has aggravated occupational imbalance which has been responsible chiefly for the evils of unemployment and overpopulation. Protection and inflation have been the twin political weapons used to promote industrialization under economic handicaps, and the more there has been overproduction, the greater has been the demand for raising the tariff wall. The subdivision of homogeneous economic regions into distinct political states, overindustrialization, underproduction in agriculture, and overpopulation have been linked together in a vicious circle in Europe from which there can be no escape until there be a fundamental readjustment of political and economic organization. In Europe, overpopulated and lacking political and economic balance, there is perpetual fluctuation of the balance of power, and struggle is perpetually renewed by the insurgent forces racialism and nationalism bringing the entire continent into periodic political upheavals.

In the continental states, where there are no artificial limitations offering obstacles to the development of natural economic regions, the problems of economic orientation are not dissimilar. The conflicting interests of different zones, sections and groups of producers must everywhere be brought into some kind of balance in the economic structure of the nation. This is especially necessary in a democratic federal state, as the United States, Russia and Britain, and India of the future. In a vast and heterogeneous nation, regional geography and ecology are central facts, and the tasks of statesmanship consist in co-ordinating the divergent lines of development and special interests of different regions and sections and bringing them all together in a common economic policy. On the one hand, the economic diversity between the regions of the USA, Russia and India is one of the strongest binders fostering a national unity operating through regional divisions of labour. On the other hand, federalism as a political experiment is bound to fail in the absence of economic interpenetration and right balancing of the interests of different regions, localities and sections.

It is well known that in the United States when the first experiments towards a confederation were launched the disparity between urban industrial interests of the Middle and New England states and the agricultural regions of the South and the West brought about a series of political conflicts which endangered unification. Opposition developed between the agricultural states who generally wanted a tariff for revenue only and those of the Middle and New England states who hoped that duties might be made high enough to protect manufacturers also. This conflict, indeed, became permanent in American financial history, a strong evidence of the divergence of economic policies of agricultural, manufacturing and mining regions, which are now being welded together with greater or less success, into a unified national policy of the Federation. As a recent American writer has observed:

> Turner's sectionalism in American history — to be carefully distinguished from regionalism — is based largely on differences in economic structure and needs. The shift of industry from the north-east to the middle states has been accompanied by changes in political beliefs, and it is noteworthy that the states to break the "Solid South" in 1928 are leaders in industrialization.[1]

---

[1] Moore, *What is Regionalism?*, Southern Policy Papers No. 10.

In India the opposition between the textile manufacturing regions in the West and the rest of the provinces early expressed itself in similar disputes relating to the rates of the cotton duties. The success of the Indian federal experiment would depend in large measure upon a balanced development of industries and agriculture as parts of a regional whole.

The Tasks of Regionalism

But regional planning is something more than economic planning. As plant and animal ecology deals with the complex and subtle linkages between different species of plants and animals and the processes of uplift of the entire biotic community of the ecological area, so regional planning deals with climate, resources and landscape, laws, customs, economic and social institutions, necessary to bring about a close harmony and progress of the human community in relation to the region's forces and possibilities. Soil, topography, climate, flora and fauna offer the fundamental life-giving essentials which bring about a regionally organized social development. With man's cultivation and industry, his understanding and use of the soil and the plant and animal resources that are bound up with one another in subtle cause and effect, relationships are blended social customs, traditions and ways of living. These give the individual easy guidance for his struggle for living and status and the community a distinctiveness essential for its survival. Sunshine and rainfall, crop and animal, man's encountering the procession of the seasons, his multiplication, distribution and circulation are tied with one another and with the pattern of culture of the region which thereby acquires stability and orientation. The region is a common and co-ordinate set of stimuli, eliciting a similarity of responses, habits and feelings which are reinforced by gregariousness, and which are moulded and stabilized into a characteristic mental type and pattern of living. The region is also a result of co-ordinate set of reactions which become crystallized into the legacy of occupations, traditions and culture. The latter direct man's impulses, interests and values along certain common channels which make life easier and smoother for the community in the region. People and resources, technology, traditions and values react upon one another, and give to the region a distinct "personality" and to the culture a distinct "areal" organization.[2] Men's lives and memories, mental patterns and aesthetic habits, institutions and behaviours are inseparable from the region, which accordingly elicits ardent pride and loyalty that sustain the human spirit. Regionalism thus is no mere geographical or economic concept; it is as wide and deep as man's collective adaptation to the needs of wresting life sustenance and appropriate human values from the bit of the earth which is the cradle of the community. Now social adaptation and selection are not sure and certain of their purpose. In the modern world man's machine technology which is a means of economic adaptation as well as his increased tempo of life, mobility, fluidity of social relations and stress of the contractual–pecuniary standard, which are mental and social adjustments to the pressures and procedures of the new technology, have brought about a serious imbalance between man, society and the region. Culture is now being uprooted from its solid, ecological base. Its norms of mechanical efficiency, competition and pecuniary valuation are associated with a reckless depletion of the heritage of the soil, trees and waters, causing a serious regional disequilibrium and aggravating the human struggle for existence. The disruption and disintegration of the region accompany also occupational disequilibrium, and disorder in man's economic, institutional and political relations. Regionalism is essentially the art of

---

[2] See *Regional Sociology*, chapter XIII.

linking ecological, technological and cultural development in terms of stability and survival of resources, community and culture. Its aim is to restore social equilibrium through eliminating the misfits of man's technology and economy as well as lags of human values and culture. Such restoration today largely lies in the regulation of giant machine organization and reduction of tempo of life, re-distribution of industry and population, re-orientation of rural and urban ways of living and a new equilibrium between people and the heritage of the region. Regional planning would not accept only the pecuniary valuation of technology and economy but recognizes human values as the ultimate product of the regional adjustment. In the region technology transforms resources and raw materials into finished goods which are converted into real income, leisure and recreation or into capital goods which are reservoirs of energy replacing the goods destroyed in the course of production. Therefore, along with the perennial flow of goods and services, a volume of capital goods or energy stores flowing one way and a stream of consumer goods and values flowing the other, we have the orientation of social, economic, educational, recreational and ameliorative institutions, permanent social products which offer easy guidance to a people in their adaptation and give to the region a distinct character, differentiating it from others till at length "it becomes, as it were, a medal struck in the likeness of a people". It is the people who unfold the individuality, the distinct culture or personality of a region by means of its roots and traditions, transforming its resources and materials for their needs, interests and values. The cultural framework is woven into the ecological skeleton of the region: it exhibits constant change, interdependence and specialization of parts, improvement or deterioration with most significant effects upon the equipment and behaviour of a people, and the naturalness and stability of its region. Regionalism aims at a continuity of this vast current of resources, energies and services for the permanence of the community through conservation and implementation, not through exploitation, and the transformation of these resources, energies and services into higher and higher values furnishing a permanent dynamics for human culture, free from the artificiality and emptiness of the technological society.

Schemes of National Regional Planning

Comprehensive schemes of national regional planning involve, therefore, a careful balancing of man's economic interests and cultural activities which aim at the ultimate values. Economically, socially and politically, regional planning gives up the narrow standpoint of price economics. Economically, regional planning seeks the goal of conservation in a reduction of the rate of disappearance or consumption of exhaustible resources and a corresponding increase in the unused surplus left at the end of a period for the purpose of benefiting posterity. It also aims at the conservation and development of local skills and aptitudes of peoples, without the degradation that the nineteenth century industrial development brought about everywhere. The social aims of regional planning are to arrest the concentration of population and industry in a few supercities or metropolises and the growth of agglomerations or "connurbations", i.e. the grouping of settlements which are attached to one another and are oriented to one big city or metropolis; to create independent little towns where a further increase of population in the region can be absorbed and people may live more harmoniously with nature and industry. Corresponding to the slum areas in the great cities there are blighted areas in prosperous river plains which used to feed the entire nation but whose farming and agricultural water supply have been ruined by decades of soil erosion, deforestation, decay and meandering of rivers. Destruction of forests, soil erosion, reclamation of swamps and canalization give rise to problems which must all be approached from the point of view of an entire river valley as a unified whole. Otherwise one province or state in the upriver areas can ruin others in the lower areas. Regional planning and co-ordination of land, forest and water resources can alone prevent increasing recurrent national losses due to desiccation, soil erosion, flood and spread of swamps and jungles, which are encountered in many agricultural states in the world today. Without some kind of regional integration different provinces and regions with their divergent interests in agriculture, irrigation and navigation range themselves in conflicting camps which may thwart national unity.[3] Deficit regions and provinces with eroded fields, choked streams and recurrent droughts can only be rescued through interregional and national cooperative planning.

The co-ordination of the tasks of agriculture, irrigation, hydroelectric development and navigation stresses in modern states the significance of contrasts and uniformities of regions. In fact, agricultural planning rests on a nationwide division of labour and interdependence of crop and resource regions; regionalism serves as the major key to both agricultural recovery and reconstruction. As the distance from the market or the cost of transport increases there is a tendency for agriculture to become more and more extensive. Marketgardening and horticulture, intensive peasant farming and largescale agricultural enterprises or plantations are arranged in concentric zones around the markets. The same idea of zonal types of culture also applies to the systems of regional and world economy, the more distant and sparsely populated regions growing food and raw materials for the industrialized and thickly populated areas. Von Thünen's

3 Mukerjee, *The Changing Face of Bengal*, p. 286.

theory of localization and Le Play-Geddes' theory of the valley section are the indispensable foundations of agricultural theory and reconstruction. Further, the sizes of agricultural units have reference to crops and agricultural practices and these would differ in different regions. Large estates extend the zone of cereal growing, peasant holdings that of stock raising and marketgardening. All these have an important bearing upon the land policy of different regions. The size of the holding, the situation of the land, distant from or near to the market, subsistence and commercial farming are all fundamental features in the movement of land rents and values. The new arts of sectional agricultural planning and farm accountancy represent the application of these ideas to agricultural reconstruction. Another line of research, which renders valuable service to regionalism, is the study of the size of agricultural units, crop and type of farming in relation to social organization, attitudes and culture of the agrarian population. Such work has been successfully carried out for cotton culture by American sociologists. Such regional or sectional surveys or plans of agricultural planning are supported and strengthened by the new movements of a more rational land utilization, erosion control, afforestation and river management which tend to be organized on a sectional or regional basis. Without regional planning, again, the dispersion of industry from the cities into the country, and the development of a decentralized and well balanced industrial structure, freed in large measure from the antagonism of classes are not possible. No doubt, class conflicts in the present political system are an expression of the modern ill balanced and centralized industrial structure, with its sudden fluctuations of employment and mass purchasing power, which can be mitigated or eliminated by the strategy of industrial and regional planning. Politically, the aim of regional planning is to utilize social and cultural traditions in homogeneous areas for building up an active citizenship. Both the Great Society and the state have through the stress of the ideal of mechanical efficiency paid little regard to local and functional groups and associations. Regional planning, instead of permitting the steam roller of centralization to obliterate all voluntary bodies would tend to make the fullest use of them for a wide variety of services, selecting institutions which have a higher community value. The recent developments of motor transport and the aeroplane, the media, telephone and the giant power and of the co-operative organization in agriculture, marketing and finance, have greatly strengthened the methods and strategy of localism and regionalism. In the democratic countries in the West there is discerned today a distinct tendency towards associating with the state a large number of voluntary bodies whose organized social services have often pioneered the way for governmental action. Adams points out that this co-operative commonwealth of statutory and voluntary bodies, local and central, has nowhere developed more than in Great Britain. It is of course far from its full expression, but

> the associative principle is enabling a great variety and richness of community effort to advance the standard of well-being, is bringing about a breaking down of class divisions and the growth of good neighbourliness and is increasing the power and usefulness of public opinion.

The introduction of regional autonomy and decentralization and exaltation of functions in corporations, professions, co-operatives and voluntary bodies can lead to the active participation of the common man in the work of the government, temper the tone of class-ridden state and favour a new ethic of service and solidarity.

The region with its characteristic agricultural conditions and structure, land tenure and policy, its distinctive social composition, its unique traditions, customs and historical events, its folk music, art and literature nourishes sentiments and loyalties, which cannot be obliterated without danger to the personality organization of its inhabitants. On the other hand, the sense of community of the region is a valuable national asset which should be cherished in order that democracy may not drift towards a wooden bureaucracy. Parochialism or the narrow spirit of the village or town has been found to be as much a misfit in this modern age of easy communication and transportation as the uniformity and standardization brought about by the centralized administration and long-range control of the nineteenth century *Leviathan* or the twentieth century totalitarian state. Many nations which have experienced the corroding and devastating effects of the formalism and impersonalism of national organizations look up to regional initiatives and experiments as giving adequate opportunities of expression for the democratic spirit of neighbourhood. As a matter of fact, democratic as contrasted with totalitarian planning largely rests on regionalism, utilizing the accumulated force of tradition and environment in natural and historical, rather than arbitrarily defined, political regions. The region thus as the focus of political consciousness not only becomes the corrective of the wastes and weaknesses of nationwide regimentation of the giant state, but also rescues the technological society, through the varied regional artistic expressions of folk culture from the exaggerated stress of pecuniary, non-humanistic values and tendencies. But the full cultural potentialities of the region as a synthesis, a living frame of the unity of folk, mind and place through labour, have not been adequately realized. These have been chiefly realized in Europe and America so far in respect of the rational ordering and co-ordination of economic activities and plans. Thus regionalism remains as yet a developing programme though indispensable in the evolution of an advanced and rationally ordered civilization.

Regionalism in Politics

As a result mostly of Le Play-Vidal de La Blache geographical movement in France, Germany and England and recently in the United States we come across practical schemes of orderly planning especially of industrial regions so as to utilize all elements in the physical environment for social wellbeing as distinct from the ruthless exploitation of particular elements, for example, coal in England and Germany, regardless of the wider social consequences which mark the stages of industrial revolution. In Germany in the Lower Rhine region, which is the most highly industrialized area in the whole country, a reformation of municipal boundaries has been taking place under the name of *Neugliederung* or *Eingemeindung* and also a better co-ordination of the distribution of coal and iron on the one hand and the export of manufactures and import trade in the most important raw materials and a considerable proportion of the food products on the other. While regional planning in Germany has been mostly industrial planning, in other countries, particularly in France and Sweden, it seeks to harmonize the interests of large industrial cities, satellite towns, country towns and villages in a common scheme in which each has its place. Historical data are used in the reconstruction of rural cultural areas, often by meticulous field surveys, which have been valuable aids in determining the areas' inherited conditions of settlement, land utilization and communications. In France, where the older regional life has persisted in most provincial towns geographers have devoted considerable attention to socio-economic regionalism, and have collaborated actively with official and unofficial bodies for these objects. Communes could now form unions or syndicates for carrying on regional activities such as canals, aqueducts and waterworks, bridges and roads, transport services, drainage and sanitation. There are thus many intermunicipal bodies which have undertaken a number of regional activities while provision is also made for interdepartmental syndicates. Municipal Chambers of Commerce are also organized for several traditional regions of French history. "Our major objective," observe Brunhes and Vallaux,

> should be sought in the rational grouping of the forces of production, of labour, of distribution, and of transport for the states of the future, so as to enable them to profit by the new forms of activity and of wealth, while at the same time respecting historical continuity.

Regional councils have now been established in France in economic engineering, judicial and educational fields, and regionalism has also found abundant expression in regional literature and other artistic expression. Along with socio-economic regionalism there is now a demand in France for the representation of natural integrations in politics and a bold redivision of the country so that each area should have a definite personality with divergent resources if possible, a welldefined central city and the legacy of a connected historical tradition. Lecoy says:

> We look forward to a second Chamber of Deputies, based upon those local groupings in which the citizen lives his true life, in which he works and thinks; upon groupings endowed with a life of their own, and constituting, in the true sense of the word, communities, because there exists between their inhabitants identities of thoughts, of interests, and of needs.

In Great Britain Fawcett has envisaged a polity based not on political entities but on ecological facts. In his *Provinces of England*, he has raised the question whether the country units developed in relation to social and historical circumstances, which have largely disappeared could be superseded by larger administrative units, more in harmony with the modern economic regions. Similarly, G.D.H. Cole has recently suggested the formation of Provincial Councils for industrial areas or "connurbations" with Regional Councils for the "Regions" within each area, while within each region there would continue lesser authorities for boroughs and districts. For the co-ordination of the different "Provinces" there should be a Federal Council including representatives of the whole area, and possessing certain overriding powers of planning and development for each portion of the country.[4] In Russia, in Italy, in Spain and in Poland the same tendency of regionalism has been followed. In Russia scientists through their intensive studies of the distribution of resources and economic patterns are devising both principles and practical policies for their co-ordinated development in terms of regional integration. In Spain Catalon regionalism has a long history. It began as a cultural movement but became definitely political, and obtained recognition from the Spanish Republic which granted Catalonia certain civil legislative powers and its own municipal administration. Similarly, Basque cultural regionalism paved the way for the desire for autonomy which received recognition leading to the creation of the most progressive communal and municipal administration in this country. The Galician movement has, however, remained mostly educational and cultural in Spain. In Poland as well a regionalism with administrative and economic aims has developed out of cultural regionalism, and there has been demand for revision of the map as well as decentralization and self-government at least in respect of cultural and economic activities and the administration of justice. In the Balkan States the conflicts between the unity of state administration and the cultural claims of regional homelands has been acute for many years due to the uncertainty in political boundaries. In the United States regionalism based

[4] "The Future of Local Government", *Political Quarterly*, October–December 1941.

on natural ecological divisions has represented even a stronger socio-economic movement, and is the natural outcome of the influx of peoples from different parts of Europe. Thus Keyserling observes:

> America is at the bottom of a new land of budding localisms, very much as Europe was at the end of the migration of the peoples, and it seems to be sub-divided into large provinces of a comparatively unified character, provinces out of which there would undoubtedly have grown in earlier days and under different conditions separated cultures.

Comparing European with American regionalism, Morgan observes:

> Regions like New England or the South are of a larger order of magnitude than those of France or Spain. It is conceivable that localisms are growing within New England or the South, and it is these which are more nearly equivalent to the regions in European countries.[5]

Besides the New England and the South, other regions with a distinctive cultural pattern are the Middle West, the Plains Area and the Pacific North-West. It is, however, only with reference to the South that Odum, Vance and others have systematically surveyed and interpreted regional culture. While sociologists in the USA have studied the localities and regions as distinct from the state, section or division as the appropriate unit of meticulous folk and cultural studies, state planning has often adopted as its unit the various ecological integrations, regions of agriculture, forestry, industry and resource patterns in general. In this country much of legislation has been increasingly sponsored by politically powerful functional groups whose interests coincide more or less exactly

---

[5] "Three Aspects of Regional Consciousness", *The Sociological Review*, January 1934.

with some geographical area. Thus the Mid-West farm bloc and the New England manufacturing group promote legislation favourable to occupational groups rather than to geographic areas and have brought the importance of such classes home to all politicians. The interstate efforts to provide labour standards and crime prevention and detection, the rise of metropolitan planning, and the emergence of at least two groups of states for planning and co-ordination purposes point in the same direction as the Tennessee Valley Authority, and lend weight to the arguments that the USA need subnational but extra-state administrative units. Vance observes:

> There are two great economic complexes that may be expected to force regionalism on the attention of the state. The first of these is the railroads, and the task is one of consolidation, elimination and unification of systems until each crop and natural resource province shall be efficiently interconnected with metropolitan centres. The second is the pressing problem of electrical power. Hydroelectric development based on the natural distribution of flowing rivers and water-power demands co-ordination of large areas.[6]

This need has actually been met by the various agencies of the national government by the establishment of more than 100 "regional" administrative areas. Several schemes have been mooted to make for a decentralized but united administration which may preserve the unique possibilities of different regions for the benefit of the nation. The federal government might divide the nation into any feasible number of regions, in each of which there might be one central office for furnishing information to inquirers and for correlating the activities of the various federal agencies operating within the region. At the other extreme, the states might be abolished and their places taken by regional assemblies with legislative authority

---

[6] *Human Geography of the South*, p. 17.

subject only to a greatly reduced national Congress and the constitutional interpretation of the Supreme Court. Both schemes have been proposed along with a host of others falling somewhere between these two. There already exist two regional planning commissions which might easily be converted into administrative bodies by the delegation of state and national powers to them. The interstate compact and the federal corporation are also offered as means of meeting the situation.[7]

In the urban industrial regions cultural change and social mobility are quick and respond easily to changed technique and scientific progress. But the regional culture of an agricultural people takes much longer or may even retain its power as the definite society, sometimes weathering several technological changes and finding itself more harmoniously in accord with later technologies than with those it resisted. Rural co-operatives and electrification or the use of cheap motors in industry are more easily assimilated to the folk culture as these increase its social and technical efficiency. Or the folk society may reflect a dominant, rather than a recessive, adaptive culture. Odum, a strong advocate of socio-economic regionalism, finds in the imbalance between folk society and the organisational–technical society the key not only to accelerated social change but also to contemporary social deterioration and senescence. He gives examples of agrarian cultures resisting the urban–industrial technology, and later adapting to newer cultural trends, or of the power of the Blacks to adapt certain language and religious form so completely as to make them his own, or in the case of a conquered people dominating the culture of the conquerers. Thus, in spite of all

---

[7] See Moore, *What is Regionalism?*, Southern Policy Papers No. 10; also Hertzler, "Sociological Aspects of American Regionalism", *Social Forces*, October 1939.

the modern technological standardization, there are evidences of increased rather than decreased folk regionalism in some instances. In India, in spite of the fact that regionalism based on affinities of language, race and caste tradition is much stronger than in most countries of the world and has left a deep impress in arts and industries, vernacular literature, religion and culture; it has been neglected as the constructive factor in economic, social and political planning. The Simon Commission, though it realized the necessity of delimiting political boundaries according to regional and cultural affinities left the problem completely unsolved. In several provinces under the newly established autonomy the provincial boundaries now offer serious obstacles to the development of natural economic regions, and various schemes for the redistribution of political boundaries are now afoot though these stress chiefly the factors of the unity of language, religion and culture.

Dissociation of Nationality from its Ecological Background in Europe

These drawbacks or difficulties are small as compared with those which attended the creation of the new states in Europe by the Treaty of Versailles. Economic nationalism here for an age neglected or thwarted the accumulated force of regional conditions and possibilities which govern natural economic orientation. Thus, the Lower Rhine and Holland form one commercial limit. Lorraine and Luxemburg form with the Ruhr district one iron and steel area. As a matter of fact the great central industrial zone of Europe covering the coal basin, which with interruptions stretches from the Ruhr to Belgium and northern France, the Saar basin, and the Upper Silesian-Polish coalfield is held together by mutual dependence for raw materials, power resources, market and credit conditions, etc. Moreover, before the war, it possessed a carefully balanced and closely interwoven currency system which practically represented a European currency unit.[8] In the map of Europe prior to the Second World War the affinities of culture and language were generally accepted as criteria for the formation of the nationality groups. Culture and language no doubt are powerful binders but these are less primary than the ecological realities and processes which represent the physical base of man's social heritage. On account of the dissociation of the idea of nationality from its ecological background the struggle between the principles of ecologic or economic orientation, on the one hand, and of political autonomy based on the likemindedness due to common language and culture on the other, will give no peace to central Europe while Russian collectivism, whose boundaries in both Asia and Europe are shifting, and which is neither assimilated nor restored to European normality always remains as a mighty challenge to European polity and culture. Ecological forces being more stable and persistent have shattered the dream of a *Mittel-Europa.* On the other hand, the multiplication of political units only on the basis of community of language and culture disregards the possibilities of greater economic integration and planning that are demanded by both free competition and rationalization. In Europe, overpopulated as she is today, chronic unemployment and overproduction in certain industries or branches of industry and stands in the way of that rational division of labour which would have created new wealth and economic opportunity, but promotes interracial hostility and race of armaments sowing the seeds of wars in the future. "The general distribution of produce", observes Josiah Stamp, "has no relation whatever to existing political areas; these existing political areas are, however, becoming

---

8 Alfred Weber's contribution to Hanns Heimann (ed.), *Europäische Zollunion.*

more instead of less insistent upon their claims to regulate such matters". Thus the logic of nationalism runs counter to the law of population in Europe.

War aggravates the symptoms of overpopulation by the destruction of wealth and deployment of capital resources, sciences, and technical skill to the production of munitions and other raw materials; it leads to the curtailment of freedom and economic opportunities for the masses of the people, and thus create overpopulation in respect of the restricted environment. It prevents that shift of occupations, which are Nature's safeguarding mechanisms for the creation of a maximum of life, and that regulates distribution of wealth which opens the door to the masses, to a new freedom and standard of living. Above all, it bolsters up a social organization and structure of population which prevent the national and international division of labour and resources which are the chief means of maintaining an optimum population in the restricted environment.

Localism vs. Centralization

The question whether society will prefer the maximum of local initiative and autonomy, even at the cost of efficient administration, to centralization is determined by technological development on the one hand which abolishes distance and targets social aims on the other. A society whose chief object is military efficiency must demand centralization and handle all vital social services through central organs. A highly industrialized community, which carries on large industrial and financial undertakings through trusts, cartels and corporations would prefer efficiency and productivity to the waste and disorder of small, independent units of production, and accept the curse of bigness, whether of corporations or of political units.

The peaceful agricultural communities of the East have preserved a characteristic social heritage of localism and regionalism in industry and art, education and collective living in a manner unknown in Europe and America. Such localism and regionalism are of course connected with diversities of races, peoples and cultures which are oriented into clans, castes, guilds and brotherhoods. Now a caste or guild in India and China mould the whole social and economic life of their region and develop a professional conscience which is an important factor in social progress. In a certain sense castes and guilds in India and China are local federations on a minute scale. There are in India caste assemblies extending their jurisdiction over a wide field from the subcaste to the whole brotherhood, inhabiting a large number of villages and extending over a region overstepping administrative boundaries. There are guilds or occupational groups arising independently or it may be out of kinship or neighbourhood relationship or an admixture of both, which have similar extending circles of authority over a whole region or community. There are, again, territorial panchayats or folk-moots in which political, ethnical and occupational elements are fused and of which the jurisdictions extend over villages and groups of villages. Group organization in the East takes the forms of regionalism and functionalism, which have kept alive multitudinous autonomous local units and united them in a loose federalism in which the central authority is a convenience rather than a state. In Europe in the nineteenth century the larger national state emerged out of the ruins of feudalism and completely subordinated or abolished all autonomous local and functional groups.

The media, apart from the steam engine and motor, now offer opportunities for reconciling the efficiency of powerful centralized government with active citizenship and responsibility in small functional and local groups; and the most vital problem of modern politics is to readjust the relation between the actual units of collective living and units of formal social control under the aegis of new technology. But the greatest obstacle to this is that those non-economic values, which are associated with localism and regionalism, are yet subordinated to the aims of political, financial and industrial power without which no nation regards itself as big or safe enough. If a people's purposes and ideals be definitely social and cultural rather than mechanical, economic and military fitness, the techniques of social planning will have to be different. The improvement of methods of communication and transport, which have enormously reduced the difficulties of maintaining contact, calls for an effective regional planning in which the intelligent and orderly pursuit of cultural aims in small intimate local groups and regions could now be reconciled with an active participation in public policies and programmes intended for the entire nation. The dangers of the past ages arising from the autonomous groupings and regions have been abolished by modern transportation and communication which have made possible an enlargement of outlook, feelings and sentiments. As a matter of fact it has been even found feasible and convenient to enlarge the field of treatment of important regional problems in the United States or France such as those of flood control, river management, and navigation, crime, education, recreation, marketing, communications and sanitation by setting up interregional administrative bodies which overstep local and political boundaries. Among the supplementary devices may be mentioned various forms of interstate agreements such as interstate commissions in the USA to consult on a number of problems and interstate compacts and ad hoc authorities, perhaps best exemplified by the interstate crime compacts, the interstate commission on the Delware River Basin and the New York Port authority. Social surveys have in that country indicated that the areal unit, suitable for dealing with a specific phenomenon such as crime does not correspond with the region, when treated from the standpoint of education, recreation, taxation or industry. Thus, various functions are being distributed or redistributed to various levels of government, and administrative areas are also sought to be adapted to these.[9] In such cases flexibility and initiative associated with localism have been combined with efficiency and intelligent anticipation of distant but achievable goals.

The chief reason why the structure of social control and government cannot be adjusted to technological changes of the modern age is that nations live in a perpetual fear of others, have made a fetish of mechanical and administrative efficiency, permitting or tolerating an excessive centralization that shatters the internal cohesiveness and solidarity of all small, intimate, local or occupational groupings and regions. The significance of the modern planning movement, which has obtained adherents in every part of the world, is that it envisages new techniques of collective social guidance and control, which by utilizing modern technology will rescue contemporary civilization from the ruthless steamroller obliteration of all vital local cultural values, interests and initiatives. But this could hardly succeed in a world, so interdependent as this, where some nations aim chiefly at military ends rendering tribute to a powerful bureaucracy or dictatorship, which now seek to impose their wills upon other peoples, and follow national goals irrespective of the interest and welfare of other nations.

---

[9] Louisworth, "Localism, Regionalism and Centralisation", *American Journal of Sociology*, January 1937.

15

Social Equilibrium

Progressive Uplift of the Equilibrium Processes

SOCIAL equilibrium like evolution and adaptation rises from level to level. Both the scene and the actors become ever new, and there is a slow succession of ever new lifeforms and balances, ever improved communities and balances of life towards an unrealized climax. Ecology has made us familiar with the idea that the equilibrium of a developing community of organisms is constantly being undermined by progressive changes in life conditions. In the life of vegetable associations each phase becomes its own executioner, and itself brings a new phase into existence until a final equilibrium is reached, the ultimate possibility under the given conditions of habitat and in the presence of the available colonizing species of plants. That stage could not have been reached but for the changes and almost invariable enrichment of the soil brought about by the early pioneer plants of the habitat which pave the way for bigger and more exigent plants making greater demands on the environment in the form of nutrients. In animal life we find the processes of equilibrium lifted to a higher level.

Plant and animal associations are bound to each other with interrelationships of feeding, reproduction, shelter and even toilet and recreation achieving for the configuration of life an equilibrium that constantly shifts. They are different phases of the same organization of life, the same natural ecological unit with some properties which may be illustrated by comparison with an organism. The integrated aggregate of animals and plants (the "bio-coenosis" to use the continental term) is, indeed, often described as an organism. If it may not be called an organism in the sense of the biologist, it is at least a whole web of life, adjusted to particular complexes of environmental factors, often a highly integrated whole, which is the nucleus of a system in the sense of the physicist. The study of plant and animal succession by modern ecology reveals that both plant and animal communities are subject to regular rules as they react upon one another and co-act in shifting the balance of the region in their favour. The region shows a progressive improvement as bare dry land becomes progressively richer and wetter and the wet lowland becomes progressively drier and eventually fitter for the *ensemble* of its inhabitants. Such changes are brought about by the mere existence and ecologic succession of plants and by the more complex and fateful influences of animal inhabitants. It is thus that the inhabitants of the region themselves reshape the region in order that they may on the whole exploit it a little more effectively. Conversely, on the region, there is succession of plant and animal communities, each one on the whole using the environment a little more effectively and harmoniously than the one before, their success consisting in their rapid multiplication and dominance over other organisms.

The Web of Life

The processes of equilibrium are thus continuously shifted to ever higher levels. A new balance is reached through tentatives and trials of various relations to the pattern, through greater abundance and metabolic activity, through intensification of competition, and through new interlinkages in the complex web of life. Man, the superdominant of life's existing communities, is now found everywhere. As he has multiplied on the earth's surface and gone to forests and prairies, mountains and lowlands, he has felled trees, burned shrubs and grasses and exterminated his animal enemies and competitors. He has been able to reshape the environment more quickly and more strikingly than the other animal inhabitants whom he has gradually replaced. The region's balance has shifted more in his favour as he has domesticated wild plants and animals for his cultivations and for animal raising, checked soil erosion and used runoff of surplus water for power and for irrigation, protected the earth's mantle of trees and grasses, selected crops, trees and animals for special protection and breeding, handled bacteria to give food to his cultivated plants, and insects to control his fieldpests and trained and managed even big rivers and watercourses. In all these efforts of conservation and regeneration, man seeks an alliance with the entire range of ecologic forces, and curbs his subtle and wholesale, quick and farreaching exploitative activities by importing new values — the thought for tomorrow, the sacrifice for inhabitants of the region yet unborn. Nature is careless about the individual but no less heedful of the species. But man's foresight and sacrifice are characterized by deliberate purpose as he clearly envisages both immediate processes and distant consequences.

The Web of Institutions

In the organization of the life community, the lives of different organisms enter into one another and the specific normal pattern of life is maintained as a co-ordinated unity. The life community with its characteristic distribution of ecologic resources and harmonic animal and vegetable populations, indeed, presents a well-defined patterned formation. As in the life community in a region there develops a complex interrelationship and equilibrium among the various organisms and a balance and rhythm of multiplication for all, so in the culture of a human community which is woven within the framework of the ecological area there is found a harmonious relationship among the social, economic, political and other institutions and traditions, establishing some kind of equilibrium for the whole community or culture. The different parts of man's institutional structure, fashioned by his twofold tools, his hands and voice, as progressively subtler and stronger implements against the struggle with the forest, prairie, and animals, are harmoniously interrelated. Man's resources, industries and arts of production and employment of labour, which his region selects, determine the balance of occupations, the status system and the pattern of group organization.

The role and authority of the family, the church, the village community and other primary groups and of secondary groups, classes and the state are largely determined by the economic system and the alignment of social and economic classes, which, again, are governed by the resource pattern and mode of land utilization of the population. The cumulative effects of climate, food and type of occupation evolve the population type which can best utilize the resources of the region. Race, food, labour and standard of living are all adapted to one another and to climate and ecological resources. Again, in the same region there is always a certain natural dependence on one another of different economic procedures that may co-exist, forestry, pastoral industry, agriculture, manufacture and trade. There is a certain amount of hostility among the various parts of the life community, and among the various sectors of the economic organization of a region, but a process of selection goes on till an approximate harmonious equilibrium is attained, and the parts and sectors live in symbiosis. The dominant economic type nourishes its distinctive group organization and modes of government and social control, its appropriate status system and scheme of social values and beliefs.

Economics, art, recreation and religion are all related to one another; the filiation is largely determined by ecological adjustments and processes. Thus culture acts as a whole bringing to bear upon the region a collective attack from the *ensemble* of technical devices and artefacts (technological culture) and from institutions, customs and beliefs and appropriating for itself the surplus of energies remaining after recoupment and adjustment of all internal conflicts as *values*.

Culture is the guardian that assures not merely a true balance between different parts of institutional life, but also between man's material and non-material social equipment and his region. The environment thus enters not merely into our bone and our flesh, but also into our occupations and satisfactions, our beliefs and faiths, into our bodies and souls.

Criteria of Social Equilibrium

The primary values that emerge out of the equilibrium between man and his environment, as interpreted by ecology, are those of social survival. In an ecological interpretation of the reciprocal influences of man and his environment expressing the maintenance of co-ordinated life, social equilibrium has for its object and its criterion social survival, which can be quantitatively measured by the density of population. The criterion of optimum in this order of equilibrium is the maximum average expectation of life from the standpoint of the individual; while from the standpoint of the community there emerges at the ecological level another criterion — the stability and continuity of resources of the region. An excessive multiplication without controls and safeguards does not assure selection and dominance. This is the insects greatest asset. A high average longevity of life in the higher grades of animals is the surest index of biological status and dominance; and longevity is defined by selection in relation to the external ecologic conditions and the needs of the species which in the case of man include proper use and conservation of resources, natural and human, for the continuity of civilization.

On a plane of higher interpretation when the same social equilibrium is comprehended in terms of costs and satisfactions, work and reward, it is the pricing process through which the equilibrium is reached. Economics, as a branch of the comprehensive science of general ecology studying the balances and mutual pressures of men, measures social equilibrium by equating prices and output, and finds a true balance in a stationary society when there are the largest aggregate wealth produced and largest per capita income or consumption of necessary and conventional (but not harmful if we do not strip our experience in the economic stage of its biological content) goods and services. A prodigious production of wealth under a system which neither assures a wise husbandry of natural resources, nor a full employment of the factors of production, nor again, an equitable distribution of wealth amenities and hazards of life is incompatible with economic equilibrium.

What for ecological interpretations are no more than blind trials and errors of experiments trying out various relationships to the organization of life as a whole; what for economics are no more than what patterns of satisfactions, resources and efforts are, from the sociological standpoint, the search for ultimate values. The social equilibrium, as sociology envisages it, is not a mere organic or economic equilibrium, but an equilibrium in which the harmony of institutions and man's varied impulses and interests, values and virtues and the range and depth of personality are implicated. Neither the organic nor the economic equilibrium, as interpreted by ecology and economics, takes account of the fullness of man's experience, however useful in some respects such partial interpretation is. Social survival, as the criterion from ecological interpretation, economic efficiency, as the criterion from economic interpretation, becomes now in the ultimate interpretation by sociology the process of compounding of interests and values in the external framework of institutions and the inner spiritual experience of personality. Sociology would express the same social equilibrium in terms of social harmony and justice in the distribution of status, property, freedoms and restraints: this from the point of view of the community. From the point of view of the individual, social equilibrium is expressed in terms of man's freedom in the pursuit of the values of life, and his rights and obligations in such pursuit are both resting fundamentally on a common social purpose. As a population by gradual increase trenches upon material resources, and inventions and organizational improvements cannot serve usefully to restore the ecological optimum of numbers, a fair distribution of wealth, economic opportunity and freedom becomes an increasingly important mode of preventing an inner dissolution and conflict and maintaining or improving the standard and expectation of life. A new orientation of occupations and of social distance between men and their pursuits maintains equilibrium in the restricted environment by the method of experiment in a concrete social situation. Social harmony, though rooted in and growing out of the soil of man's adaptations to the region and economic relations with fellowmen, however, embrace timeless and spaceless relations, expressing the unity of an all-inclusive personality. The conception of social equilibrium as a biological and an economic reality is an abstraction of great practical use for certain limited practical ends, but it misses the full significance of the social reality.

On the social and cultural level, the principles of adaptation, economy and justice are identical. Ecological equilibrium is attained in and through economic equilibrium, and when the maximum social welfare and justice are attained, economic equilibrium is also reached. Social harmony and justice are final and all-inclusive, implying a condition of equilibrium between man and the environment, and between man and the pattern of groups and institutions realized through a reconciliation of the demands of living, economic power and social values in the successive levels of ecology, economy and the state.

Disequilibrium, Inherent in the Modern Economic System

Economic equilibrium in modern economic society is a price and income scheme with continuous flows of money, goods and services, which are stable. Such a scheme depends for its smooth working on the legal and social framework of property rights and socially recognized freedoms in respect of specific resources and to make exchanges of group rights and duties. The latter, again, depends upon political and sociological processes and relations within the community. The state as the organ of the supreme coercive authority of the community as well as the family, the guild, the village community, the class, the profession and corporation, which all exercise social control and regulate the use and exchange of the freedoms allowed by the laws, represent the *ensemble* of structures, rigid or flexible, which impose an extra-economic valuation on the so-called economic freedom, and thus practically limit economic advantage in exchange. The flow of money, goods and services, therefore, is naturally liable to change due to ecologic, economic and sociological causes. Changes in the quantity, position or form of resources such as land, coal and other minerals which diminish gradually or suddenly through use, climatological cycles, whose effects are more profound and far reaching, affecting every sector of economic life through agricultural fluctuations, cause disharmony of prices and output. A sudden increase or decrease of population also establishes a disequilibrium. Changes in the mechanical–

technological system through the accumulation, wear and tear and decay of fixed instruments of production or through new inventions or, again, through monetary policy and regulation and over saving, hoarding and "waste" of money, similarly cause fluctuations. A war scare or a speculative fever upsets the general equilibrium of output. A nation's change in foreign policy and political alignment or the irrational elements in the international situation create incompatibilities in equilibrium conditions. A prolonged political uncertainty at home or international complication abroad may engender a sense of insecurity in property and investments and perplexity regarding the movement of prices. High taxation, increase of debt, strain on credit, inflation of currency, withdrawal and impounding of gold, and uncertainty in business enterprises are all linked together in a vicious circle of disequilibrium of credit, finance and industry. Other psychological factors are represented by changes in fashion, taste, and mode of living or changes in the attitude towards the future or between labour and capital, which cause disequilibrium.

The modern technical organization of industry is such that a nicety of balance cannot be achieved through easy or prompt readjustment, when one sector of the economic life changes more rapidly. For the lack of elasticity of the system, which prevents the changeover and conversion of the fixed capital and machinery and of specialized labour, the lack of adaptation of wage and interest rates to new conditions are largely responsible for many particular disequilibria which are inherent in the present industrial structure. Similarly the present social–legal framework of the modern industrial society with its free exchange, wage system and lack of security causes a maldistribution of expenditure between production goods and consumption goods, a disequilibrium of distribution of economic power and advantage in exchange and a chronic disharmony between the interests of the entrepreneurial class which dictates the course of production and those of society as a whole. Here, again, we find imbalance inherent in the present scheme of exchange and of personal and property rights. The rational determination of the distribution of status and property remains the greatest socio-economic problem of the modern industrial society. Its psychological and ethical counterpart is how to subordinate instrumental and economic to intrinsic social and moral values and develop an ethical socialized type of the individual who may be in greater accord with the rational, impersonal society in which he has to live and move.

The Scheme of Social Status and Values

Society constantly changes its scheme of social status and values, which precondition, surround and overreach man's biologic and social adaptations, economic ends and the laws of exchange. Through class conflicts and political struggles the distribution of coercive authority in the community changes, and this brings about changes in the concepts and institutions of property, contract and exchange reflecting a new balance of economic power and system of status. Through laws and public opinion, through economic planning, the "framework of freedom" and the flow of goods and services are constantly being changed. Such change is made inevitable through a new social gradation, a new class consciousness involving political alignments, a new equilibrium of power in the state, which redistribute status, property and freedoms and restraints to make exchanges. All through, society tends to establish an equilibrium between man's biologic drives and his environment through the institutions of status, property, freedom and restraints. In a regime of social co-operation, status, property and restraint imply not merely an equilibrium between the individual's appropriative instincts and his scarce means, but also an equilibrium between economic interests and social welfare and justice — a condition of equilibrium between men and goods, and men and men and their reciprocal services and efforts. The system of distribution of status, property and freedom and controls in any society accordingly reflects its scheme of ultimate values, its rational planning of the social and legal conditions which will enable men to seek and find what are worth seeking and finding. Through the coercive and ameliorative functions of the state, through a scheme of progressive taxation that applies the principle of equi-marginal satisfactions and substitute returns, through new economic restraints, through new socially recognized economic rights and duties, through an inchoate public opinion as regards what is fair and reasonable in exchange, in wages, interest and profits and other increments and values, the industrial society now seeks an economic equilibrium by subordinating the exchange system and market relations to the norms of social welfare and justice what the masses are now convinced have been disregarded in and banished from the economic sector of culture.

It is culture which is the true monitor of the social equilibrium that it comprehensively and finally interprets and seeks as man's freedom in the pursuit of the higher values and as harmony and justice in his relations to fellowmen. The present redistribution of status, property, economic freedom and restraints, discernible in the modern economic society, with a view to attain social harmony and justice, is the move towards both the condition of equilibrium in society and right conduct of the individual in exchange. Where an orderly adjustment and move towards the social equilibrium are thwarted by various social, economic and political factors, industrial unemployment and strife, spread between poverty and wealth, individualism, class consciousness, submergence of the *elite* and middle classes and weakening of the political structure become chronic symptoms of social disequilibrium. A civil war, fought with or without arms, class rule whether by labour or capital and dictatorship soon pave the way to social equilibrium. Those who seize control of the machinery of the state can retain control and can alter the society's framework of rights and liberties and distribution of status and economic power, because their policy represents the rationalization of social welfare and justice that the orderly processes of political, economic and judicial procedure could not assure the community in the condition of grave disequilibrium.

The social equilibrium expressed in terms of social harmony and justice can be quantitatively expressed though with grave inadequacy for many practical purposes; the criterion of optimum that may be adopted here is the maximum agreement in political matters, i.e. relating to the use of economic power and wealth for the community, or the maximum recognition of man's rights, which express the respect for the worth of each individual and the will of the community to produce the maximum of social welfare or the minimum social distance between groups and classes. Such quantitative measurements and comparisons could give us guidance as regards definite social situations favouring to a greater or smaller extent the achievement of a co-ordinated unity of social relations. But these could only be used when we do not require to see more deeply and neglect the qualitative aspects of social situations. For the social situation in modern urban–industrial society, social harmony and justice posit a new constructive kind of social idealism which promotes an ethical socialized type of individualism and a collective sharing of the opportunities and risks of the modern industrial system and which would defy quantitative expression. Our interpretations of the equilibrium must rise from level to level through physical science, biology, psychology, economics and ethics in order that we may gradually include all elements in our experience, and may obtain a complete or perfect representation of it.

Towards Greater Wholeness

The trend of evolution is for the configuration of life to attain greater and greater wholeness, solidarity and permanence through intimate and subtle linkages. What is haphazard in Nature's trial and error, what links together the various parts of the life community — the great vegetable and animal aggregations — blindly in a more or less stable equilibrium of the region, becomes purposive in culture. Nature's subtle and intricate balance is upset by a sudden increase of metabolic activity in one part, a storm of breeding of one species of animals, a famine, pestilence or a sudden invasion of the habitat by some alien species of plants and animals. Some sectors of the living world, whether plants, animals or men, change more rapidly than others. Physical conditions also undergo gradual and sudden transformation and even shift, as do those of the biotic environment. All this destroys the existing equilibrium and routine of life of the inhabitants of the region, which elicits nature's regulative mechanisms until the habitat and inhabitants again settle down into a smooth and harmonious working system. Similarly in the institutional life and relations of man, there are jerks and pulls caused by an invention, an importation of an alien culture trait, a differential rate of change in different sectors of culture, a shift of political power among the classes, or a change of ideologies and morals. Under ordinary circumstances the social balance, like the biotic, is not disturbed by minor lags and fluctuations which are mediated and absorbed. But when an imbalance in the pattern of culture springs from a sudden catastrophe like a devastating war or a revolution, political or technological, which affects every part of culture or forms a series of gradually accumulating improvements or maladjustments between the parts, as for instance, between economics and ethics, or between religion and science, man sets about reconstructing his culture pattern, finding out anew a nice balance in the changing world. Economic history exhibits the sociological succession of human and institutional relations, which is even more variegated than the ecological change and succession in their external scene. Around a postulated well balanced culture pattern, harmoniously woven in the ecological framework of the region that delights the artist, law giver and religionist, gather beliefs, attitudes and values which act as the sieve of selection of customs, institutions and personality traits.

Man always thus consciously seeks a harmonious relationship between his economic toil and the scarce and fateful resources of the region, between his efforts and technology and his material satisfactions and rewards and economic values and the ultimate values of truth, beauty and goodness. Any maladjustments between parts of his nature and culture not only disturb the co-ordinated wholeness of culture, but also cause strains and stresses in the personality. Now the ultimate values represent the very substance of co-ordinated wholeness that man can apprehend. It is these which man strives to objectify in the scheme of property making and using, in status, freedom and restraints, and in the balance he establishes between the cultural or intimate and the ecological or contractual phases of social relationship and behaviour, between divisible economic values and indivisible social aims, between rights and duties. Man's rights of health, work, freedom and education, security of life and compensation for accident, of fair wages and decent housing and standard of living indicate how far the economic organization serves as a means to ultimate values. These latter represent the norms for the solution of all imbalances, conflicts and misfits at the various levels of social adaptation. More than that these embody themselves in the creative experiences of religion, art and literature. Religion and the fine arts search for and renew in man's concrete relationships and behaviour these ultimate values. It is through a new spirituality and artistic expression that mankind today is bridging the social distance between the classes, denuding individualism of its unethical and anti-social features, and forging affective bonds between men who remain anonymous and invisible in the city, the nation and the world state.

The Great Society and the World Community break down without a universal art and religion. Man no longer cherishes allegiances to his small communities, his primary groups and neighbourhoods which have disciplined and humanized him in his past social evolution; while neither law nor external social restraint or pressure can be a substitute for his primitive affective attitudes in the system of social control. It is to an ardent, wide-minded art and religion that modern man has to look for in finding out his real role and status in the city, the nation and the international community where he has so far escaped from the sense of social obligation by making his relationships so fractional and impersonal. Social equilibrium thus enlarges with the configuration of life itself, presenting a dynamic equilibrium of the lesser and simpler with the greater and more complex co-ordinated wholes until these cross the boundaries of time and space and become identified with the totality of experience of the personality, which is essentially of an organic or "holistic" character.

The Mechanisms of Social Equilibrium

Social phenomena are so reciprocally interdependent that an analysis which seeks to reduce these to a few limited and simple elements becomes too superficial and mechanical. To explain, say, law, politics and religion in terms of ecology and economics is to fall into the errors of geographical and economic determinism. It is true that ecologic adaptations and economic processes remain relatively constant determining influences of culture. But such influences are transformed in society into possibilities. In the give-and-take between the less constant and more elusive non-material and the more constant and more definite material sectors of culture, climate and agriculture, resource patterns and economic types mingle silently with the mind and ultimate values.

Culture thus refashions and assimilates the habitat into itself. The arts of production, the division of the economic classes and the status system become a part of society's framework of rights and duties, their significance being thus linked, in society's newer and subtler linkages, with ethical and spiritual ideals. The causes of the various social phenomena, which are none the less ecological and economic, cannot accordingly be supplied by ecology or economics alone. In a theory of social causation and equilibrium it is fundamental to remember that phenomena which though strictly ecological, biological or economical to all appearances, actually depend upon other social phenomena. This is also the reason why the effects, if any, abstracted out of social phenomena became cumulatively and progressively greater and more widespread (Tarde's laws), easily upsetting an established social equilibrium and bringing into existence restorative counter-social phenomena.

Finally, social effects work upon the minds of the individual through progressive stages and mechanisms. At first there is a modification of patterns of instincts and interests as the preliminary towards the attainment of a new social adjustment. Certain new urges come to dominate and emerge in the foreconsciousness while others are repressed or baffled and appear in sublimated forms or rise in open rebellion against the self and society. Groups then form representing episodes in the individual's efforts to attain an equilibrium. Such groups express and partially satisfy the new urges and urge combinations, and help towards the blending of urge patterns and the integration of personality.

A biological event such as a sudden increase of population or a catastrophic epidemic which sweeps away considerable numbers changes the established balance of occupations. This gradually modifies instinctive patterns of behaviour, habits and interests. A new culture trait such as an invention, social or technical, similarly upsets the nicety of balance of established patterns of behaviour and leads to a reorientation of urges, desires and interests. This, if persistent or supported by similar traits, tilting the instinctive patterns in the same direction, leads to the formation of new groups expressing a new set of desires and interests. As one invention after another is introduced, the imbalance in instinctive patterns results in the gathering together of new interests and values around appropriate social institutions. Social institutions condition and reorient human behaviour more forcefully than groups or a floating mass of new desires and interests, and help more successfully towards removing the maladjustment of human nature with the environment. The formation of institutions represents the last step in the readjustment of urges and interests and of the personality social process towards the social equilibrium. These crystallize in traditions and sentiments, elicit group loyalties, develop moral codes and compete with other institutions including the state in individual or group pattern making and in bringing about a new equilibrium of power and system of status. Institutions, representing as these do patterns of aids to adjustment of economic interests and of social values, are society's most effective and smooth working mechanisms to absorb changes or congeries of changes and to administer towards the social equilibrium. These are "presentations" to the individual of systems which resolve his inner conflicts and build up his personality in the changing *milieu*.

Social Equilibrium, an Integral Personality-Social Experience

Man's adaptation is one single process and the abstractive neglective procedure, which strips it in terms of biological or economic significance or values by conceiving successive stages and levels is adopted simply as concession to our imperfect perceptions. The view of blind organic drives or impelling economic interests as something segregated from social values and traditions, institutional codes and standards and moral sentiments, and entering into the mind from outside is, indeed, the legacy of the over simple nineteenth century materialism. This regarded man's personality and institutional life as something merely added to a picture which is otherwise interpreted physically or biologically. In social experience what are significant are not stages and levels but the co-ordination of all the elements of experience in the unity of the active, self-conscious personality.

Social equilibrium is achieved through the personality process which is cultural, and neither ecological nor economic in origin, and reflects a culturally derived integration or pattern. The latter aims at a co-ordinated wholeness of living through the realization of personality in the society and of society in the personality, which implies the ascription of the ultimate values to human relationship and the social process. The process of social equilibrium as reached through the integration of ultimate values in the concrete social situation by the striving, suffering, loving personality is a concept which will bring the social sciences nearer the solution of the problems of a chaotic and imperfect society. It will give a superhuman direction to what on account of an unfortunate division of knowledge we regard as organic and mechanical adjustments in the biological and economic levels. The unified, synoptic interpretation which only can do justice to social experience as revealing reality will enable us to import truth, beauty and goodness into our incomplete trials and errors of life, into our struggle with the fast tempo and tenuous, fractional relations of the mechanical–technical system, into our unsuccessful achievements for harmonizing between the ecological, economic and deliberate and the cultural, instinctive and integral forces and relations. Human interactions and groups will embody more the indivisible and ultimate common value attitudes that are embodied in the threefold chord of truth, beauty and goodness "not lightly broken" and that art and religion express rather than the divisible, instrumental values that underlie purposive, contractual groups and associations. Thus, man's relationship to fellowmen will be revealed not by their particular ends and means nor by their reciprocal pledges or contracts, but by a commonness of the spirit, compelling a mutual sharing of the rewards and hazards of life, and carrying with it the exhalting feeling of the expansion of the personality. Man's "good" stands for a sharing which increases its range until it comprehends the whole universe. His true "knowledge" increases, common insight and mutual understanding. His appreciation of "beauty" increases intelligent and discriminating sympathy. Thus, in mystical experience the objective and cosmic values of truth, goodness and beauty are linked together by the feature or function which all have in common in contributing to one inclusive system of co-operative life. The development of this impersonal, a cosmic mysticism expressing itself especially in new spiritual attitudes in the fine arts and social work will weave a new pattern of bonds between man and fellowman in the modern age of indirect human contacts and invisible social relationships, and humanize the deliberate, fractional and economic phases of conduct and relations in our mechanical, anonymous and unrighteous society. The imperfection of social equilibrium remains, and will ever remain, always inciting man's highest efforts and aspirations to establish a progressive series of organic and personal wholes, in Nature, in the social community and in beyond the human, extending from the organic and regional adaptations and economic advantages to the highest levels of spiritual creation. The true realization of inclusive wholeness in the active self-conscious personality in love and sacrifice for fellowmen will establish truth, beauty and goodness in our unintelligible, imperfect and disharmonious world. Thus all that is holy will be present with our social strivings and the stuff of dreams and ideals woven into our failures and disappointments.

Index